...acio uob fernãdo guttriz cartã donationis ...firmit...nis de er
...tis ⁊ in cultis. uineis pratis. riuis mõtib; ex... ...omnu
...⁊ hereditario inpptuũ habeas tu. ⁊ tua posteritas. Hec aũt here
...nfregerit. sit maledict⁊ ⁊cũ iuda traditore ininferno dãpnat...
...⁊ ept. x. kł fbr. ⊂Ra. oᵃ. cᵃ. Lxxxᵃ.vii. ddefonso impatore reg...

Sig + num
ipato + ris

drnaldus eps infede sce mai...

Qz ꝓ ses fuer p

⊂omite don d põtius senior...

Ponz de menerba

⊂omite don ramiro de absto...

# TRUE TO THE LETTER

800 Years of Remarkable Correspondence, Documents and Autographs

*Non cercare nulla che non ti venga da Te*

*Luigi Pirandello*

*Rio de Janeiro 15. IX. 1927.*

# TRUE TO THE LETTER

800 YEARS OF REMARKABLE CORRESPONDENCE, DOCUMENTS AND AUTOGRAPHS

## PEDRO CORRÊA DO LAGO

Preface by

### CARLO GINZBURG

with over 450 illustrations
in color and black and white

ed alla persona, a cui sono scritte. La supplico de'
miei rispetti alla Sig.a Contessina Orsi, e di darmi nuove
della sua salute, che desidero, e spero ristabilita.
Cosa faranno l'anno venturo del nuovo Teatro in
Bologna? Sarà la stessa società dell'anno passato
in opinione di far gli onori del suo paese?

Il Sig.r Marchese Francesco Albergati è stato qualche
mese ammalato per causa dei medicamenti. ora
che non si medica sta molto meglio. egli ha
risolto di ritornarsene al Canada. Mi ha fatto una
proposizione amorosa per vantaggio di mio Nipote.
e può essere, ch'io mi disponga a lasciarlo andare
con lui, appoggiato ad un'amico suo, negoziante
affaricco. Il Paese è felice per chi ha voglia di
lavorare; ed un giovane, che ha talento mediocre,
e docile temperamento si può fare la sua fortuna.
S'ciò succede, il nome Albergati farà in più parti
del mondo l'onore ed il bene della mia casa.
Del sesto Tomo della mia nuova edizione, ella vedrà
alla Testa della Commedia, intitolata la Guerra,
una legenda, che rende qualche Giustizia a questo
Cavaliere di Lei parente. Sono ossequiosamente
di V.e.        Parigi li 10 Xbre 1765. Umo: Devo: obbmo
                              Umilis: dev: obbl: Servitore
                                   Carlo Goldoni

*For Bia*

# CONTENTS

mon cher Baudelaire

J'ai reçu les Paradis artificiels & vous
en remercie. Le livre est bien annoté. Si vous
êtes curieux de annotations, venez le voir ce
soir ou un autre.

En somme, la chose qui en fait
intéressé. l'art bien conduire & très étrange.
Voila.

Bonjour

Feydeau

autographe d'autant
plus curieux que je n'ai
pas du tout demandé
à m. Feydeau
son opinion.

Samedi.

# PREFACE  *Carlo Ginzburg*

reud wrote that, as money does not belong to the world of childhood desires, it does not give any pleasure in itself. Collecting, however – which demands a massive investment of time, energy and money – is a very different matter: it springs from an impulse, the roots of which reach right back into childhood. All of us collected something when we were young, whether it be stones, shells, postcards or stamps, but for some people this impulse actually gets stronger the older they get. This was the case with Pedro Corrêa do Lago. The word 'pleasure', which occurs so frequently during his introduction to this book, reveals a great deal in this context. The search for pleasure may drive the collector to the exclusiveness of possession, but in Pedro's case it brings a totally different delight – that of sharing the wonders of his own collection with others.

A few years ago, I had the privilege of seeing many of the items reproduced here. My most vivid memory of that extraordinary morning is the passion with which Pedro Corrêa do Lago spoke about the documents in his collection, and my own enthusiasm as I stood admiring them and listening to him. Today, as I take another look at this selection of pieces, I can't help wondering what lies behind my own reactions. How can one explain the fascination that autographs exert over us?

This question is answered by P.-J. Fontaine, the author of the oldest known manual on autograph collecting (Paris, 1836), who talks about those documents that were never intended for public scrutiny: when an author 'writes a confidential letter which he presumes no one else will ever see, he does so without polish, without affectation, without preconception, and the heart – to use Abbé

Zanotti's expression – is revealed in all its nakedness, as it really is.'

Anyone reading these words today will inevitably recall Baudelaire's *Mon coeur mis a nu*. Chance, the capricious god that directs the steps of seekers and collectors, willed it that Pedro Corrêa do Lago's collection should include the note from French novelist Ernest Feydeau that is reproduced here (left), on which Baudelaire scribbled a phrase beginning with the word 'autograph'. Feydeau thanks the French poet for sending him a copy of *Les Paradis artificiels* (1860), which he describes as 'well executed and very strange', and says that he has made some notes: 'if you are curious about the notes, come and see them this or any other evening.' Baudelaire has underlined certain passages, including the word 'curious', which he takes up again in his own comment: 'autograph all the more curious as I never asked M. Feydeau for his opinion anyway.'

He obviously didn't intend this ironic remark to be seen by anyone other than himself. Can we therefore deduce that it expresses 'without polish, without affection, without preconception' Baudelaire's feelings towards Feydeau? That would be an over-hasty judgment. On the one hand, Baudelaire reacted very favourably towards Feydeau's novel *Fanny* (1858), and wrote both to French literary critic Charles-Augustin Sainte-Beuve (who had also written a favourable review) and to Feydeau himself: 'There, to be sure, is a good book, compact, solid, which has all its components well assembled and which will last.' On the other hand, in a letter to his mother, Baudelaire expressed a very different opinion: '*Fanny*, immense success, repugnant book, arch-repugnant'. That was undoubtedly Baudelaire's real opinion, and the praise delivered both to Sainte-Beuve and to

Feydeau would have been motivated by opportunistic considerations. Furthermore, the scorn and intolerance towards Feydeau that Baudelaire always manifested to his friends seem to be reflected in his comment at the bottom of the note reproduced here.

However, the simple fact that he underlined certain passages in Feydeau's letter, and the vigorous marks that he made with his pencil when reading it, may sow just a few seeds of doubt. In actual fact, Feydeau's notes on his book must indeed have aroused Baudelaire's curiosity, because he did finally get to see them, and in a letter to his publisher, Poulet-Malassis, described them as 'horribly numerous and very amusing… I must confess that some of them are useful, and I shall transcribe them into my copy'.

Thanks to Freud, we now accept that there are elements of ambiguity in most human relations, if not all. No doubt, this is why, when Baudelaire read the note with pencil in hand, and underlined the common word *voilà* three times, it seems to us anything but common. Thus the reproduction of an autograph provides clues that no critical edition can possibly supply. As Pedro Corrêa do Lago recalls, the poet Lamartine once defined the autograph as the 'physiognomy of thought'. The word 'physiognomy' evokes not only the portraits – often magnificent – that are to be found in this collection, but also the gestural element of the handwriting, which is doomed to disappear through the impersonal nature of the typewriter and the computer. (It is rare for a technical advance not to be accompanied by a loss.) The shock conveyed by the autograph may perhaps be explained as follows: it reminds us that behind the immateriality of the content, which guarantees its reproducibility, there exists (or existed) the real bodies of men and women.

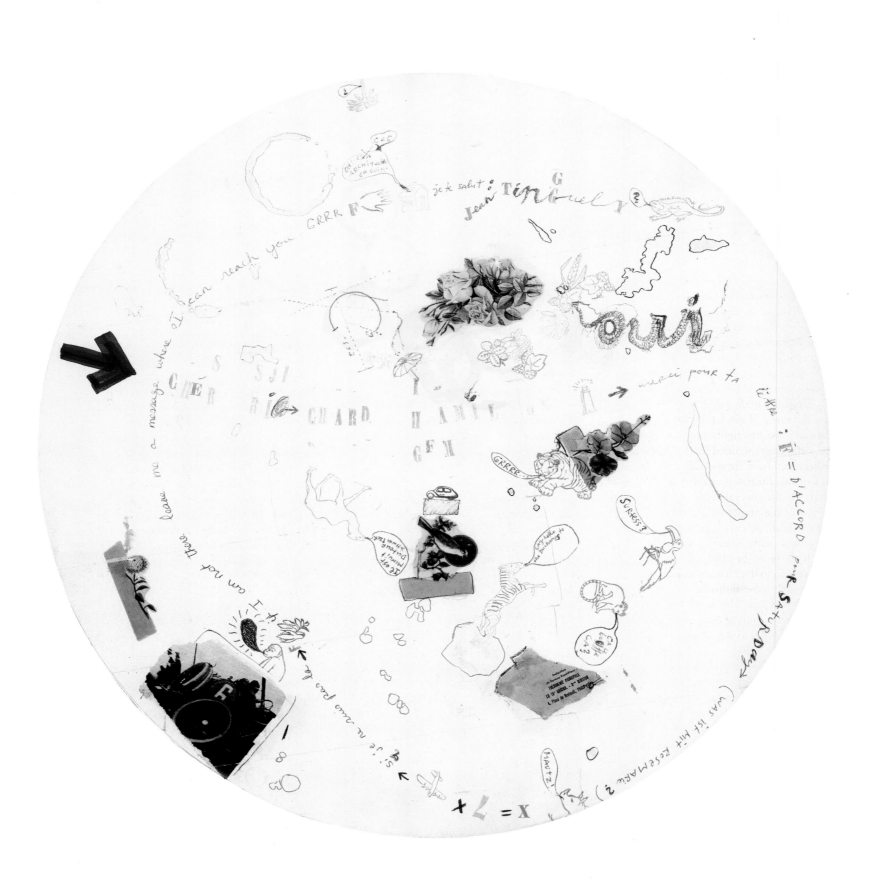

'If I am not there leave me a message where
I can reach you.'
Jean Tinguely, autograph document signed.

*Quit that of "Autographs", dear young Lady; that is a weak pursuit, wh* can lead you to nothing considerable! —*

*T. Carlyle*

# A PASSION FOR AUTOGRAPHS

For thirty-five years, collecting autographs has been a source of enormous pleasure for me – a pleasure I hope to share with my readers through this book. It contains three hundred and fifty out of some thirty thousand items that I have been fortunate enough to gather together over the years.

There are many publications dedicated to a vast range of specialist subjects, from toy cars to paperweights, but apart from a few manuals intended for the experienced collectors, I have always been struck by the lack of any illustrated volume that could convey to the general public all the seductive powers of autographs – the charm and the subtle yet potent magic of the letters, documents and photographs which can touch our hearts by bringing back to life the events and the characters that have enriched the past. If this book ignites a spark or two, I shall be delighted, but my main aim is simply to convey the pleasure of searching, acquiring, studying and conserving the pieces of paper that go to make up a fascinating world. I hope also to give a little insight into the nature of this passion, which others may not share but the attractions of which they may at least come to understand and appreciate.

The first advice that one might give to a beginner is to choose a favourite area rather than reaching out in all directions. Specialization increases one's chances of assembling a collection that will be more significant and less demanding. There are, for instance, exemplary collections that focus exclusively on French or English literature, 19th-century music, Impressionist painting and so on, and the principle of following a single thread is one that I would wholeheartedly endorse.

Nevertheless, for reasons that I myself am not really able to explain (though the main one is probably that I am interested in all sorts of things at the same time), I have gone against both this principle and my own common sense, and opted for diversity – or what one might call a disciplined eclecticism: this general collection embraces a raft of different fields. There was never a conscious decision to collect everything, and it is only with hindsight that I can say that my speciality is simply temporal: I looked for items related to the people I found most interesting in Western history and culture from 1500 onwards, though I sometimes went back even further in time.

The result is a collection whose most striking quality may indeed be its ample range. It builds up a panorama encompassing centuries of handwriting, from medieval kings right through to the Beatles, and it includes most of the outstanding figures of history, literature, the sciences, music and art. I am told that very few collections cover such a wide area, and certainly this is why various friends as well as my publisher feel that it could form the subject of a general illustrated work that has long been missing from the field. This book does not pretend to illustrate the 'ideal' collection – that, of course, would be impossible. However, whether or not the reader is familiar with the worlds it uncovers, it will offer him or her a selection of documents from different ages and areas of human activity that often show great men and women in a new light.

Some collections specialize in a single type of autograph: manuscripts, letters, official documents or photographs. Once more I must confess that I am attracted to all these categories, the diversity of which will be dealt with in the next chapter. Sometimes these

forms of autograph may even take on an aesthetic quality, all the more so if they emanate from an artist – whether amateur or professional – as is the case with the letter reproduced opposite, by the Swiss sculptor Jean Tinguely (1925–91). It has been drawn on a paper tablecloth from a café, and still bears the imprint of the glasses. Tinguely was writing to the English pop artist Richard Hamilton (b. 1922), using a mixture of different languages and styles of handwriting. It is without doubt a particularly striking example of the autograph as a work of art, though there will be several more in the course of this volume.

Another interesting piece is by the Scottish-born essayist and historian Thomas Carlyle (1795–1881), reproduced above. In 1872, he wrote in a Victorian album: 'Quit that of "autographs", dear young Lady; that is a weak pursuit, which can lead you to nothing considerable!'

If this epigraph has been highlighted here, and has been chosen to open a book in praise of autographs, this is partly because the meaning of the word 'autograph' is commonly mistaken. Most people understand it as being synonymous with a signature, and they think of a scrap of paper hastily signed by a pop or film star. The hunt for such scribbles is certainly limited in scope, and if Carlyle was indeed referring to the prey of the autograph-hunters, then he certainly had good cause for his scepticism. But those who collect autograph manuscripts and documents are a different breed. For them, the word 'autograph' goes back to its derivation and means 'written with one's own hand'. Even in painting, it refers to a work that is executed entirely by the artist, without the help of a pupil. Strictly speaking, some people would confine the term to manuscripts, but although the words may be complementary, they are often understood as different things.

We might say, then, that while all signatures are autographs, not all autographs are signatures. Indeed, ordinary signatures are generally the least interesting items, since they convey nothing. A letter, on the other hand, or an historic document, or even an inscribed photograph will deliver a message, which may in itself be richly complex. This is the exciting quest that has given rise to our book – the quest for the unusual item which may move us by its content or by its sheer quality. It may seem surprising that such items are still sometimes available on the open market instead of being preserved in museums, archives or libraries, but many of them belong to private collections which get broken up – for instance, when someone dies – and put up for sale, thus enabling private individuals to enhance their own collections.

Autograph-lovers have been around since ancient times. Roman scholars Cicero (106–43 BC) and Pliny the Younger (c. 61–113 AD) apparently owned quite remarkable collections, and Pliny even complained about the rarity of letters written by Julius Caesar (100–44 BC). Roman biographer and historian Suetonius (c. 69–122 AD) describes his emotions on actually holding in his hands some poems written by the Roman emperor Nero (37–68 AD). The Chinese poet and calligrapher Mi Fu (1051–1107) said: 'I desire neither honours nor wealth, but only the handwriting of the masters.' Unfortunately, no notable autographs have come down to us from antiquity. It was not until the Renaissance, at the very earliest, that certain men of influence such as the French statesmen Duc de Sully (1560–1641) and Jules Mazarin (1602–61) became aware of the value of manuscript documents, and took steps to preserve them. Their collections formed the basis of the great libraries, and for the last four hundred years the work of private collectors has played a major role in the conservation of this written heritage.

French essayist Michel Eyquem de Montaigne (1533–92) 'conserved the writing' of his friends and of people whom he admired, and so did Johann Wolfgang von Goethe (1749–1832), Queen Victoria (1819–1901), and – in more modern times – Austrian writer Stefan Zweig (1881–1942), former US president Franklin D. Roosevelt (1882–1945) and software pioneer Bill Gates (b. 1955). There have also been many anonymous collectors who have rooted out and ensured the survival of important items ever since the middle of the 19th century,

when this particular market became established in Europe. It was then that the collectors, the dealers, the experts and the auctions became a part of the cultural scene.

Today, the autograph market is substantial, and every year there are tens of thousands of collectors chasing after millions of items, big and small, all over the world. The most active centres are in the USA, Britain, France and Germany, but there are other dynamic markets elsewhere, particularly in Europe, where countless auctions take place, and dealers and libraries regularly sell items from their stock.

Although people often talk of the investment value of autographs, you will rarely find collectors who are concerned with financial gain. They collect simply for the pleasure of collecting. There are many factors involved in this passion: a taste that is inborn or acquired in childhood; the enthusiast's curiosity, formed by a chance reading, or by a journey; a particular cultural or intellectual approach. However, a major part is played by the emotions. Collectors often talk of the thrill they get when they acquire an autograph letter, as if they were establishing a new and intimate relationship with an admired personality, or perhaps with their favourite author. Of course it is personal taste that directs one's choice, and a collection will always centre on personal interests and inclinations. French writer Émile Herzog (1885–1967), better known by his pseudonym André Maurois, described this mixture of reason and emotion when talking about a famous collection: 'when it is of this quality, it…becomes a work of art, erudition and love.'

Every letter, even the most insignificant, is a touching relic of the person who wrote it – a tangible link that defies the passage of time. Holding it in your hands is unquestionably the closest contact you can possibly have if the person is no longer with us.

This 'meeting' takes place through the intermediary of the paper which the person has touched and to which he or she has devoted some seconds, minutes, hours. The paper has frozen this moment of time in the life of the writer. The pleasure of possessing it contains a certain sweet fetishism, tinged perhaps with an element of indiscretion; we are reading words that were intended for someone else, but the collector will somehow feel that he or she is really the ultimate, secret addressee.

Autograph letters have been described as 'fragments of time past', 'impressions of the heart' and 'slices of life'. Holding a document from, say, the 12th century is rather like

▲ Madame de Staël, autograph letter signed, 1809, with autograph inscription by Thomas Jefferson on the back.

travelling in a time machine: I can imagine this same piece of parchment lying on a large wooden table hundreds of years ago, when a Spanish king draws a cross in lieu of writing his signature. For an enthusiast, such pieces open windows onto whole areas of the past, recapturing events which would otherwise be lost from memory and of which they are often the sole surviving witnesses. Historians and biographers are well aware of this, and have always used such manuscripts as primary sources. The more revealing and important the content, the more precious the document, both for the historian – whose only concern is to acquire information – and for the collector, who will be emotionally stirred and stimulated by the touch and associations of the object itself.

Naturally, all collectors aspire to items of indisputable historical or artistic value – the content of which may modify an historical viewpoint or give insight into an author's way of thinking. But these are becoming rarer and rarer on the open market, as the majority have already been acquired and now have a permanent place in public institutions. This is particularly true of such favourites as Wolfgang Amadeus Mozart (1756–91) and Ludwig van Beethoven (1770–1827).

The collector is forced to turn to seemingly ordinary texts, which will perhaps reveal something unexpected or even humorous, but which his or her predecessors may have regarded as unimportant. The beauty of such a text can often escape someone who has not studied its context, but the passionate collector will discover its hidden charms. Many such pieces appear in this book. Frequently, limited means have prevented me from acquiring major items whose importance is far more obvious and therefore far more attractive to wealthier purchasers.

Famous American collectors have pointed out that the autograph is the least valued sector of the art market. For the equivalent of a single mediocre Impressionist drawing, one can buy several exceptional autographs. With a comparatively modest budget, one can still build up a very substantial collection in certain fields, but it is important to know one's subject, follow one's instincts, avoid fashionable trends, learn to read between the lines, and seize those opportunities that others have failed to notice.

These first few pages contain a selection of pieces that have attracted me for various reasons, all of them bound up with the range of emotions these autographs can arouse. An autograph poem by Paul Verlaine (1844–96), such as the one reproduced centre left, is interesting in its own right, but its history gives it an extra dimension. This is the signed manuscript of the very first Verlaine poem ever published, *Monsieur Prudhomme*. It is a sonnet he wrote when he was eighteen – at that age fellow poet Arthur Rimbaud (1854–91) had already composed his masterpieces – and it is the work of a beginner who had none of the precocious talent of his future friend. Nevertheless, it is an important text, because it marks an early stage in his career, and the many variations between the manuscript and the final printed version.

Envelopes, even when they are signed, are generally the poor relations in the autograph family, but here too certain circumstances may increase the value tenfold. The autograph envelope reproduced above was penned by the writer Franz Kafka (1883–1924) and contained a love letter to his fiancée Felice Bauer. The original correspondence is no longer available to collectors, but the envelopes (scattered some twenty years ago) enable us to acquire something apparently very simple but in actual fact quite exceptional, because Kafka autographs are extremely rare; once more it is a thrill to hold a piece of paper that once contained a love letter from the great author.

The document reproduced below left is also revealing. At first sight it may seem like a rather dull piece of official bureaucracy, but on closer inspection it turns out to be a curious aspect of a great philosopher's work: Georg Wilhelm Friedrich Hegel (1770–1831) was Rector of the Royal University of Prussia, and here he has twice signed a certificate attesting that a student does not belong to any secret societies.

Opposite is the last page (recto and verso) of a letter written by the French writer Madame de Staël (1766–1817). This too is remarkable for more than one reason. Firstly, the text itself is very fine; secondly, the addressee is Thomas Jefferson (1743–1826), third president of the United States and formerly US minister to France. A line that Jefferson has added on the back, in order to classify the mail, increases its value. Thus the document combines the autographs of two great figures and is of interest both to French and American collectors. Madame de Staël's literary talent is evident when she declares in this letter: '…from one end of the Earth to the other, everything that concerns love of liberty and of justice owes you homage. If I were not the daughter of [French financier and statesman]

▲ ▲ ▲ Franz Kafka, autograph envelope signed, 1912.
▲ ▲ Paul Verlaine, autograph poem signed, 1862.
▲ G. W. F. Hegel, document signed twice, 1830.

M. Necker, I should think my name to be too little known for you to recall it, but I am sure that you love my father because you comport yourself as he does.'

There are many other such items which are close to my heart and which stand out in a rather long collecting career. This is a passion that began very early in my life, when I was eleven years old. At the time we were living in Brazil, and my interest in collecting was very much a hobby. I had an album of autographs which I had asked for personally, and I was content with that.

In 1970, the year in which I turned twelve, I followed my diplomat father to Europe, and had the idea of writing to people whom I admired in order to get their autographs. To my surprise, hundreds of replies followed: letters, signed photos and plain signatures, all of which were fascinating to a young boy and made waiting for the postman a source of permanent excitement. Nowadays, celebrities are pestered to such a degree that most of them ignore this kind of request, but during the 1970s they were still amazingly accessible.

My debut, however, was far from promising. I wrote to the English writer J. R .R. Tolkien (1892–1973), author of *The Lord of the Rings* (1954–55), who at that time was nowhere near as famous as he is (posthumously) today, and to French film director François Truffaut (1932–84) after I had seen his *L'Enfant sauvage* (1969). A letter from Tolkien's secretary brought me a swift refusal on the grounds that he had been so swamped with requests that he had made it a rule never to send anyone his autograph. A two-month wait brought me nothing at all from Truffaut. I was deeply disappointed and convinced myself that my splendid initiative would never bear any fruit. But then, shortly before Christmas, a large envelope arrived. It contained the illustrated book of *L'Enfant sauvage*, together with a personal inscription (above left). I was exultant, and unquestionably I owe my continued passion for autographs to the kindness of Truffaut. My false start could certainly have snuffed out my enthusiasm.

It was around this time that a great childhood friend, Michael Guttmann – today a famous violinist – offered me a remarkable piece that belonged to his father and reinforced my devotion to the cause. It was a postcard (above right) signed by the Norwegian composer Edvard Grieg (1843–1907). He hated portraits of himself, but he did occasionally sign them, though not without registering his disapproval. On this card he wrote: 'A horrible portrait of Edvard Grieg', but he also took the trouble to add

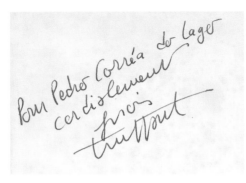

a couple of bars of music, which makes the autograph all the more precious.

At thirteen, I discovered by chance that the items I thought I could only acquire by asking directly or by letter – or which were given to me by friends of my parents – were also available from specialist dealers. In 1971, I shyly entered the office of John Wilson in London (he was then an expert at the start of his career, and is now one of England's leading lights), and made my first purchase: a small envelope written by Queen Victoria.

Many other modest acquisitions followed, within the range accessible to a teenager's pocket-money, and then at sixteen I returned to Rio de Janeiro, where I still live. In the course of countless journeys to Europe and the USA, I have subsequently made contact with a wide circle of dealers, and it is from them that I have purchased the finest items in my collection. This has had a decisive influence on my whole way of life for the last thirty years and, almost without my realizing it, has taken over many of my choices, my cultural interests, and even – in a manner that was totally unexpected – my professional career.

The fact that I am Brazilian and live in my home country has of course affected the direction in which my collection has proceeded. Living so far away from the major markets and suppliers, I have turned increasingly to Brazil for my sources. The lack

of real competition here has helped me in the last twenty years to assemble what may well be the largest private collection of Brazilian autographs, and the first part of this – amounting to more than fifteen thousand pieces – is now exhibited at a state-run museum in Rio Grande do Sul. However, I continue to be fascinated by personalities from all over the world, and I try to obtain the quality items that sometimes come up for sale in Brazil, which many foreign celebrities visited in the course of the 20th century. Indeed several of the documents presented here are connected with Brazil.

A few years ago, another large general collection, containing several outstanding pieces, was split up and put on sale. It was the work of a film director of Greek origin who was married to a Swedish lady, and it reflected their own personal lives. The autographs of their compatriots – relatively rare on the international market – added a degree of originality to a collection that otherwise consisted of the most sought-after names. I should have liked to meet this couple, and indeed many other enthusiasts whose interests are similar to my own, but strangely enough I have only happened to make contact with dealers (some of whom are themselves collectors), and my quest has for the most part been pursued in solitude. Thus I have rarely been able to display my passion, and this may be why I welcome the chance to devote a book to my collection – which has now become too big, almost in spite of myself. I hope that this volume will interest not only my fellow enthusiasts but also those readers who share my fascination with Western culture, and who might find these documents entertaining or even inspirational.

About a hundred texts accompany these autographs, which have come down to us from more than a hundred and fifty outstanding men and women. The selection has been dictated by their popularity among collectors from all countries, although there are some notable absentees owing to the fact that their autographs are unobtainable or prohibitively expensive. Naturally any principle of selection is bound to be controversial. Presidents of the USA would certainly have been more numerous had this book been written by an American, and composers and philosophers would have taken up a great deal more space had the author been German. It is always difficult to decide who to put in and who to leave out, and while certain celebrities may enjoy a greater international fame than perhaps they deserve, there are other great men and women whose reputation has failed to spread beyond the borders of their homeland. I have tried, however, apart from a few rare exceptions, to focus on people whose fame is universal. In so far as collectors tend to have precisely the same interest as the general public in those outstanding personalities whose lives and stories exercise a permanent fascination, I believe I have come close to achieving my aim: despite the limitations inevitable in choosing people and items from a single collection, most of the names most treasured by collectors are in this volume.

David Schulson, the American dealer who is perhaps the greatest modern connoisseur of European autographs in the USA, would have preferred to see more 20th-century celebrities, such as Elvis Presley (1935–77) or Bob Dylan (b. 1941). Other friends, however, have advised me to expand the section dealing with older manuscripts. I can only hope that between these two poles I have managed to achieve a reasonable balance.

I have organized the book according to a fairly flexible chronological pattern, with each text covering from one to three people who are linked because of certain affinities or because the document itself brings them together. In general, the reader will find a full-page reproduction on the right-hand side, which aims to convey the feeling

of holding the original document in his or her hands. The commentaries vary in length, for no particular reason other than the relative importance of each autograph and person. All the letters, portraits, drawings and photographs are original pieces that form part of this collection, and the majority of the manuscripts are published here for the very first time. The transcriptions and translations at the end of the book are intended for those readers who might be interested in a complete record.

The descriptions of the featured pieces themselves and of the incidents they relate to are naturally a reflection of the tastes that have shaped the collection as a whole. Just as a library will reveal the intellectual orientation of its owner, autographs will faithfully mirror the instincts and the personality of the collector. Stefan Zweig, for instance, is someone who fascinates me for a number of reasons: firstly, I admire his books; secondly, he too had a passion for autographs (and wrote some wonderful lines on the subject); thirdly, he died in Brazil. His entry visa for his first visit to Brazil is reproduced above. Thanks to the royalties he earned during the 1920s, Zweig was wealthy enough to acquire the documents he loved most – those that revealed the birth of a work of art. He wrote: 'The only thing that can give us a slight idea of the intangible process of creation is the pages of a manuscript, and above all those that are not destined to be published – the still tentative sketches, riddled with corrections, and out of which, little by little, the true, definitive form is crystallized.'

▲ Stefan Zweig, autograph document signed, 1936.

Writers' manuscripts are a growing passion among scholars, and have even become a subject for study, particularly in French universities, where they are used to analyse what Goethe called 'the genetics of writing'.

Collecting autographs, which Lamartine (1790–1869) saw as representing 'the physiognomy of thought', is a gentle, discreet occupation which has long suffered from being less visual than collecting works of art. By comparison with books, which are almost always published in large numbers, generally the manuscript has the advantage of being unique, but its silent power lies above all in its ability to evoke the dreams, joys, hopes, dramas and disappointments of distant figures.

To end this prologue, let me once more turn to Stefan Zweig: 'How can we capture the mysterious moment of transition when a line, a phrase, a melody passes from the invisible to the material, if not in the original writings of the great masters, whether the fruits of great effort or written in haste?'

# THE AUTOGRAPH IN ALL ITS FORMS

Just as museums, libraries and universities jealously guard their manuscript treasures, private collectors are always on the hunt for new autographs in whatever form. The diversity is evident from the group of documents reproduced on the page opposite, varying in their nature and their format, and all taken from the collection on which this book is based. This chapter will set out to present the most common types and the different categories of autograph liable to come on the market, in accordance with the current hierarchy of forms and the interests of the collectors.

The great collectors of the past had a much wider choice than today and could acquire the most prestigious manuscripts – those that reveal an artist in the very act of creating a work. Thus Stefan Zweig was able to obtain drafts of masterpieces by Goethe, Friedrich Schiller (1759–1805), Honoré de Balzac (1799–1850), Lord Byron (1788–1824) and Stendhal (1783–1842), as well as manuscript versions of great symphonies by Mozart and Beethoven. Today, such autographs are far rarer, and only the most subsidized institutions and a handful of billionaire individuals can afford them.

Nevertheless, there are still thousands of pieces in circulation that are fascinating enough to attract the enthusiast. They are scattered all over the world in their different categories: manuscripts, autograph letters signed, signed documents, signed photographs, and signatures. Supply and demand dictate the value, but it is always the content that regulates the degree of interest. It is through their judgment of the importance or the tone of the content, and through their ability to place an item in its context and recognize its hidden significance, that the real connoisseurs are to be distinguished from the dabblers, who would overlook it out of carelessness or ignorance.

For Europeans the uniqueness of the content generally used to compensate for any imperfections in the document itself, but this is changing. Nowadays, American sales catalogues detail folds or creases in the paper, especially when they coincide with the signature. However, even now, the current obsession with the actual condition of a piece is not the same with autographs as it is with books and photographs, where a less than satisfactory appearance can cut the value by up to ninety-five per cent.

Even though personal taste plays a major role in the make-up of a collection, there are certain points on which all enthusiasts would agree: everyone dreams of acquiring a poem from Charles Baudelaire's (1821–67) *Les Fleurs du mal* (1857), in perfect condition and covered with his corrections; a page from Byron's *Don Juan* (1819–24) or Goethe's masterpiece *Faust* (1808–32) will do just as well, or a letter from Rimbaud to Verlaine containing his views on poetry, or from American poet Ezra Pound (1885–1972) to Irish writer James Joyce (1882–1941) discussing the latter's novel *Ulysses* (1922), or from Pablo Picasso (1881–1973) to Henri Matisse (1869–1954) on the subject of modern art, or a love letter from the French Emperor Napoleon (1769–1821) to Josephine de Beauharnais (1763–1814).

A few years ago, one great collector went to a public sale and managed to acquire a letter from French painter Paul Gauguin (1848–1903) concerning the crisis that drove Vincent Van Gogh (1853–90) to cut off his ear. Another bought a letter in New York: Tsar Nicholas II (1831–91) was informing his prime minister that he had just received a visit from a monk who had greatly impressed him. The name of the monk was Rasputin (1872–1916). Recently, autograph letters from Francis I of France (1494–1547) to the Holy Roman Emperor Charles V (1500–58), and from Napoleon to Louis XVIII (1755–1824) were put up for sale, but such letters are considered to be national treasures and must not leave their country of origin, and so in this case the French State exercised its pre-emptive rights.

It has often been said that new information technology will kill off the autograph. Perhaps it will, although during the last hundred years the telephone and typewriter have already cut the number of handwritten messages significantly. Faxes will certainly not be seen as autographs, nor will emails – even if they are the authentic words of the sender. There is no doubt that methods of writing have changed dramatically and are still changing. However, this will only add to the value of autographs: manuscript messages from future celebrities will become rarities and, as such, all the more precious to collectors.

Public institutions remain the main buyers, and, while the number of private collectors is on the increase, it seems almost certain that interesting pieces from the past will also continue to become rarer, and therefore more expensive. Tastes have changed enormously over the last thirty years, and they also vary considerably from one country to another. New forms of documents, such as signed photographs, have appealed to enthusiasts.

In this section, we shall take a look at the different forms of autograph, reproducing dozens of the most desirable pieces. The figures here are different from those that appear in the main body of this book.

The autograph letters signed, reproduced here, are examples of different types of correspondence from the golden age of pen and paper. Prior to the 16th century, autograph letters are very rare, but after 1500 messages exchanged between monarchs were sometimes in their own hand. This is certainly the case with the letter from Philip II of Spain (1527–98) reproduced above. It dates from 1579 and is addressed to Philip's uncle, King Henry of Portugal (1512–80), whom he was to succeed the following year, thereby uniting the two kingdoms. The political content is important: Philip is demanding a key position for one of his allies.

Above right, there is a very formal message written by Frederick the Great (1712–86) to a prince. Rather paradoxically, the interest of this piece lies precisely in the thinness of the content, since the young King of Prussia manages to write twelve lines that say virtually nothing. It is worth quoting one long sentence to convey the tenor of this magnificent piece of waffle: 'I felt this feeling when seeing you in Berlin and it will never leave me, I beg you to be persuaded of this and to believe that on all occasions I shall derive a sincere pleasure in convincing you of these feelings, being for ever, my dear cousin, the very good and very affectionate cousin of Your Royal Highness….'

Letters written by the great chemist and scholar Antoine-Laurent Lavoisier (1743–94) are rare. The one reproduced above left – in which he is writing about his land –

is a fine example of an 18th-century autograph letter signed.

When a piece deals with the subject that has made its author famous, it takes on an extra dimension of interest. The letter reproduced above was written by French chemist Pierre Curie (1859–1906), who was run over and killed by a cart just eighteen days later. The great scientist is talking here about a measure of radioactivity and mentions the word 'radium', which is the veritable icing on the cake for all Curie collectors. The premature death of Pierre made his autographs considerably rarer than those of his wife Marie (1867–1934), who survived him by almost thirty years.

For a collector, exceptional contents make the best autograph letter, but there are a few other qualities that can really add value. It should be in perfect condition, and the text should be on one page or on two separate pages, as this makes it easier to display – and therefore all the more desirable.

Written at a time when most authors were already almost exclusively using typewriters, the letter reproduced above, by German novelist Thomas Mann (1875–1955), is exemplary in its clarity: the headed notepaper identifies the person, the signature is very legible, and the writing is in the centre of the page. Furthermore, the content itself is out of the ordinary: one year before his death, the great writer is thanking the president of the Argentinian Pen Club for organizing a conference on his work that is to be held in Buenos Aires.

While the letters of Mann are relatively easy to come by, those of his contemporary, the great philosopher Ludwig Wittgenstein (1889–1951), are extremely rare, which means that content tends to be secondary. The letter reproduced above right contains a friendly message and also has the virtue of bearing a clear signature, which makes it all the more attractive. Another rarity is letters by the most

famous 20th-century Japanese writer, Yukio Mishima (1925–70), who committed suicide at an early age. The letter on the right is a response to a foreign publisher, asking him to contact the author's agent.

Even when they are very short, some autograph letters can be astonishingly revealing. In the 19th century, brief messages were often written on visiting cards, such as the one reproduced below right (or the one on page 148, from French sculptor Auguste Rodin to a pupil). This is from the German archaeologist Heinrich Schliemann (1822–90), who excavated the ruins of Troy at Hisarlik in Turkey and is here inviting a young English colleague – Arthur Evans (1851–1941) – to dinner. It was Evans who, at the turn of the 20th century, made another sensational discovery: Knossos in Crete.

Autograph letters signed, such as those on the following pages, can be in all sorts of styles and formats. English novelist D. H. Lawrence (1885–1930), for instance, was in Italy when he wrote the letter on page 18 (above right) on a single sheet folded in two, which allows the first and last pages to be viewed at the same time.

▼ Thomas Mann, autograph letter signed, 1954.
▲ Ludwig Wittgenstein, autograph letter signed, 1940.
◄ Yukio Mishima, autograph letter signed, 1965.
► Heinrich Schliemann, autograph note signed, c. 1885.

Collectors prefer letters to be written in ink and signed with the author's full name. If they are in pencil, or are signed only with the first name or with initials, the value generally drops unless the content is special. Certain 20th-century celebrities, however, did tend to use their initials, including the great English economist John Maynard Keynes (1883–1946) (above left) and the French composer Erik Satie (1866–1925) (centre right). The intertwined initials of the latter form a monogram which is as desirable as any complete signature – particularly on such a card, as it contains an invitation to the pianist Ricardo Viñes to dine at Madame Edwards's (Misia Sert) in the company of Picasso and 'A. Paul Hinn-Air, the celebrated critic' (Satie's witty name for Guillaume Apollinaire). When a famous person's autographs are particularly rare, such as English poet Alexander Pope (1688–1744), even a letter of three lines can be considered a find (below right).

Typewritten letters are usually less attractive than those that are handwritten, but as always it is the content that is all-important and may determine the value of the piece. This is certainly the case with the letter from Carl Gustav Jung (1875–1961) reproduced on the opposite page (above left), in which the statement that 'My mind doesn't function

▲ John Maynard Keynes, autograph letter signed 'JMK', 1935.
◀◀ D.H. Lawrence, autograph letter signed, 1916.
◀ Erik Satie, autograph letter signed 'ES'.
▶ Alexander Pope, autograph letter signed, c. 1720.

PROF. DR. C. G. JUNG

KÜSNACHT-ZÜRICH
SEESTRASSE 228

February 1st 1949.

Mr.P.M.Shankland,
Short Film Production,
Zonal Office Information Services,
HAMBURG MOHLENHOF.
63 HQ CCG BE BAOR 3.

Your Ref.ISZO/FILM/SEP/45

Dear Sir,

Your proposition is indeed most interesting, but
it will be equally difficult to translate such a thing as my
ESSAYS ON CONTEMPORARY EVENTS into the language of the film.
I must confess that I have not the slightest imagination in
this respect. What I think I would do would be : I should give
my little book to a number of better-class writers that are
interested in the film and I should even start a competition
among them in order to see what kind of dramatic phantasies
they develop while reading the Essays. My mind doesn't function
along these modern ways, but I could imagine that a fertile and
dramatising mind could get the necessary kick out of my peculiar
way of looking at things.

I'm going to hand your letter around among my
colleagues here and if something turns up that might be of
use to you I will let you know.

Yours very truly,

C.G. Jung.

---

THE WHITE HOUSE
WASHINGTON

February 24, 1943.

Dear Mr. President:

I am sending herewith a photograph
taken of us on my recent trip. I thought
you might like to have a copy.

With my warm regards,

Always sincerely,

*[signature]*

His Excellency
Getulio Vargas
President of the United States of Brazil.

Enclosure.

---

**LOAN AGREEMENT**

THE GALLERY OF MODERN ART INCLUDING THE HUNTINGTON HARTFORD COLLECTION   COLUMBUS CIRCLE   NEW YORK 10019

Request for Loan from:   M. and Mme. Dali
Port Lligat — Cadaques
Prov. de Gerona, Espagne

Exhibition:   Salvador Dali 1918 – 1965
To arrive no later than   December 1, 1965
To be returned   March 14, 1966 Return address: ?
Shipment via:   Lenars & Co. Paris ?
To be insured by:   Lender ☐   Borrower ☐      through: Lloyds of London, Ltd.
Credit line if different from above:

Are photographs available?   Please send one and bill The Foundation for Modern Art, Inc.
Is a photoengraving available?   Black and white size      Color size

| Museum No. | Artist | Exact Title & Date | Medium & Support | Dimensions Height 1st | Insurance Valuation |
|---|---|---|---|---|---|
| 180.65.17 | Salvador Dali | AUTOPORTRAIT AU COU RAPHAELIQUE | huile s/toile | 53 x 41.5cm. | 40.000 |

KINDLY FILL IN THE MISSING DATA, THANK YOU.

*[signature Salvador Dali]*

return one copy to:
THE REGISTRAR
GALLERY OF MODERN ART
2 Columbus Circle, N.Y. 19, N.Y.

Lender's Signature *[Gala Dali]*

Title

Date
Telephone: 212-LT-1-2311

Please See Reverse Side

The Foundation for Modern Art, Inc.

---

along these modern ways' takes on special significance coming from the pen of the father of analytical psychology.

As far as 20th-century politicians are concerned, autograph letters are generally very rare, especially from their period in office. With some American presidents, there are barely a dozen known examples. This is not, however, the case with Franklin D. Roosevelt (1882–1945), even though the majority of his letters were typed. The one reproduced above right, on headed White House notepaper, is striking because it is addressed to his Brazilian counterpart, President Getúlio Vargas (1883–1954).

Finding one document containing the signatures of a famous couple is far rarer than one might imagine. A fine example can be seen on the left: an authorization for the loan of a painting signed jointly by Salvador Dalí (1904–89) and his wife Gala in 1965.

Some letterheads can add interest to a piece even if the content is nothing special. The letter on page 20 (above left), from the Futurist Italian poet Filippo Tommaso Marinetti (1876–1944), is written on the notepaper of the magazine *Il Futurismo*. It features a reproduction of the famous 'fist' by Futurist painter and sculptor Umberto Boccioni (1882–1916) – a key symbol of this important artistic and literary movement, which was founded in Italy in the

▼ Carl Gustav Jung, typewritten letter signed, 1949.
▲ Franklin D. Roosevelt, typewritten letter signed, 1943.
◄ Salvador Dalí and Gala Dalí, typewritten document signed, 1965.

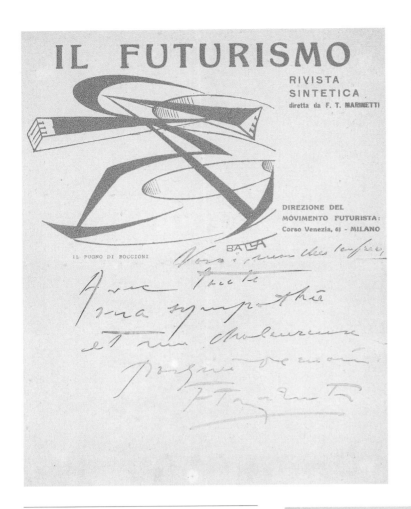

▲ Filippo Tommaso Marinetti, autograph letter signed, c. 1925.

◄ André Breton, duplicated letter signed, 1922.

► Walt Whitman, printed literary quotation signed, 1890.

*Salut au monde !*
What cities the light or warmth penetrates I penetrate those cities myself,
All islands to which birds wing their way I wing my way myself.

Toward you all, in America's name,
I raise high the perpendicular hand, I make the signal,
To remain after me in sight forever,
For all the haunts and homes of men.

*Walt Whitman*

early 20th century – drawn here by the artist Giacomo Balla (1871–1958). Thus an ordinary thank-you note from the founder of the movement becomes a particularly attractive item for a collector.

To a lesser extent, this is also the case with the letter above right, which is signed by André Breton (1896–1966), the leading light of the French Surrealist movement, and is written on the notepaper of the magazine *Littérature*. Breton is reminding his correspondent that his subscription is about to run out – a message that would have been of far less value to us had it been written on ordinary notepaper.

In the 20th century, great writers were often asked to sign literary typescripts. Today, these are the most common form of signed extract or quotation, although of course the passage is far more attractive if it is entirely handwritten. The very fact that such extracts are written from memory, are generally neat and tidy with no corrections, and are frequently well known makes them attractive. Even when they are in printed form, quotations signed by the author can be of great interest, like the Goethe piece on page 84, for instance, or the famous poem *Salut au monde!* by the American Walt Whitman (1819–92) (opposite below), which has a bold signature written in ink.

The most prestigious form of autograph, however, remains the original manuscript of a great literary or musical work, where all the corrections, deletions and additions allow us to trace the thought processes of the author or composer. These first drafts are becoming rarer and rarer on the open market, although there are a few in this book. Collectors have been forced to turn to other types of manuscript – copies made for the printer or, later, for admirers, or even the corrected

proofs revealing the final stages of the creative process.

Two such specimens are reproduced above. The first (top) is a manuscript prepared for the printer, in which the young Truman Capote (1924–84) has copied out his original text without any of the corrections. This great American novelist was barely thirteen years old at the time, and this is his first known work – a three-page short story entitled *Our Parrot is Proud of Her Vocabulary*.

Printed proofs, on which the author may have made his last-minute changes, are equally desirable. The example reproduced here (below) is by Balzac. He used to make so many corrections even at this stage that he

▲▲ Truman Capote, autograph manuscript signed, 1937.
▲ Honoré de Balzac, corrected proofs, 1843.

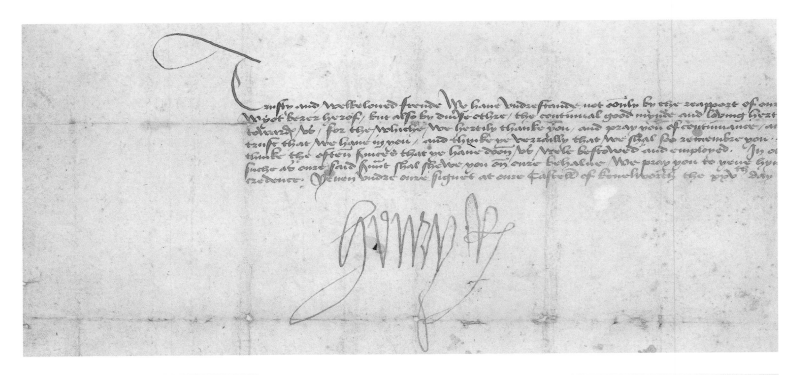

▲ Henry VII, document signed, c. 1495.
► Hirohito, document signed, 1931.

was known as the 'terror of the typographers'. These proofs of *Ursule Mirouet* are annotated and signed by Balzac on the first page ('Make a revision of this page, de Balz.'). They contain relatively few corrections, as this is the final version of a published novel which he was revising in preparation for the 1843 edition of *La Comédie humaine*. All the same, these pages show how thoroughly and methodically Balzac read and corrected the proofs of successive editions of his novels, unlike many authors who never look back at their published works.

With historical figures, the autograph is generally in the form of a signed document. Heads of state validate vast numbers of official letters and documents simply by signing them, and many of these have been kept by the families concerned, who may eventually put them up for sale. In this way, it is even possible to acquire autographs of political figures from the 15th and 16th centuries, whereas the original writings of authors, artists or scholars from the same period – whose signatures were confined to private correspondence – are for the most part virtually unobtainable.

Above is an official letter signed *c.* 1495 by Henry VII of England (1457–1509); here the King is praising the conduct and loyalty of one of his vassals. The right-hand margin has been cut off, and so the actual date is missing. The full signature of this king (here 'Henry R') is very rare, because he generally wrote only his initial.

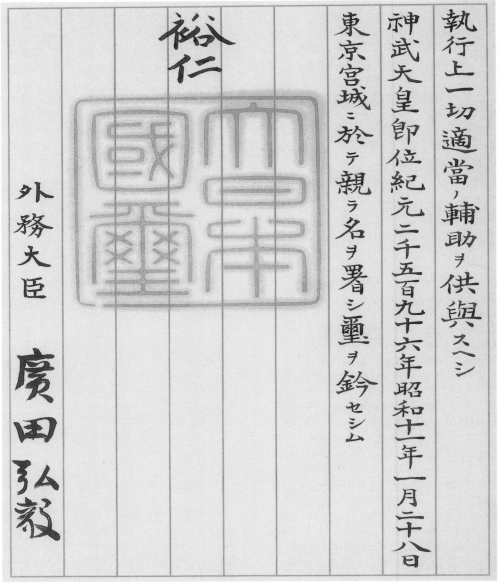

▲ Louis XIV, letter signed, 1686.
► Gregory XIII, letter signed, 1581.

Opposite (right) is the final page of a document signed in 1931 by Emperor Hirohito of Japan (1901–89), confirming the appointment of a Brazilian consul to Yokohama and bearing the Emperor's signature just above the seal. Japanese collectors cannot get enough of the rare autographs of their rulers.

Documents signed personally by Louis XIV (1638–1715) – the so-called 'Sun King' – are considerably rarer that one might expect, bearing in mind the length of his reign. Above is an official letter addressed to Pope Innocent XI (1611–89), which Louis XIV did sign in his own hand. This was not always the case, even when he was writing on state business to other monarchs. He actually employed a number of secretaries who were authorized to imitate his signature on most documents, and his successors did the same.

Many collectors try to obtain a complete series of monarchs' signatures – the British and the French are particularly keen to do so – but rarity makes such collections very difficult to assemble. The document reproduced on page 23 (below right) was signed by Gregory XIII (1502–85). He gave us the Gregorian calendar and his historical role makes him a popular choice, but once again such documents are difficult to obtain. This has meant that, over the last fifty years or so, very few collectors have attempted systematically to acquire autographs of all the pontiffs since 1400. Rosine and Renato Saggiori – to whom we owe a great deal of our knowledge about autographs – are the exception: they have been able to put together a more or less complete series, which is a unique accomplishment for private collectors.

Among all the personal documents, cheques have a little niche of their own. For almost two centuries now, most famous people have had occasion to sign them, and some collectors even specialize in them. Such pieces are relatively affordable, are more interesting than plain signatures, and in certain cases can be quite valuable. The four cheques reproduced in this volume cover a period of one hundred and forty years, during which time the use of this kind of document became more and more widespread. The oldest is the one signed by English poet Percy Bysshe Shelley (1792–1822), dated 1818 and reproduced on page 98. Then comes a cheque for five pounds, made out to himself and signed by Charles Dickens (1812–70) just one year before his death. The third cheque was made out by American composer George Gershwin (1898–1937) to the publisher Alfred Knopf in 1929, and the fourth is signed by Hollywood icon Marilyn Monroe (1926–62), in settlement of her telephone bill of $12.18. Cheques written by such prominent people can take a place of honour in any collection, and some – for instance, those bearing the signatures of George Washington (1732–99) and Abraham Lincoln (1809–65) – regularly fetch record prices in the USA, where certain enthusiasts such as bankers concentrate on financial documents.

Envelopes are less popular and tend to be regarded as a minor form of autograph, particularly when they are unsigned. Occasionally, however, they can be significant, as is the case with the envelope

◀◀◀ Charles Dickens, autograph cheque signed, 1869.
◀◀ George Gershwin, autograph cheque signed, 1929.
◀ Marilyn Monroe, typed cheque signed, 1957.
▶ Anton Chekhov, autograph envelope, 1904.

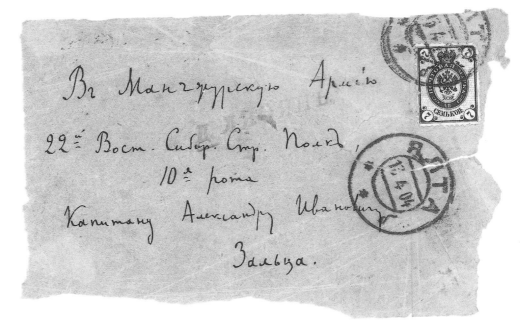

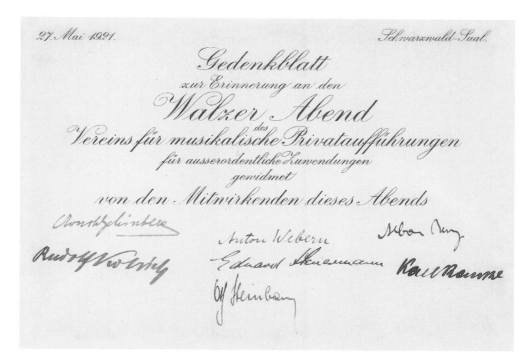

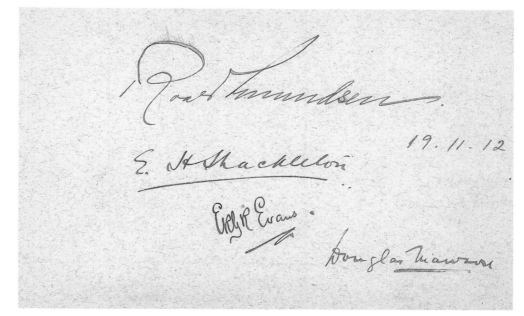

addressed by Franz Kafka to Felice Bauer (on page 11). The same may be said of the one on the opposite page (below right), addressed by Anton Chekhov (1860–1904) to a young soldier in the Manchurian army. The playwright's widow, actress Olga Knipper, who was a great interpreter of his female roles, gave it to an Argentinian admirer two years after her husband's death. Chekhov autographs are very rare, and this one – written in the year of his death – is still a prized specimen of his handwriting.

The least attractive autograph for a collector is a simple signature on a card or a scrap of paper. But this form can be well worth acquiring if the signature belongs to a particular kind of celebrity – for instance,

someone who rarely signed anything. The signature of Chinese soldier and statesman Mao Tse-tung (1893–1976) (top left) is one of those rarities. It was obtained by the wife of a politician during a visit to China, and was written on her notepad. Mao's skill at calligraphy was a feature of his popularity in his homeland, and the Chinese were able to admire his writing on large posters. The vigour of the signature gives us some idea of this particular quality.

The signature of the American aviation pioneer Wilbur Wright (1867–1912) (below left), who died long before his brother Orville (1871–1948), is also much in demand in the USA, where there are many collectors who are interested only in signatures – the most

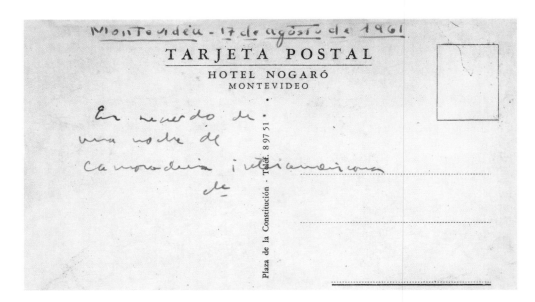

affordable of the various forms of autograph – and often put them in frames together with portraits of the signatories.

A far less common variation on this form is a combination of signatures on a single document, which can be extremely desirable. For instance, the invitation to a musical soirée on page 25 (above right), which brings together the names of three great atonal Austrian-born composers: Arnold Schoenberg (1874–1951), Anton Webern (1883–1945) and Alban Berg (1885–1935). One very rarely finds these three signatures together, and so this piece is altogether exceptional. Similarly, the two great rivals in the quest to conquer the Antarctic, the Norwegian Roald Amundsen (1872–1928) and the Briton Ernest Shackleton (1874–1922) could only join forces on the same page of an album (page 25, below right). The two explorers signed at different times, and the page also contains the signatures of two fellow English polar explorers named Evans and Mawson.

Signatures may be combined because the people concerned happened to be in the same place at the same time, but sometimes a collector may spend years gathering together on a single sheet the signatures that he or she considers valuable. For the last twenty years, many American collectors have been trying to combine the signatures of all the living ex-presidents of the USA, who have become more numerous in recent times than at any other period in history.

The piece reproduced top left is unusual and important for several reasons: it unites the signatures of the 'big three' of the Paris Peace Conference in 1919 – the US President Woodrow Wilson (1856–1924), the British Prime Minister David Lloyd George (1863–1945), and the French Premier Georges Clemenceau (1841–1929) – as well as that of Marshal Ferdinand Foch (1851–1929). Just this combination alone, rare in itself, would make the piece interesting, but almost thirty years later the family that owned it asked President

Harry S. Truman (1884–1972) to add his own signature, which he did with the comment: 'It is a very great pleasure to sign the page with these great men.'

Along with signatures, but more highly prized by enthusiasts, are inscriptions, often written on the flyleaf of a book, but also on plain cards or sheets of paper. Inscriptions may be important, particularly when the dedicatee is also famous. Collectors have become more and more attracted to what the Americans call a good 'association', i.e. a piece that links together two or three well-known names. About fifteen years ago, all records were broken at a public sale of a first edition of *Les Fleurs du mal* which bore the following inscription: 'To Eugène

▶▶ Woodrow Wilson, Ferdinand Foch, David Lloyd George and Georges Clemenceau, signatures, and Harry S. Truman, inscription and signature, 1919–47.
▲▲ Ernesto 'Che' Guevara, postcard inscribed and signed, 1961.
▼ Martin Luther King, inscription and signature, c. 1961.
▲ Bertolt Brecht, autograph quotation signed, 1955.

Delacroix, as a token of eternal admiration, Charles Baudelaire'. Most inscriptions, however, are devoted to unknown recipients, like the one opposite (below left) from American civil rights leader Martin Luther King (1929–68) to an English Catholic priest. If they should also include a particular thought or a literary quotation – as is the case with the inscription by German playwright Bertolt Brecht (1898–1956), also reproduced opposite (below right) – then of course that will add an extra dimension. Among the mythical figures of the second half of the 20th century, autographs by Ernesto Guevara (1928–67) are very rare and in high demand. His tiny signature, 'Che', appears under three handwritten lines (opposite, above right): 'In memory of an evening of inter-American camaraderie', Montevideo, August 1961.

Just as authors often copy out thoughts or quotations in albums or for inscriptions, so too do composers and musicians. Since the early 19th century, they have taken to writing out a few bars as the most polite response to requests for an autograph.

During the Romantic period, it was regarded as a tasteful occupation for young (and even not so young) ladies to keep albums in which they collected contributions from the great artists, writers and musicians of their time. The higher the lady was on the social scale, the longer the 'contribution'. For more than a hundred years, from around 1820 until 1930, this fashion produced millions of lines and bars from all the great writers and composers. It was only after the Second World War that the custom died out.

Nowadays, music is perhaps the domain that attracts the largest number of collectors worldwide. It is a universal language which can be understood just as well in Europe, the USA and Japan, and musical scores in the handwriting of the great composers are extremely popular. The finest pieces are fought over tooth and nail by museums, universities, libraries and private collectors all over the world. Complete manuscripts of major works are far beyond the reach of most enthusiasts.

On this page are two musical quotations of different character. That of Arturo Toscanini (1867–1957) (above right), written in Montevideo in 1903, shows the famous young conductor going to a great deal of trouble writing several bars on the page of an album. The single bar signed by the Russian composer Sergei Prokofiev (1891–1953) c. 1930 (below right) offers a striking contrast.

◀ Arturo Toscanini, autograph musical quotation signed, 1903.
▶ Sergei Prokofiev, autograph musical quotation signed, c. 1930.

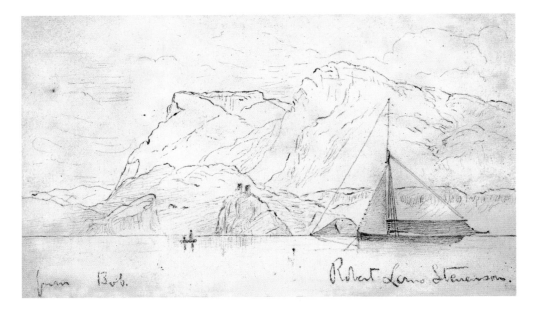

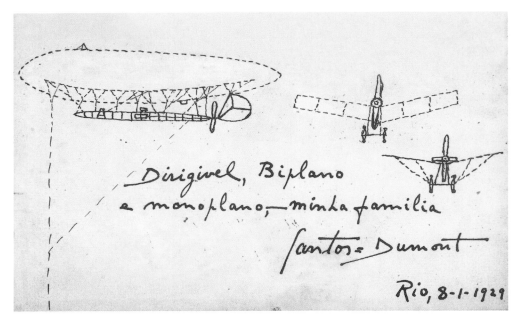

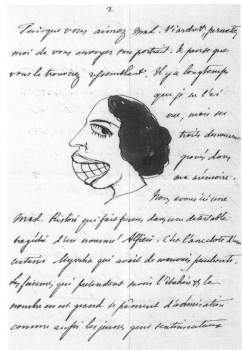

▼ Robert Louis Stevenson, signed drawing, c. 1890.
◄ Alberto Santos-Dumont, signed autograph drawing with inscription, 1929.
▲ Prosper Mérimée, autograph letter signed, with drawing, 1855.

A single note, however, is enough to increase the value of a composer's signature tenfold.

The autograph comes closest to being a work of art in itself when it is combined with a drawing or a photograph. Some writers are also gifted artists, ranging from amateur to virtuoso. Such works used to be regarded as minor, but nowadays there is a great deal of interest in them, and over the last twenty years or so several important books have been devoted to them. Until then, with the exceptions of the French writers Victor Hugo (1802–85), Jean Cocteau (1889–1963) and Antoine de Saint-Exupéry (1900–44), whose talents were generally recognized, authors' drawings had merely been the subject of curiosity.

The most avid collectors now seize on pieces in which authors, artists and sometimes even scientists and musicians embellish their writings with illustrations. Before photography became so popular, drawings were the principal means of fixing an image, and this is why there were so many amateur artists during the first half of the 19th century. Scottish author and poet Robert Louis Stevenson (1850–94), for instance, author of *Treasure Island* (1883) and *Dr Jekyll and Mr Hyde* (1886), was one of the great 19th-century novelists who loved to draw. The detailed landscape (above left), which is difficult for us to identify now, contains a very precise outline of cliffs, with a sailing boat in the foreground. Perhaps it was a familiar sight to the recipient of the picture.

Below that, on the left, is an album page drawn by the Brazilian aviator Alberto Santos-Dumont (1873–1932), who describes his inventions as his 'family': the airship, the biplane and the monoplane. In France

he was recognized as having accomplished the first officially monitored flight of a machine heavier than air in 1906, but for the last fifty years his accomplishments were systematically downgraded in the USA in order to push forward the claims of the Wright brothers.

Prosper Mérimée (1803–70), the author of *Carmen* (1846) – which inspired French composer Georges Bizet's (1838–75) famous opera – was a fine artist, who sometimes expressed his ideas through cartoons. The illustrated letter reproduced above right, addressed to an English lady, contains a cruel portrait of the famous singer Pauline Viardot: 'Since you like Viardot so much, allow me to send you her portrait. I think you will find it's a good likeness. It's a long time since I last saw her, but her features remain engraved on my memory.' A number of French authors from the Romantic period, such as Alfred de Musset (1810–57) and George Sand (1804–76), were almost as gifted as Mérimée and practised their art assiduously.

As far as professional artists are concerned, collectors are usually on the lookout for signed drawings. An American enthusiast, for example, succeeded in acquiring a single sheet (opposite, below right) on which the creators of Snoopy (Charles Schulz), Batman (Bob Kane), the Pink Panther (Fritz Freleng) and

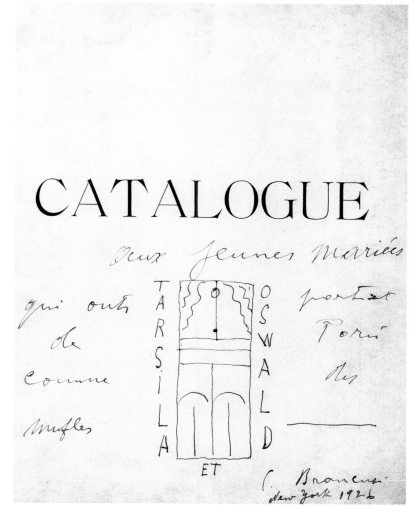

Woody Woodpecker (Walter Lantz) had drawn their iconic characters, which are among the most popular of the 20th century.

Autograph collectors regard an artist's drawings as a good alternative to a manuscript, because it has the same material basis – paper – and also follows a particular pattern. There are many artists prior to the 19th century whose letters are extremely rare, but a signed or unsigned drawing can sometimes compensate for the absence of a text. It is no coincidence that the great autograph collectors of former times were also frequently great collectors of drawings.

The magnificent grisaille wash drawing above left, representing Robinson Crusoe on his desert island, is of such quality that leading experts in the field are now in agreement that it is an early work by the great English writer and artist William Blake (1757–1827), whose autographs are now virtually unobtainable. There are two other known drawings of Robinson Crusoe by Blake.

Above right, Constantin Brancusi (1876–1957) has inscribed the flyleaf of the catalogue for a New York exhibition in 1926. He has decorated it with a drawing

reminiscent of *The Kiss*, one of this Romanian sculptor's major works depicting an entwined couple. Brancusi was amusing himself by identifying the male figure with his friend Oswald de Andrade (1890–1954), the Brazilian poet, and the female with Oswald's wife Tarsila do Amaral (1886–1973), a well-known Brazilian painter. The inscription, in somewhat broken French, reads: 'To the young married couple who have left Paris like skunks.' Brancusi autographs and drawings are rare, but those based on a work as important as *The Kiss* are even more unique.

The ubiquity of the image in the 20th century revolutionized culture, and inevitably had a profound effect on the tastes of autograph collectors. For the last thirty years, the increasing popularity of signed photographs, which had previously not been held in particularly high esteem, has made the best examples into extremely appealing objects. The value of this form of autograph has increased rapidly in recent times, and there are some enthusiasts who devote themselves to it exclusively. It must therefore be given its proper place in this book, in order to reflect a new and very clear trend among

▼ William Blake, drawing, c.1785.
▲▲ Constantin Brancusi, autograph message with signed drawing, 1926.
▲ Charles Schulz, Bob Kane, Fritz Freleng and Walt Lantz, signed drawings, c.1990.

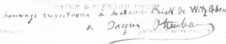

modern collectors all over the world. The following pages contain photographs by various artists, some famous and some forgotten, and will convey the degree to which the custom of dedicating portraits has expanded since the 1860s.

An American journalist has suggested that the photographs which celebrities chose to inscribe had to correspond to the image they had of themselves, or show them 'as they wanted to be seen'. This may not always be the case, but it is true of the majority of portraits reproduced in this book.

From the 1860s onwards, photography enabled the general public – for whom the price of a painting would have been prohibitive – to gain access to portraits that were both affordable and perfectly accurate. Families and friends were seized by a collective obsession as they set about exchanging portraits in the *carte de visite* format. Albums presented a vast parade of parents, children and relations, but also of contemporary celebrities, whose images were published and sold in large quantities by studios such as Disdéri and Nadar. The idea of enhancing these images with the signature of the celebrity appears to have mushroomed at the same time, and so along with the *carte de visite* format, the autograph took on a new dimension linking image to handwriting.

Thanks to this new craze of the 1860s, modern collectors are now able to find signed portraits of great men and women who died a century and a half ago. On this page you will see a selection of photographs all in the same format and signed by some of the great names of the 19th century: above left, Mayer and Pierson's full-length inscribed portrait of the composer Jacques Offenbach (1819–80), whose operettas were extremely popular during the Second Empire; above right, the English poet Robert Browning (1812–89), whose signed photographs are attractive to many collectors; below left, a portrait of the great Hungarian composer Franz Liszt (1811–86); and below right a rare photograph of the American author and philosopher Ralph Waldo Emerson (1803–82).

From the 1890s, the popularity of the postcard gave collectors a new medium through which to gather the signatures of great figures. The photographs were no longer original prints but photomechanical reproductions,

▼ ▼ Jacques Offenbach, signed photograph c. 1860.
▲ ▲ Robert Browning, signed photograph, c. 1865.
▼ Franz Liszt, signed photograph, c. 1865.
▲ Ralph Waldo Emerson, signed photograph, c. 1868.

and all over the world people started writing to celebrities and asking them to sign postcards. In this way, fans who lived thousands of miles away from their heroes could nevertheless acquire their signatures.

The postcard signed by French writer Jules Verne (1828–1905) (above left) was taken from an original negative by Paul Nadar (1856–1939) – the son of Félix Tournachon (1820–1910), whose pseudonym was Nadar – and reproduced as a photogravure. Thanks to the popularity of his books, Verne's autographs are in demand all over the world. This is also true of his contemporary Leo Tolstoy (1828–1910) (above right), perhaps the most famous novelist of his time. During the last few years of his life, the Russian novelist responded conscientiously to most requests for his autograph, and he signed this one for a Portuguese admirer. Even the great Irish dramatist George Bernard Shaw (1856–1950) – whose malevolence towards autograph collectors was legendary – did occasionally relent (below left), and the postcard (below right) signed by the American artist Andy Warhol (1928–87) shows that the craze had still not died down in the 1960s.

Photos embellished with forged signatures are a relatively new phenomenon, and are generally restricted to the worlds of film, sport and pop music. With other forms of forged document, however, the means are not available to everybody. It is easy enough to copy a simple signature and put it on a photograph or cheque, but to copy someone's handwriting in a complete letter, for example, is an immensely complex task. Apart from the problem of the handwriting itself, the text must not contain any anachronisms, the paper must belong to the correct period, and the ink must be of the right colour and composition. This level of skill frequently eludes the forgers. Any such undertaking would only be worthwhile if one expected to sell the document for a high price, but this in turn will drive the forger into making the contents unusually interesting – sometimes too interesting – and such autographs may then seem too good to be true, arousing the suspicions of the collector.

Detecting forgeries requires a trained eye and experience. Suspect pieces will almost certainly be in a script that looks like it has been drawn rather than written, is sometimes even shaky, and betrays the conscious efforts of the forger. The big scandals – which have been quite uncommon – date mainly from the 19th century except in the USA, where clever 20th-century forgers succeeded in creating high-quality letters of historical and literary interest.

In the most sensational affair of recent times, the documents were offered not to collectors but to the press. These were the famous Hitler diaries which were 'discovered' in Germany during the 1980s – a find which was trumpeted to the world by a popular news magazine. Kenneth Rendell – perhaps the leading autograph dealer in America – proved for one of his own country's magazines that the writings attributed to Hitler could not be authentic, and the German journalists were forced to admit to one of the most calamitous media blunders of the 20th century.

▼▼ Jules Verne, signed photograph, c. 1900.
▲▲ Leo Tolstoy, signed photograph, c. 1906.
▼ George Bernard Shaw, signed photograph, c. 1925.
▲ Andy Warhol, signed photograph, c. 1968.

Some 19th- and 20th-century pieces have a double attraction – they are portraits photographed by well-known photographers and signed by their famous subjects. The following pages contain a few of them, and there are a number of others within the main body of the text. The adolescent playing the violin (overleaf, above right) is Xie Kitchin,

one of Lewis Carroll's (1832–98) favourite models. On the back of the photograph, the famous author, whose real name was Charles L. Dodgson, has written an inscription to the young girl's mother, dated 1876, and has signed it 'the Artist' – a clear indication that, as an accomplished photographer, this is precisely what Carroll considered himself to be.

Above left, the portrait of the Comtesse de Castiglione (1837–99) is one of a famous series taken over the course of forty years by Pierson, Napoleon III's (1808–73) favourite photographer. Dated 1895, when this famous courtesan's beauty had already faded, it has an inscription on the back in pencil for the suitor to whom it was dedicated. Underneath the portrait, La Castiglione has written 'A la montagne!' [To the mountains!]. Although it is unsigned, the quality of this portrait and its inscription make it quite remarkable.

During the 1870s, a new format of photographic portraits swept Europe and the USA: cabinet cards. These did not supplant the *carte de visite*, which remained in fashion at the beginning of the 20th century, but they broadened the choice and were twice the size.

Opposite (above left), in this format, is an inscribed portrait of Sarah Bernhardt (1844–1923), undoubtedly the most admired actress of her time, posing on stage *c.* 1885 and photographed by the Nadar studio

▲ Pierson, photograph of the Comtesse de Castiglione, albumen print with pencil inscription on the back and below the portrait, 1895.
◀ Lewis Carroll (Charles L. Dodgson), Xie Kitchin playing the violin, albumen print inscribed, 1876.

▲ Nadar, Sarah Bernhardt on stage c.1885, inscribed and signed by Sarah Bernhardt, c.1885.
◄ Arnold Genthe, portrait of Jack London, signed by the photographer and the author, c.1905.
► Man Ray, portrait of Paul Valéry, signed by the photographer, and inscribed with autograph verse and signature by the poet, c.1920.
►► Frederick Evans, portrait of Aubrey Beardsley, signed by Beardsley, c.1896.

(when Félix's son Paul had already taken charge of all the negatives).

Portraits of celebrities taken by great photographers are tempting more and more photograph collectors, who are almost as numerous and often wealthier than autograph-lovers, since prices on the photography market are generally higher. The value of a piece relates more to the quality of the original print than to any autograph by the subject, and in this respect it appeals to a very different kind of collector. In such cases, inscriptions and signatures do not affect the price of the print, which may be signed by both the sitter and the photographer, as in the example above right of the American novelist Jack London (1876–1916) taken by his compatriot, the great photographer Arnold Genthe. It is the same with the portrait (below left) of Paul Valéry (1871–1945) taken by Man Ray (1890–1976), arguably the most famous photographer of the 20th century. This photograph, signed by Man Ray, bears a beautiful inscription in verse by Valéry:

*Je suis jeune il est vrai, sur ma photographie…*
*Hélas! Bien fol est qui s'y fie!*
*Ce monsieur frais et net, Fabre, m'est étranger,*
*Paul Valéry*

[I am young, it is true, on this photo of me…
Alas! He who trusts it is mad as can be!
This fresh clean man, Fabre, is a stranger to me,
Paul Valéry]

Above is a photograph of Aubrey Beardsley (1872–98) taken by the English photographer Frederick Evans (1853–1943). This original print – not signed by the photographer – shows the illustrator, famous for his work on the books of Oscar Wilde, at the age of twenty-four. Barely two years later he was dead, and his autographs (particularly signed photographs) are extremely difficult to get hold of.

After the 1860s, countless highly competent photographic studios became established in Europe and the USA, and even

if they had no artistic pretensions, many of them acquired a good reputation through the high-quality finish they gave to their portraits. This is certainly the case with the three portraits reproduced here, and even if the photographers are not as well known now as those on the previous pages, nevertheless they produced fine work in their own specialized field.

The inventions of Thomas Edison (1847–1931) and Alexander Graham Bell (1847–1922), two Americans born in the same year, revolutionized the lives and habits of people living at the end of the 19th century. Edison's gramophone and incandescent light bulb and Bell's telephone symbolized the technical advances of an age which regarded such progress as the be-all and end-all. The large and very official-looking photograph of Edison (above right) is one of the best-known portraits of him, and is typical of the formal poses favoured by American portraitists. It bears his famous 'umbrella' signature, with the flourish above the name, and it shows him at the age of fifty-seven, at the height of his fame, when more than a thousand patents had been issued in his name. The magnificent photograph of

Bell (above left) was taken by Harris & Ewing, a studio in Washington which was patronized by American presidents for almost one hundred years.

The photographer Civitadini does not figure among Italy's top names at the beginning of the 20th century, but his portrait of the famous writer Gabriele D'Annunzio (1863–1938) (right) deserves a place in the highest ranks of formal portraits during that period. It is dedicated to an ambassador with whom D'Annunzio was on close terms, marking the tenth anniversary of the 'Great Flight', which he had undertaken in 1918; the aviator poet had flown over Vienna to drop more than 400,000 leaflets on the enemy capital. D'Annunzio was one of the great letter-writers of the 20th century. There are vast numbers of his letters, often fascinating, but they remain extremely popular among Italian collectors, who have become more numerous and more active in the markets over the last few decades.

Photographs with signatures and inscriptions on the back are generally less prized than those signed on the front, simply because the full effect cannot be taken in at a single glance. Nevertheless, some are of great

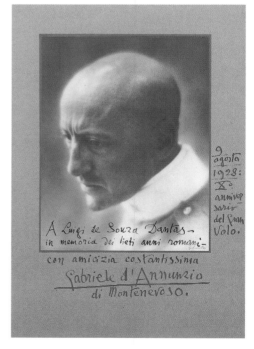

▼ Alexander Graham Bell, signed photograph, c. 1915.
▲▲ Thomas Edison, signed photograph, c. 1900.
▲ Gabriele D'Annunzio, inscribed and signed photograph, 1928.

interest as certain celebrities only signed their portraits on the back. On this page is a portrait of the Danish author Hans Christian Andersen (1805–75), whose cabinet card is remarkably well preserved. The photograph was taken in Copenhagen *c.* 1870, and Andersen dedicated it with a friendly inscription to an English admirer. Signed photographs of Virginia Woolf (1882–1941) are extremely uncommon and, in the circumstances, even a portrait signed on the back has become a highly desirable piece. This is even more so when – as with the

portrait reproduced above – it is one of the best-known likenesses of her.

An original print on a postcard, on the other hand, such as the amusing portrait of Josephine Baker (1906–75) above right, is bound to be signed on the back and is still very attractive for collectors. At the time – in the 1930s when she was at the peak of her fame – the great singer and dancer was touring Europe on an Italian liner. For quite some time now, many American collectors have been specializing in Afro-American celebrities such as Baker.

▶ ▶ Hans Christian Andersen, signed photograph, *c.* 1870.

▶ Virginia Woolf, signed photograph, *c.* 1939.

▲ Josephine Baker, signed photograph, *c.* 1932.

▼▼ Cole Porter, signed photograph, c. 1955.
▼ Frank Sinatra, signed photograph, c. 1939.
▲ Pelé, signed photograph, c. 1960.
◄ Gagarin, Popovich, Nikolaiev and Leonov, signed photograph, c. 1962.

Certain areas of activity are particularly popular among young collectors, who tend to be attracted by the media celebrities of the time – for instance in sport or pop music. Their fame is often local and almost always ephemeral, but some do achieve lasting and universal renown. This is true of certain footballers, boxers and racing drivers, whose portraits are always in demand internationally. Edson Arantes Do Nascimento (b. 1940) – better known as Pelé – is one such figure, and the photograph above is dedicated to a trainer whom he regarded 'as a father'. Other markets are consistent but limited to their country of origin – such as baseball, which fascinates Americans (who pay huge sums for the best pieces), but leaves the rest of the world indifferent.

For twenty years, the conquest of space made Russian and American astronauts into household names. After the 1980s, however, their exploits began to seem less sensational and the fame of the pioneers and their successors faded away. Great names like Yuri Gagarin (1934–68) and Neil Armstrong (b. 1930) have remained in demand, but the majority of space explorers are no longer of any interest except to specialists, nearly all of whom are American. Gagarin was the first man to travel in space, and the Soviet Union exploited his image to the full. He and the other Russian space pioneers travelled all over the world and sometimes signed group photographs like the one on the left, showing Gagarin, Popovich, Nikolaiev and Leonov.

The great names of rock and pop music arouse worldwide interest, and the manuscripts of famous songs that have appeared on the market in the last ten years have raised record prices. Premature death

has added considerably to the value of autographs by Jimi Hendrix (1942–70), Janis Joplin (1943–70), Jim Morrison (1943–71), Bob Marley (1945–81), and even Elvis Presley and John Lennon (1940–80). A single page of the lyrics of *Nowhere Man*, one of Lennon's hits of the 1960s, recently fetched just under half a million dollars at a public sale. Autographs of Bob Dylan and Paul McCartney (b. 1942) consistently maintain their value, as do those of the Rolling Stones (who along with the Beatles have a section of their own in this book, on pages 264–265). The rock and pop market is so well established that the big British and American auction houses conduct regular sales.

Among the singers of earlier generations, the popularity of Frank Sinatra (1915–98) was matched in the USA only by that of Bing Crosby (1904–77), who preceded him by a few years. Along with Irving Berlin (1888–1989), the best-known American composer in the 1940s and 1950s was undoubtedly Cole Porter (1891–1964) (above, far left). Autographs and especially signed photographs of all these celebrities remain very popular.

Many autograph collectors are fascinated by the cinema, perhaps because they feel close to the actors who have been immortalized by the silver screen. Letters from the great stars, however, are rare, and generally the only autographs available are in the form of album pages or signed photographs. The biggest names of all have usually employed armies of secretaries to deal

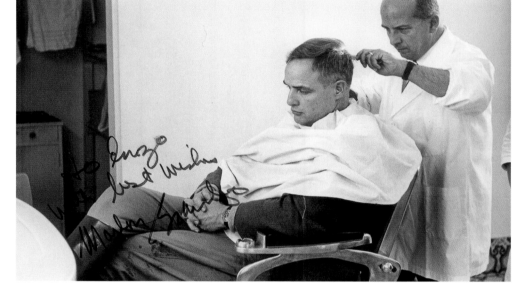

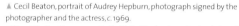

▲ Cecil Beaton, portrait of Audrey Hepburn, photograph signed by the photographer and the actress, c.1969.
◀ Henri Cartier-Bresson, portrait of John Huston, inscribed and signed by Huston, c.1960.
◀◀ Humphrey Bogart, signed photograph, c.1940.
▶ Marlon Brando, signed photograph (by Bob Penn), c.1965.

with demands for inscribed photographs, but the majority of these do not bear autograph signatures. Almost all the 'signed' portraits of Jean Harlow (1911–37), for instance, were actually signed by her mother.

Since 1975, some very convincing forgeries have been produced in the USA, especially in California. This is an area where one needs to take very great care, but the best portraits are of such high quality that they are well worth the high prices paid by many collectors, particularly in America.

The photographs reproduced on this page include two more that have been signed by famous photographers. The portrait of Audrey Hepburn (1929–93) in *My Fair Lady* (1964) (above left) was taken by Cecil Beaton (1904–80), who designed the costumes for the film, and whose signature in red pencil can be seen directly underneath the photograph. The inscription to a Swiss friend of the actress is written on the mount. Above centre is a portrait of the American film director John Huston (1906–87) taken by Henri Cartier-Bresson (1908–2004) and inscribed by Huston to a colleague.

Humphrey Bogart (1899–1957) and Marlon Brando (1924–2004) have become almost mythical figures for critics and the general public alike. Authentic Bogart autographs are rare, but the one top right was dedicated personally to a Brazilian journalist during the 1940s. Brando was notoriously

unobliging to his fans, and signed almost exclusively for friends. He dedicated the photograph above to Enzo, his Italian hairdresser, seen here hard at work during the filming of John Huston's *Reflections in a Golden Eye* (1967).

Directors are generally far less popular than actors with the majority of collectors. The few, mainly European enthusiasts who are interested in the great directors can still acquire quite outstanding pieces for relatively modest prices. Undoubtedly this is one of the most rewarding areas for any cinephile just starting out as a collector.

In the second half of the 20th century, contracts signed with producers seem to be the most common form of autograph by American actors and directors. As in the rock and pop market, these are a solid investment and form a 'genre' in themselves. In the USA

there are auctions devoted exclusively to the cinema.

As can be seen here, there is a wide range of celebrities whose signed photographs are available to the collector: singers, politicians, writers, actors, composers, artists and even philosophers – almost all the great names of the 20th century have at one time or another, with good or less good grace, given in to the demands of their fans and their friends.

The portrait overleaf (above left) of the winner of the Nobel Prize for Literature in 1982, Gabriel García Márquez (b. 1928), shows that even authors are subjected to the constant pressures of stardom. His inscription on a photograph taken in Stockholm on the occasion of the awards ceremony refers to 'that horrible day'.

Enthusiasts much prefer original prints to printed copies. The least popular photographs

▲ Gabriel García Márquez, signed photograph, 1982.
◀ Dmitri Shostakovich, signed photograph, c. 1955.
◀◀ Heitor Villa-Lobos, signed photograph, 1955.
► William Faulkner, signed printed photograph, c. 1964.
►► Martin Heidegger, signed photograph, c. 1965.

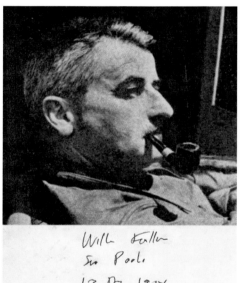
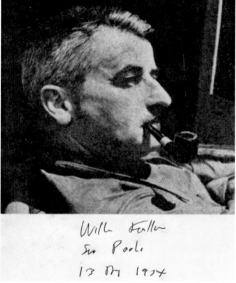

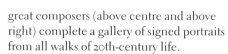

are those cut out of newspapers or magazines, as the technical quality is generally extremely low. But signed photographs taken from books are more acceptable, as with that of William Faulkner (1897–1962) below left. This was obtained by a Brazilian admirer when Faulkner visited São Paulo in 1954. The portrait to its right is signed by Martin Heidegger (1889–1976), who was arguably Germany's greatest 20th-century philosopher and whose long life yielded quite a large number of autographs.

Pieces signed by the Russian composer Dmitri Shostakovich (1906–75) are popular among admirers of his work, which occupies an outstanding place in the history of 20th-century music. Equally in demand are autographs by the greatest South American composer, the Brazilian Heitor Villa-Lobos (1887–1959). The photographs of these two

great composers (above centre and above right) complete a gallery of signed portraits from all walks of 20th-century life.

While we are on the subject of photographs bearing the signatures of contemporary celebrities, we must turn to the vexed question of the autopen. This diabolical gadget holds a pen and reproduces the signatures of American presidents from the last forty years. Their signatures, written in ink after a model autograph of each president, can only be identified as the work of the autopen if one specimen is superimposed on another: they will be absolutely identical in every detail, which can never happen if the signing is by hand. These machines can sign thousands of documents and photographs a day, and are now used all over the world by public figures. Unlike facsimiles, which are printed, these

inked autopen signatures deceive many collectors, especially in the USA, and they are beginning to appear on the scene in Europe as well, most notably in signatures purporting to come from Queen Elizabeth II of England (b. 1926). Facsimiles are also a problem for collectors, as much with letters as with photographs, because some of them can be of a very high quality. One must be wary of impersonal messages, especially thank you notes apparently handwritten by 20th-century statesmen such as Winston Churchill (1874–1965) and Charles de Gaulle (1890–1970), and signed photographs without an inscription.

Portraits signed by heads of state or government are often official photographs that have been presented to dignitaries or foreign ambassadors. They are rarely given on demand, and so they are not available to

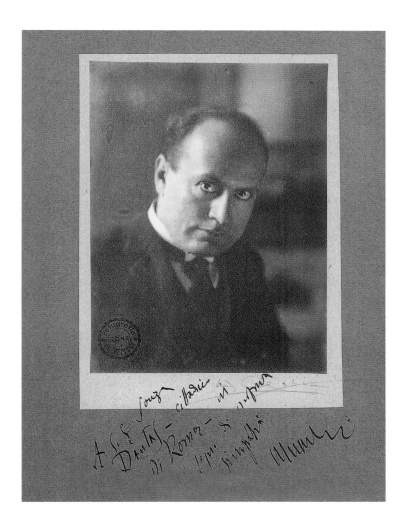

collectors until or unless the families of the recipients decide to sell them, which usually happens one or two generations later.

Most collectors, including myself, stay clear of autographs by Nazi leaders, but there is a group that specializes in this subject. Conversely, other 20th-century dictators such as Joseph Stalin (1879–1953), Juan Perón (1895–1974) and Benito Mussolini (1883–1945), who for more than twenty years made their mark on the history of their respective countries, are represented in this book. Some of the official portraits of these controversial figures may be interesting in themselves, like the photograph of Mussolini reproduced above left, which is dedicated to an ambassador who had become a personal friend and who is addressed as 'citizen of Rome'.

De Gaulle, even before coming to power in France, signed some portraits in England during the Second World War, and the one reproduced here (above right) was taken by a photographer in Edinburgh. His signed photographs are difficult to find, and he is one of the few political figures of 20th-century France whose autographs are still very much in demand.

Pope John Paul II (b. 1920) is a unique phenomenon. He is more popular than most of his predecessors (with the possible exception of John XXIII), and yet strangely his autographs are still relatively rare despite his immense workload throughout his long pontificate. He signed the colour portrait (below right) in his native language on the occasion of his visit to Poland in 1983.

Demand for the autographs of politicians tends to be much less consistent than for those of musicians, artists, scientists and writers of the same period. Collectors tend to lack interest in the political personalities of the last few centuries, other than the major historical figures, most of whom are represented in this book. They are accompanied by a wide range of fascinating characters with whom the reader will briefly come into intimate and sometimes quite unexpected contact.

▼ Benito Mussolini, inscribed and signed photograph, c. 1924.
▲ ▲ Charles de Gaulle, signed photograph, c. 1943.
▲ Pope John Paul II, signed photograph, 1983.

# ALFONSO VII *of Spain* 1104–1157

# ALFONSO IX *of Spain* 1171–1230

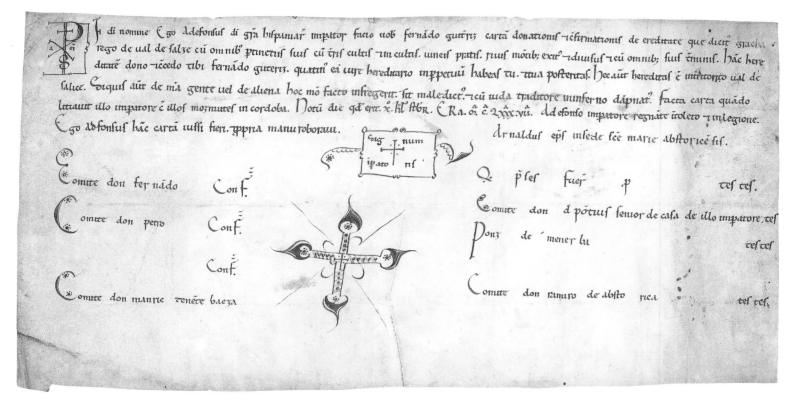

Documents signed by medieval monarchs are extremely rare, simply because the monarchs themselves were often illiterate. Their signature was not essential for the validation of decisions made in writing, which were sometimes ratified simply by scribes or notaries. For a long time charters were authenticated by a seal rather than by the sovereign's own hand.

The documents reproduced here would already be remarkable just for the fact that they date from the 12th century, but they are all the more exceptional because they actually bear the signatures of the two kings. Alfonso VII was King of Castile and León from 1126 until 1157, and made the Moorish kings into

his vassals. The 1149 parchment (above) gives him the title Emperor of the Spains (*Hispaniarum imperator*), referring to the fact that he united the two kingdoms under the same crown. There is a cross inscribed in a cartouche which a notary has certified as being signed in his own hand ('*signum imperatoris propria manu*'). The text itself confirms the rights of the Guterriz family to their land, and pronounces a curse on anyone who defies this decision, condemning them 'to hell along with Judas, the traitor'.

Alfonso IX of León has himself drawn the magnificent lion after which his kingdom is named. This authenticates the parchment reproduced opposite, referring to the rights

of a monastery. Grandson of Alfonso VII, Alfonso IX inherited only the kingdom of León, and it was he who founded the University of Salamanca in 1220 together with his son, the future saint Ferdinand III (1201–52). The latter was canonized in the 17th century, and was responsible for the final reunification of the two Spanish monarchies in 1230, having inherited Castile from his mother and León from his father.

▲ Alfonso VII, document signed on parchment, 1149.
► Alfonso IX, document on parchment, signed with a drawing, 1193.

[In] nomine domini nostri ihesu christi amen. Ego Alfonsus dei gratia rex legionis et gallecie per hoc scriptum perpetuo ualiturum notum facio presentibus et futuris. quod do et concedo pro amore ihesu christe concedo deo et monasterio de arcas. et uobis comitisse dōne aça... pri. et successoribus uestris in perpetuum. hereditatem que uocatur uineiro cum totis suis terminis et directuris nouis et antiquis. ut tam nos quam monasterium de arcas illam hab... uos in secula seculorum. Hoc autem facio pro remedio anime mee et parentum meorum. et quia par... ...ceps effica desido oronum que in iam dicto monasterio domino seruient. Siquis igitur de meo uel alieno genere hoc meum factum infringere... iram dei et regiam indignationem incurrat. et pro ausu temerario pariat parti regie penam... ... Facta carta apud beneuentum ... Era millesima cc. xxxi. Ego rex domini alfonsus hoc scriptum quod fieri iussi proprio robore confirmo.

...po compostellano archiepiscopo existente.

Manrico legionis episcopo.
Johannes ouetensis episcopo.
Lupo astoricensis episcopo.

Gondisaluus ... domino petro uela cancellario.

Comite Gomez ...
Comite Froila ...
Johannes fernandi regis maiordomo.
Petro fradi ... maiordomo.

# CHARLES V *of France* 1338-1380

# CHARLES VI *of France* 1368-1422

# KING EDWARD IV 1442-1483

During the 14th and 15th centuries, European monarchs began to sign some of their own correspondence, as well as important administrative documents. As far as French kings are concerned, the oldest signatures one can hope to find are those of Charles V and his son Charles VI (who went mad *c.* 1392). Such documents, however, are extremely rare, and in the last fifty years only two or three have appeared on the market. The two parchments reproduced above bear the signatures of the father and the son.

In England, Edward IV and his successor Richard III (1452–85) are probably the first monarchs whose signatures are accessible to collectors. However, fewer than ten have become available in the last forty years, and most of those were on documents whose content was somewhat bland.

This is certainly not the case with the letter opposite, written on paper and signed in Latin by Edward IV. It is addressed to the Duke of Milan and accredits the King's envoy Robert Chamberlain Miles.

▲ ▲ Charles V, document signed on parchment, 1378.
▲ Charles VI, document signed on parchment, 1386.
► Edward IV, document signed on paper, 1482.

Serenissime princeps consanguinee et amice car. Salutem et prosperorum successuum incrementa. Obsecutus est nobis quplures annos comiter proba animose et fideliter Dns Robertus Chamberlayn miles. Et quoniam dictum Robertum ob merita in nos sua intime familiarem et nobis optime carum habemus: apprime rogamus Serenitatem vestram si istic se receperit. habet enim in aco terras omnia res intuitu dignas ad principis palacia visere). Velitis eum prosequi quoddam favore ppuo est enim vetasto sanguine nobilis eques strenuus re militari peritus et nobis ut supra maiorem in modum acceptus. Quicquid benefici aut favoris in eum contuleritis id ome in nos collatum existimabimus possimus in eum benefici aut favoris immemores mus q. Valeat memorata Serenitas posfeliciter ex urbe nra Londoniar xxii die Maij Anno dni 1482.

Ricardus R. dei gracia Rex
Anglie et Francie et dominus Hibernie

*I, the King…I, the Queen*

# ISABELLA I *of Spain* 1451-1504

# FERDINAND II *of Spain* 1452-1516

These two Catholic monarchs are mainly remembered as the patrons of explorer Christopher Columbus (1451–1506), but their reign also saw the expulsion of the Moors and Jews in 1492, and the division of the New World between Spain and Portugal through the famous Treaty of Tordesillas. The document reproduced above was signed by both monarchs in June 1494, three days after the treaty had been ratified and less than a year after Columbus's return to Spain. It refers

to the new laws of navigation imposed by this treaty – laws which were of particular relevance to Columbus.

Opposite is a letter signed by Isabella alone in 1500, concerning the purchase of *azulejos* (glazed tiles) from Seville for the Alhambra in Granada, and ordering the chamberlain Sancho de Paredes to pay the two suppliers a sum in excess of ten thousand *maravedis*. Some fifty years ago, the discovery of several hundred documents, in excellent condition, signed by the Queen and

addressed to her chamberlain, brought fresh supplies to a market in which her signature was legendary for its rarity. Items that bear the signatures of both monarchs are much more scarce, especially those whose contents go beyond the daily routine. According to Spanish custom, sovereigns did not sign their first names, but used the formula 'I, the King' and 'I, the Queen'.

▲ Ferdinand II and Isabella I, document signed, 1494.
▶ Isabella I, document signed, 1500.

La Reyna

Sancho de paredes mj camarero yo vos mando que de los tryzientes ochenta e syete mill e qui̇nj̇
entos mrs que vos por mj mandado resçebistes del tesorero morales enla çibdad de sevilla de
ys e pagueys luego a herna martinez vanquero ocho mill e setecientos e quarenta e dos mrs
e medio los quales el ovo de mj por çaso de ocho mill e dozientos e setenta e çinco azulejos quel
ovo dado por mi mandado enla dicha çibdad de sevilla para traer a esta çibdad de granada de los quales
los vijmill e quinjentos e çinquenta e seys son de marca mayor que se venden a vijblancas cada uno que son mjll
mjll e dozientos e quarenta mrs los otros quatro mjll e setecientos diez e nueve he son de mar romjño
que se venden a blanca e media cada uno que son vijmjll e quinjentos e çinqu̇enta e siete e medjo ansi son
todos juntos los suso dichos ocho mjll e setecientos e quarenta e dos mrs e medjo Con ansi mjsmo los
otros mjll e quatroçientos e diez mrs para que los de bernjñolo vez espartero por noder de
e seras en que se fizo el dicho azulejo e dad el nervo al dicho herna mjnjs vijlazio los dichos
mrs e tomad su carta de conosçimj̇ento delos que vijn be de vos ala qual E vnesa mj cedula mando a los
mjs contadores mayores de cuentas que vos esçiaban e pasen en cuenta todos los suso dichos mrs a
los escrivanos de mj camara que vos los descargen de donde vos los tiene vij cargados fecha en el
alhambra de granada a xxv dias de agosto de mjll e quinientos años

yo la reyna

por mandado de la Reyna
fernand de çafra

Conosco yo hernand martines cambiador que resçebi de vos Sancho de paredes camarero de la
Reyna nra señora los ocho mjll e setecientos e quarenta e dos mrs que de la sus posi
ço de çierto azulejo segund se contiene en esta cedula de su alteza suso escripta e otrosy
mjsmo con eso que resçebi de vos otros mjll e quatroçientos diez mrs para dar al dicho lopez
espadero por los quatro azulejos e çiertas obras que hizo para las del dicho azulejo de manera
que son por todos diez mjll e çiento e çinquenta dos mrs medjo e por que es verdad les dicho
vos dí esta carta firmado de mi nonbre fecha en el alhambra de granada
a xxv dias del mes de agosto de mjll e quinientos años

por que se den al dicho azulejo viij V. de xlij m por çierto azulejos que ha dado en juan x por noder de çafra para esta çibdad

*...fifty ducats for the excellent master of painting*
*Raphael of Urbino.*

# RAPHAEL

## 1483-1520

Having been commissioned by Pope Julius II (1443–1513) to decorate the Vatican library, Raphael (whose full name was Raffaello Sanzio) went to Rome in 1508. He spent the last twelve years of his life there. Leo X (1475–1521), who succeeded Julius II in 1513, put him in charge of a major project for the collection of antique marbles and inscriptions, as well as making him architect of St Peter's. Under this pontiff, no expense was spared when it came to works of art, and the Vatican accumulated a vast quantity of treasures.

In 1516, Raphael painted the frescoes of the Camera dell' Incendio for the Vatican chambers. The document reproduced opposite dates from this year: in the name of Leo X, the chancellery of the Holy See is paying the painter for work done in the Vatican chambers. At the bottom of the page, the artist's own handwriting declares: 'I, Raphael, painter, have received the fifty ducats for this month of June.'

Such receipts containing one or two lines are the only specimens of Raphael's handwriting that have been available to collectors for the last hundred years or so. About a dozen are known, but even these documents have been disputed. Some specialists have put forward a theory that a 19th-century forger may have added the lines attributed to Raphael at the bottom of a batch of authentic receipts. But most experts agree that these words are genuinely written in Raphael's hand, and several of these receipts form part of large public collections, and are reproduced in their catalogues.

▶ Raphael, 17th-century French engraving, after original self-portrait of the artist.
▶▶ Raphael, document with autograph line signed, 1516.

RAPHAEL D' VRBIN:

Ipse Raphael pinxit.

P. Stent excudit.

Ferdinandus ponzettus
archidiacon⁹ surrentin⁹ &  Sᵐⁱ dñi pp ᵍnalis
Came̅ apſice presidens  Thesaurarius

SPectabilibus viris dño Augustino chisio & socijs pecuniaᵤ aluminū Sᵗᵉ
Cruciate depositarijs. Saluᵗ. in dño. Auctate ñri thesaurariatus officij vobis
tenore pñtium commicтim⁹ & mandamus. Quatenus de dictis pecunijs penes
vos existentibus. Soluatis duc. quinquaginta de carl̄. decem pro duc. ad
rationem monete ueteris excellenti pictori magistro Raphaeli de vrbino pro
eius prouisione /a/ Sᵐᵒ dño ñro ei assignata p vnum mensem inceptum die
prima mensis junij proxime preteriti in operibus picture palatij Sᵐⁱ dñ ñⁱ
nec non p coloribus necessarijs. Sicut apparet p cedulam manu. r. d. J.
magistri domus Sanctitatis sue & nobis exhibitam.
Quos sic solutos i uris computis admictemus
Datum Rome i Cama aṗtica die p̄ mensis july . 1516. pontᵘ ῦ Sᵐⁱ dñi ñⁱ
LEONIS  pape      X            anno        tercio
                                      duc . L . de carl̄.

                        Visa C. Blondub


Jo raphaello dipintore ho receuto li duc. cinquanta
p questo mese de junio.

*The lawyer Fernando de Rojas...who signs it...in his own hand.*

## Fernando de ROJAS

### C. 1465-1541

In the course of this book, we shall frequently be commenting on the rarity of a person's signature, but in the case of Fernando de Rojas this piece really is unique. The full-page document reproduced here is currently the only known text in the hand of the great Spanish author.

His *La Celestina*, published in 1499, is one of the classics of Spanish literature, but very little is known about his life. All we know is that he came from a Jewish family that converted to Catholicism, was a lawyer, and lived for a long time in Talavera de la Reina, where he married a woman from the Alvarez family, who were related to the Avilas. The document reproduced opposite was written and signed by a lawyer named Fernando de Rojas in 1509, in Talavera, where the author of *La Celestina* had already been living for several years, and it concerns the property of a member of the Avila family.

It seems highly unlikely that two lawyers of the same name and with links to the Alvarez and Avila families should both be residing at the same time in this little town. Although there is no authenticated specimen of Rojas's handwriting – or even of his signature – with which this document might be compared, the circumstantial evidence suggests that this is indeed a unique and genuine piece, and an important discovery for the history of Spanish literature.

The pages reproduced above and opposite come from the same legal document. The former was not written by Rojas, but he did pen and sign the latter. Out of the three signatures at the bottom, his is on the far left.

During his or her research, a collector sometimes benefits from an extraordinary stroke of luck: he or she might happen to purchase a piece of no apparent significance, only to discover later that it is something

exceptional. This was the case in Madrid, in 1979, when this document was sold as part of a lot containing old papers and parchments, and clearly the vendor – a specialist bookseller – had not bothered to look carefully at them. It is published here for the very first time.

◄ List of goods belonging to the Avila family, manuscript on paper, 1509.
► Fernando de Rojas, autograph document signed, 1509.

En XXX dias de mes de agosto de quinientos e ... años ... dias
... honrrados Pº matheos de talabera e de ... nombre de los sobre dichos
... herederos de ... orden ... como testamentario e
fue el ... de aquella ... e ... que de la una parte e de la
otra ... quentas ... de ... el ... de aquella de la otra
... juntamente ...
... que ... testamento hizo e ... e ...
... todo lo ... e ... papeles ... la suma de
... e lo ... de hallo que la ... e ... quentas ...
... los herederos por ... mill e dozientos ... que ...
to mas ... ... que ... e hizieron los ...
... que ... e ... e pagaran ... todo ...
... de agosto en que ... ... e ... de ... e hizo
... tomando por testigos la ... e que ... al bachiller
... de ... e dita ... villa de talabera ... juntamente
lo firmo ... e los ... nombre ... e ... que ... mas ...
... mill e trezientos e ... e ...
veynte mill e ... e ... e ...
to lo firmaron ... los ...

# CAESAR

## Cesare BORGIA

### 1475-1507

The model for Niccolò Machiavelli's (1469–1527) most famous work *The Prince* (1513), Cesare Borgia – along with his sister Lucrezia (1480–1519) and his father Pope Alexander VI (1431–1503) – is the best-known member of this Italian (originally Spanish) family. This is perhaps the most famous of all Renaissance families on account of the monstrous excesses, real or imagined, that are attributed to its members.

There can be no doubt, however, that Cesare was an extremely brutal man, even by the violent standards of his time. It is also a fact that he was cultured and a great patron of the arts. Appointed bishop of Valencia at the age of seventeen, and made cardinal one year later by his father, he resigned the post at the age of twenty-three to become a soldier. Louis XII of France (1462–1515) had also made him Duke of Valentin. He died in combat.

His letters and documents are extremely rare. The one reproduced opposite bears his first name, printed in its Latin form, together with his curious monogram in the lower section, which was meant to serve as an envelope, perhaps in order to identify the document for future classification.

This handwritten piece is dated 1503, and has the ornate signature of Cesare, who had just been made Duke of Romagna by his father. It confirms the appointment of Gianpietro da Imola as curate of the Castle of Mordono.

► Cesare Borgia (as the Duke of Valentin), 17th-century French engraving.
►► Cesare Borgia, document signed, 1503.

# CAESAR

borgia de francia dei gra dux Romandiole Valentieque princeps
tiadine et Vrenasii dns plumbini et c: Ac s. r. e. confalonerius et capitaneus gnalis Fideli nostro
Andree somusperii molen castri nri morodini Vicario Salut: Fidei que sinceritas qua erga
nos et statum nrm grerum comprobaris: et in ipso officio qd hactenus laudabiliter exercuisti acce
pimus bene gesta nos inducut ut tibi reddam ad grm liberales: Atq ideo te Andream infradch
dicti nri castri Vicarium ad Trimestre a fine prmi offici inchoandu cum honoribus omnibus fa
cudis facultate noduno Salario et rmolumentie cosuetie putur tenore resirmimus mandtes
omibz ad quos spectat grrmie te cotinuaret diduz officim p te ipm et no p aliu p mittentes
tibi parent obediat et sfauorib assistant oportunis: ac de Salario et rmolumentis prodictis nsso
dente: et fructat ab his qbus incumbut cogitis temporib respondet Dat c crome in confilio
nro Ano dm millesimo qngentess tertio Ducatus vero nostri et romandiole ptmo.

# QUEEN ELIZABETH I

## 1533-1603

Elizabeth I and her father Henry VIII (1491–1547) are perhaps the most famous of all English monarchs prior to Queen Victoria. Her mother was Anne Boleyn (*c.* 1507–36), Henry VIII's second wife, whom the King had beheaded. Elizabeth's situation was made all the more precarious by the fact that her parents' marriage had not been recognized by the Pope, and so the Catholics considered her illegitimate. Her half-sister, Mary Tudor (1516–58), re-established Catholicism in England on her accession to the throne, and Elizabeth had many enemies in the court who tried to discredit her with the Queen. If the latter had not died prematurely, it is quite possible that her younger sister could have been executed. During the ten years that preceded her accession, she was forced to deal with a series of plots against her, as well as many false accusations of treason.

The document reproduced opposite is a particularly striking one, as it is dated 20 November 1558, the very day that Elizabeth came to the throne. Her sister had died three days earlier, and one can well imagine the relief of the new sovereign when she summoned her Council for the first time. Her inexperience was such that she forgot to add 'The Queen' after her name, in the manner of her sister, or even an R (for *Rex* or *Regina*) as her ancestors had done and she herself would also do henceforth. Here she is confirming the appointment of Edward Saunders, who had already been the principal judge of the realm 'in the time of our deceased sister the Queen late dear Mary'.

▲ Elizabeth I, 17th-century French engraving.

► Elizabeth I, document signed, 1558.

Quene Elizabeth ... 17 ... 1558
... 24 ...

## Elizabeth

By the Quene

Trusty and welbeloved we grete you well Lating you witte that our will and
pleasure is ye contynue the exercise of thoffice of our Attourney generall in your Cort
as ye did heretofore in the tyme of our derest Sustor te Quene late dec[eased] ... doing
and exequting all maner of thinges to the same office apperteyning as amply as you were
wont to do untill ye shalbe otherwise advertised from us in this behalf And these
our [letters] shalbe your sufficient warrant and discharge in this behalf Yeven
under our Signet at our Manor of Hatfeild the xxth day of November the
first yere of our reign

# Saint VINCENT DE PAUL 1581–1660

## Saint FRANÇOIS DE SALES 1567–1622

The signatures of Catholic saints are rare to the point of being unobtainable prior to the 16th century. Most of these people did not become famous until after they were dead, and so their writings were not preserved. Saint Vincent de Paul and Saint François de Sales were exceptions, because both were famous during their lifetime – the former for his charitable works, and the latter as bishop of Geneva. Although their signatures are far from common, there are a number of known specimens, and these are attractive pieces to collectors. The letter from Saint Vincent de Paul, reproduced on this page, was dictated to his secretary, but the last lines and the signature are in his own hand. He is confined to his bed, and is giving a worker leave to go to the assistance of his mother.

The document reproduced opposite is quite extraordinary in so far as it confers official status on the signature as a relic. Stuck onto a fragment of a theological manuscript written in Latin by Saint François de Sales, there is another text dated 1677: members of the clergy certify that this is the signature of the saint – who had died some fifty years before – and they recognize the fragment as a sacred object of worship.

Cutting up the manuscripts of saints in order to make them into holy relics does not seem to have been common practice. This very rare example is all the more precious as it appears to be the only one of its kind to have come on the market for many decades.

▲ Saint Vincent de Paul, 18th-century French engraving.
► Saint Vincent de Paul, letter signed, with additional autograph lines, 1654.
►► Saint François de Sales, autograph manuscript, c. 1610.

In Nomine Dñi Amen. fidem facio per præntes Ego Rotus
pub[licus] inf[ra]s[crip]tus qualiter die undecima mensis July 1667. Pontif[icat]us
SS.mi in Xp̃o Patris et D.N.D. Clementis, divina providentia Papæ
Noni Anno eius p.mo Reu.dus P[ate]r Antonius Ægidius Gallus
Ord[in]is Minimo[rum] S.ti Francisci de Paula Professus et Corrector
Ven[erabilis] Conventus SS.mæ Trinitatis in Monte Pincio de Alma Vrbe
mill[esim]o Rosario co[nventuali] et Reu[erendus] P[ater] Joannes Franciscus Arzauus de
Civitate Aquen[si] in Provincia Provinciæ Sacerdos Professus
d[ict]æ Religionis in d[ic]to Conuentu degens, nec non aliis omni meliori
modo medio eor[um] Jurament[o] tactis Pectoribus more Sacer-
dotali dixerunt et declararunt suprad[ic]tam Schedulam a b
utraq[ue] parte Scriptam, et huic p[rese]nti folio alligatam, fuisse,
et esse Scriptam propria manu Sancti Francisci
de Sales, et p[ro]ut[ali] simili Jurament[o] tact[is] p[ec]tore reco-
gnouerunt et quilibet eorum recognouit per similitudinem
non solum p[re]dicto Sed omnia alio meliori modo &c Jn
Quor[um] fid[em] &c Act[um] Romæ La[u]dæ Supradicta

Ita est Pa[te]r M[aest]ro D[omi]n[ic]o Sim[in]is [...] Em[inentissi]mo[rum] &c R[everendissi]mo D[omi]no D[omi]no Card[ina]li Vicar[io] [...]
[...] fr[ater] Maria Sim[in]is p[ro] me ut fidem

Nos Marius Miseratione divina Episcopus Sorven[sis] S.R.E. Cardinalis Ginettus SS.mi D[omi]ni N[ostri] Papæ
ac in Vrbe Romaneque Curiæ eius dis[tric]tus Judex ordinarius &c Vniu[er]s[is] fidem facimus et att[est]a-
mur suprad[ic]to[s] P.P. Marium Pont[...] Sim[in]is Rorü et Antonium franciscum Maria Sim[in]is eius
Administratorem de p[rese]nti et qui[...] m[od]o neg[otiis] sub p[...] in eo[rum] sub[scrip]t[i]s[?] et publicanis fuisse
et esse Nost[ri] Tribunalis Notar[ios] publicos legales authenticos ac fide dignos ac tales
q[u]ales sese faciunt eorumq[ue] scripturis tab[...] publicis q[...] similibus p[ro] Jud[ic]e et extra jus
adhibita[m] fuisse ac de jure plena[m] ad hiberi fide[m] ... [S]D data[m] Romæ ex Æd[ibus]
nostris hac die ij July 1667

[signatures]

*...[The Dutch] have just sent...a very powerful fleet to the bay of Todos los Santos in order to attack the town of San Salvador....*

## Peter Paul RUBENS

### 1577-1640

Of all the artists of the 17th century, Rubens had one of the most brilliant careers. Quite apart from his artistic genius, he had a character, culture and intellectual curiosity that made him the friend of princes and of the other great personalities of his time, as well as being an influential diplomat on the European scene – especially in the late 1620s. His studio was probably unique in the number of assistants that he employed and in the importance of the commissions he received. He was immensely famous for more than half his life, executed or supervised the production of more than 3,000 works, and was one of the most prolific artists of all time. He represented Archduchess Isabella, the regent of Flanders, during some difficult peace negotiations, and their friendship brought him into contact with the monarchs of Spain and England.

It was in this context that Rubens – universally admired as an artist and respected as a courtier (despite his relatively humble birth) – left Antwerp on a diplomatic mission to Madrid in August 1628. In June, before his departure, he wrote the letter reproduced here. It is in Italian, and is addressed to the historian Pierre Dupuy (1582–1651), Louis XIII's (1601–43) librarian in Paris, with whom Rubens corresponded between 1626 and 1629. The letter reads like a fascinating journal: he is commenting with great acumen, but in line with his own interests and political views, on the main events happening in Europe. It is worth quoting some of his remarks: 'The surrender of Trino was extremely strange. The Duke (of Mantua) imposed a tax of seven thousand pistols on the citizens, and allowed the Jews to be robbed by the soldiers. This decision resulted in a greater loss for the Christians than for the Jews, because the houses of the latter were full of objects that

the Christians had pawned for sums of money that the Jews are allowed to lend at high rates of interest.'

The most interesting political comment, however, is his prediction – which was later to be confirmed and which shows just how well informed Rubens was – that 'according to certain rumours' the Dutch were going to invade northeastern Brazil, which was then in Spanish possession. 'These states are conducting a disastrous war against the King of Spain, subsidized by private financiers, especially those of the West India Company, and if I am not mistaken they have just sent a very powerful fleet to the bay of Todos los Santos in order to attack the town of San Salvador, which they had already taken once by treachery.'

In Madrid, Rubens was to be received by Philip IV (1605–65), who was an enthusiastic admirer of his work but had doubts as to whether his aunt, the regent Isabella, had been wise to choose an artist for the role of diplomat. The King actually wrote to the regent on 6 June 1628 (naturally without Rubens knowing, and just five days after Rubens's own letter to Dupuy): 'I am not pleased that you are involving a painter in matters that are of such importance. You can well understand the degree to which this could compromise the reputation of my kingdom, and how much damage it could do to our prestige if we make so lowly a person our representative with whom foreign envoys are meant to discuss affairs of major import.' After his arrival in Madrid, however, Rubens's exceptional charm and intelligence completely reversed the king's opinion, and the following year he even entrusted the artist with another mission – this time to London.

Rubens was a prolific letter-writer for that period, but most of his letters are now kept in

▼ Peter Paul Rubens, 18th-century French engraving.
▲ ► Peter Paul Rubens, autograph letter signed, 1628.

public institutions, and fewer than half a dozen have appeared on the market since the Second World War. The letter reproduced here was sold in the USA in 1922, and resurfaced during the 1990s. Even the greatest collections of the 19th century had none of Rubens's letters – or at most one, which would generally not be as interesting as this.

Baya de todos los Santos per Inquatoriss di nouo della Città di S. Salvador presa da loro contra il suo costume fatta assai vilmente. E non auendo altro farò fine con baciar a VS Real SL suo fratello humilmte le mani

d'Anuessa il primo di Giugno 1628

Di VSSSma molto Illustre

non lo scrissi a VS la settimana passata perche mi trouai in un viaggiretto fuori della strada per poter compiere colla nostra corrispondenza

Seruitor Affmo
Pietro Pauolo Rubens

*I have nothing but praise for the care that you are taking over the discipline of my army, sparing not even those that belong to you....*

# LOUIS XIII *of France* 1601-1643

## *Cardinal* RICHELIEU 1585-1642

Louis XIII has often been described as a weak man, dependent on Cardinal Richelieu for all important decisions. This image has undoubtedly been reinforced by the novels of Alexandre Dumas (1802–70), which made Richelieu, the King and his wife Anne of Austria (1601–66) household names all over the world. It is certainly true that Richelieu had more power than any other French minister, and that, for example, he forced the King to have his favourite Cinq-Mars executed for treason. However, a document such as the one reproduced here (above right, and opposite) proves that Louis XIII did sometimes impose his will against the wishes of the minister.

For many people the ban on duelling is one of the most memorable of Richelieu's measures, but this correspondence shows that the sovereign knew how to use his power in order to grant exceptions. The episode is all the more significant in that it concerns a man-at-arms who was close to the cardinal, La Meilleraye, 'guilty by way of the duel he fought against a cavalryman from La Rochelle'. The King pardons him with the following words: '…valuing as I do the courage of La Meilleraye, who committed this fault only [through] ignorance and courage, I lift the penalty imposed upon him by the judgment made against him, and desire that he resume his post in order to serve as he has done before.'

Nevertheless, the King is at pains to reassure his 'cousin' the cardinal that he approves of the actual principle which his decision has overturned in this case: 'I have nothing but praise for the care that you are taking over the discipline of my army, sparing not even those that belong to you, and I am greatly pleased by this example.'

The second page of a letter dictated to a secretary in 1630, and bearing Richelieu's own signature, is reproduced above left.

▼ Cardinal Richelieu, 17th-century French engraving.
◄◄ Cardinal Richelieu, letter signed, 1630.
◄ ► Louis XIII, autograph letter signed, 1628.

seruir comme auparauant, et n'estant la
presante a autre fin je prieray toujours
Dieu quil vous conserue en sante aussi
long temps que je le dezire.

LOUIS

à Paris ce xiij Mars
1628

A Mon cousin le card.
de Richelieu

*Send some new workers immediately....*

# PETER *the Great*

### 1672-1725

Peter the Great (Peter I of Russia) was the first Russian monarch to establish personal relations with other European states, and he played an all-important role in the effort to modernize his country. By opening it up to the West, he sought to bring Russia the benefits of the progress that was being made there. The most memorable of all his initiatives remains the foundation of the new capital, St Petersburg, which 'revealed' Russia to the rest of Europe.

The letter reproduced opposite was dictated to a secretary in Russian, and signed by the Tsar. It was written in Moscow, seven years before his death, and is addressed to a Colonel Henning, who was in charge of a canal-building project. Peter the Great is evidently annoyed at the delay in the work, and is asking for immediate reinforcements for the work teams. The letter is dated 30 December 1717, and demands that the water should be flowing by February. (The following year he sent William Henning – who was one of his most competent men – through Germany, France and Italy to draw 'the most curious and most useful machines' and to sign up qualified workers.) On the right is the address page, bearing the red wax seal of Peter the Great.

This letter was written at a particularly difficult time for the Tsar. Two months earlier, when he returned from a long journey to France, he learnt that the heir to the throne, Tsarevitch Alexis, had fled and sought asylum in Naples. The Tsar persuaded his son to return by promising to pardon him. On his return, however, the latter was seized on charges of conspiracy and beaten to death, probably on his father's orders.

▲ Peter the Great, 18th-century French engraving.
►►► Peter the Great, letter signed, 1717.

Господинъ половникъ

По совѣршатеи строениемъ привода
ехали оныя досмотрѣ осамде
те стна, етѣ дабы надъ втедеаб
числе о егорала та стна i воды
пити.

Петръ

Wъ пошаъ дв 30
декабря 717

*...received...for copies...and memoirs...inserted...*
*into the 3rd, 4th and 5th [volumes] of the encyclopedia....*

## Charles de MONTESQUIEU 1689-1755

## Denis DIDEROT 1713-1784

Diderot and Montesquieu (whose full name was Charles-Louis de Secondat) were two of the great names in the Age of Enlightenment. Montesquieu, however, played no part in the publication of the *Encyclopédie ou dictionnaire raisonné des sciences, des arts et des métiers*, which was the most ambitious project since the Gutenberg Bible. The encyclopedia, under the direction of Diderot and French mathematician, scientist and philosopher Jean Le Rond d'Alembert (1717–83), took from 1751 until 1772 to complete.

The two documents reproduced here date from 1753 (opposite) and 1754–55 (above), at a time when success was already guaranteed. The encyclopedia had attracted an unprecedented 4,000 subscribers.

Above, in a note that is written entirely in his own hand, Diderot acknowledges receipt of 450 pounds from the bookseller Le Breton (who had commissioned the project) for texts inserted into the third, fourth and fifth volumes. There is no precise date, but the fifth volume appeared in 1755, and so it is likely that this receipt was written in the same year, or the previous year.

The letter from Montesquieu (opposite) is addressed to one of the team working on the encyclopedia, the scholar La Condamine (1701–74). Unlike his friend Montesquieu, who had raised but failed to fulfil hopes that he would take part in the project, La Condamine provided many articles and notes, mainly for the first few volumes.

It is often difficult to ascertain whether Montesquieu's letters are in his own hand. The author of the *Lettres persanes* (1721) and *L'Esprit des lois* (1748) employed secretaries whose handwriting was often similar to his own. Although the signature on this letter is undoubtedly his, a slight difference in the colour of the ink suggests that the text was dictated. The letter comments on reactions to La Condamine's candidacy for the *Académie française*, which Montesquieu himself had proposed with the support of the philosopher Condillac (1715–80). 'The proposal was very favourably received, and *cum elogio*'. In line with a strategy that had been honed by his allies, Montesquieu reminds the candidate not to talk to Buffon. La Condamine did not, however, gain entry to the Academy until 1760. The letter finishes with an affectionate message: 'I embrace you with all my heart, my dear La Condamine, whom I also love with all my heart.' The address page bears a fine impression of Montesquieu's seal.

▲ Denis Diderot, autograph document signed, 1754–55.
► Charles de Montesquieu, letter signed, 1753.

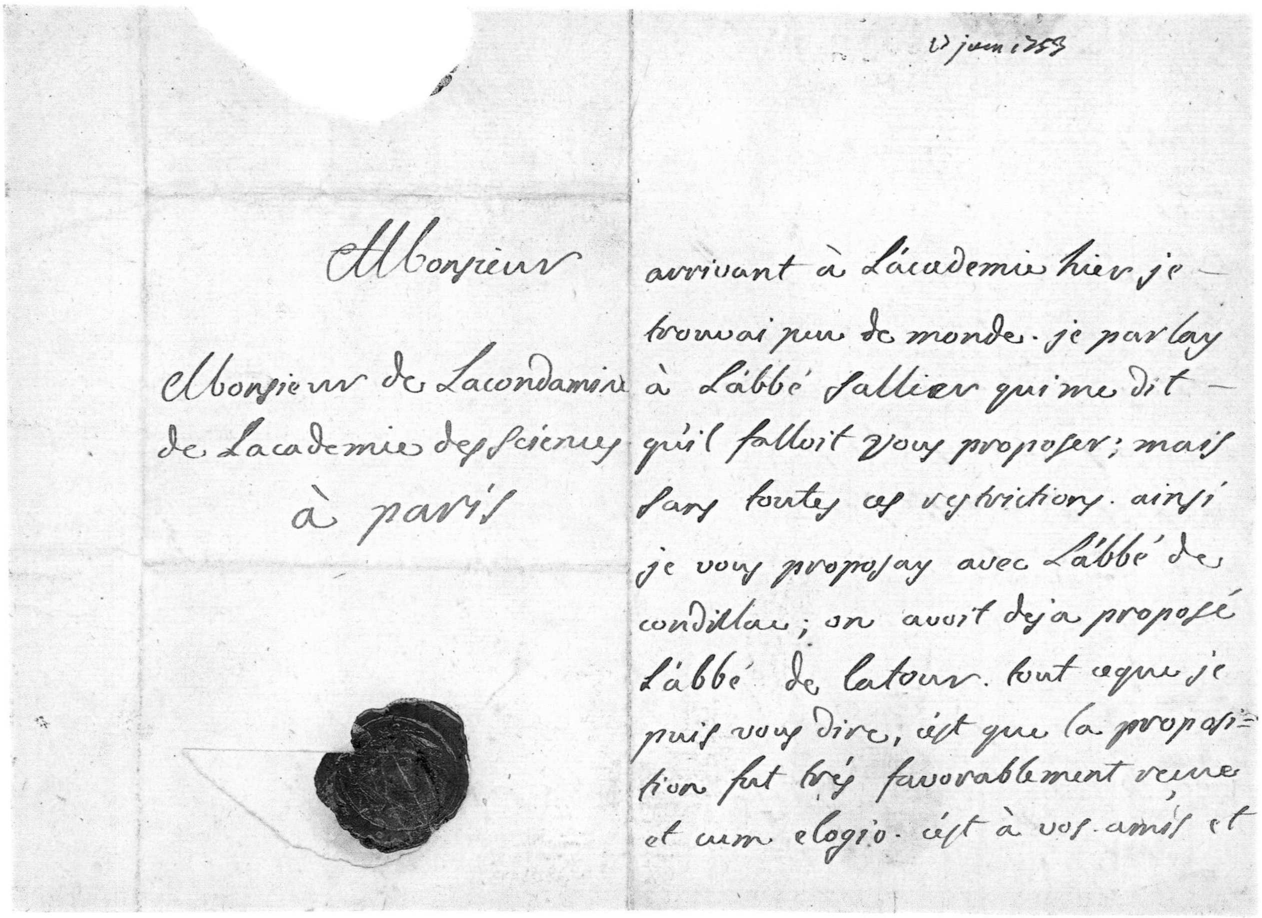

17 juin 1753

Monsieur

Monsieur de Lacondamine
de Lacademie des Sciences
à paris

arrivant à Lacademie hier je
trouvai peu de monde. je parlay
à Labbé Sallier qui me dit
qu'il falloit vous proposer; mais
sans toutes ces restrictions. ainsi
je vous proposay avec Labbé de
condillac; on avoit deja proposé
Labbé de latour. tout ce que je
puis vous dire, est que la proposition fut tres favorablement reçue
et cum elogio. c'est à vos amis et

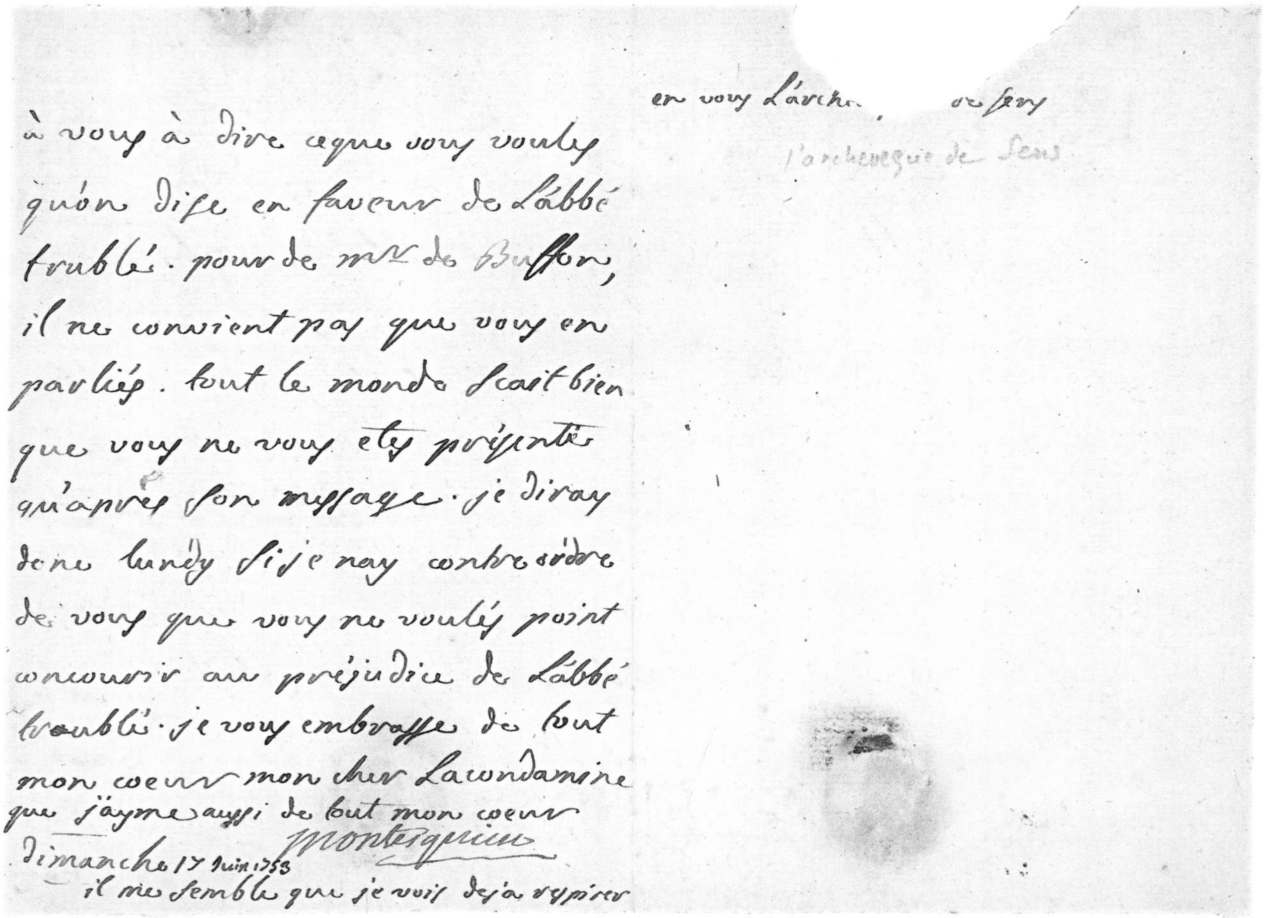

à vous à dire ce que vous voulez
qu'on dise en faveur de Labbé
troublé. pour de mr de Buffon,
il ne convient pas que vous en
parliés. tout le monde scait bien
que vous ne vous etes présenté
qu'apres son message. je diray
donc lundy si je n'ay contre ordre
de vous que vous ne voulés point
concourir au préjudice de Labbé
troublé. je vous embrasse de tout
mon coeur mon cher Lacondamine
que j'ayme aussi de tout mon coeur
Montesquieu
dimanche 17 juin 1753
il me semble que je vois deja respirer

en vous Larcheveque de sens
l'archeveque de Sens

*I beg you to be so kind as to give eight cups of wheat to Madame François, baker at Ferney....*

# VOLTAIRE

## 1694-1778

In 1758, at the age of sixty-four, Voltaire (the assumed name of François-Marie Arouet) retired to Ferney, a village on the Franco-Swiss border, where he led a tranquil life in the company of his niece, Madame Denis. When he wrote this letter in 1772, he had already been one of the most famous men in Europe for some twenty years. Every little movement or action was watched and noted, and the Genevan painter Huber captured his daily life in a number of watercolours, drawings and paintings, from which engravings were made that were sent all over the continent. (The watercolour depicting a dozing Voltaire, right, was done in the manner of Huber.)

The French soldier, poet and courtier Chevalier de Boufflers (1738–1815), after a visit to Ferney, reckoned that in the light of 'his expenditure and good deeds...he is the king and father of the country where he lives...'

It is against this background that one should visualize the great philosopher, at the age of nearly eighty, taking up his pen at the request of his baker. He 'begs' a neighbour to supply wheat to 'Madame François, baker at Ferney, who has great need of it in order to practise her trade'.

Boufflers's observations take on a vivid reality in such a context. This plea from the 'Lord of Ferney' confirms his role as a benefactor – albeit on a modest scale – to the people of his village.

▲ Voltaire, 18th-century French engraving.
► School of Huber, Voltaire asleep, French watercolour, c.1765.
►► Voltaire, autograph letter signed, 1772.

Monsieur

je vous supplie de vouloir bien
accorder huit coupes de bled a
la femme francois boulangere
a ferney qui en a une extreme
besoin pour fournir ses pratiques
je vous serai tres obligé.

jay l'honneur d'être avec
un attachement respectueux
Monsieur

votre tres humble
et tres obeissant
a ferney 19 nov.ᵇ 1772    serviteur voltaire

*You have everything needed to make a husband happy, and so...it is your sole aim to please him, to be of use to him, to attach him to you, to amuse him and to have no other thought or purpose but him....*

# MARIA THERESA *of Austria*

## 1717-1780

This long, handwritten letter from Maria Theresa of Austria was addressed to her daughter Marie Caroline, future Queen of Naples. The first few pages, which would be regarded today as 'politically incorrect', reflect the virtuous principles that a mother would try to inculcate into her daughter during the 18th century. We know that Maria Theresa wrote similar letters to all her daughters prior to their marriages, including Marie Antoinette (1755–93). Undoubtedly, though, she considered Marie Caroline to be shrewder than the future Queen of France, since she lavished on her all the remarkable advice that is contained in this letter.

The beginning alone is illuminating: 'You have everything needed to make a husband happy, and so at this time it is your sole aim to please him, to be of use to him, to attach him to you, to amuse him and to have no other thought or purpose but him...no moods, no impatience, always merry, always tender – those are the only bonds by which we can gain and maintain the respect and affection of our husbands, who alone are able to make us happy, as far as one can be happy in this world, as you well know.'

Despite these detailed recommendations, Marie Caroline did not heed her mother's advice. Capricious and scheming, she set out to dominate her husband, and became the true power in the kingdom of Naples – at least until Napoleon forced her husband to abdicate in 1806 (an episode described in a letter from Napoleon to Talleyrand, page 89).

◀ Maria Theresa, 18th-century Austrian engraving.
▶ Maria Theresa, autograph letter signed, 1768.

*Luxembourg ce 8 de may*

Madame ma chere fille, je vous ai ecrit le 5
par la poste vous faisant bien mon complimens
sur l'arrivée dans votre roijaume et aupres
de votre cher Epoux je souhaite que celle ci vous
trouve plus epouse mais sa femme et alors
vous aurois accompli parfaitement tout
votre penible voijage et le dificile de ce nouveau etat, que Dieu vous accorde si heureux
et si benit qu'etoit le mien vous avez tout
pour rendre heureux un epoux c'est donc asteur votre unique but de lui plaire de lui
etre utile de l'amuser de l'atacher a vous
et de n'avoir d'autre pensé et objet que lui
vous avez un parfait model devant vous
c'est votre belle soeur point d'humeur point
d'impatience toujours gaije toujours douce
voila les seules liens par lesquelles nous pou-
vons gagner et soutenir l'estime et la
tendresse de nos epoux qui seules peuvent
nous rendre heureux autant qu'on le peut
dans ce monde vous savez bien

qui me tient encore a coeur, ce sera un moment
dificile mais qui est a prevoir et ils ne vous
quitteront pas sans vous avoir donné des lumieres ou conseils que vous scauroit sur tout
s'ils pouvoit vous trouver une Dame comme
la j'aar car tout homme et a tout age a
besoing de conseil et il est heureux si on trouve
un vrais amis encore plus vous a votre age
avec l'esprit et le feu que vous avez et l'inexperience du monde ils vous sacrifient sans
cela d'etre absents de leurs tendres enfants et etat
et ils ne peuvent l'etre trop long tems a cause
de tems c'est donc ce moment que j'ecause
encore qui m'occupe tres sensiblement a cause
de vous vous ne saurez jamais leur montrer
toute votre reconoisance et sensibilite mais
il ne faut pas s'abbandonner a une tristesse
outrée cela pouroit deplaire a votre cher mari
qui doit vous tenir asteur lieu de tout
et fixer vos desirs et bonheur je vous donne
ma chere et aimable fille ma benediction
se continuent pour vous et suis toujours
l'Emp: se porte tres vore fidelle chere
bien au barat j'en ai des nouvelles marie therese

qu'il n'y a rien de parfait dans ce monde
et que chaque etat a ces peines mais les aijant
passez tous je peux vous asseurer que celui
d'un bon mariage est bien a preferer a tout
les autres et qu'il porte avec soi des consola-
tions dont les autres sont privez ainsi ma
chere et bien aimable fille courage tout comen-
cement est dificile le bon Dieu vous a bon
appelle et choisir pour cet etat suivez exac-
tement les voies de la divine providence
et plus de regrets pas meme des pensez sur
ce que vous avez quité c'est peu de choses en
comparaison de ce que vous avez asteur a
soigner et dont le bon Dieu vous at com-
pensé a moi pour vous animer a faire vos
devoirs et pour consoler une vielle chere qui
vous aime bien tendrement mais qui en a tout
toutes les raisons car vous avez surpassez mon
attente par votre conduite dans tout ce voijage
ainsi importez vous toute l'approbation et
des coeurs par ou vous avez passez et ce que
cette petite gene que vous vous est donné
n'est pas bien recompensée par l'approbation

generale, par votre propre satisfaction car vous
devez la sentir celle qu'on at quand on fais
son devoir et la consolation que vous m'avez
donné et a tout votre famille d'avoir reussit
si parfaitement, mais ne vous orgueillisez pas
reconoisez votre foiblesse devant Dieu que sans
sa divine asistance vous n'auriez put en
venir a bout et sans les bons conseils de
mad: de paar que vous avez suivit si bien
n'est ce pas un grand don de Dieu que tout
les gens qui sont meme que peu de tems avec
vous vous aiment tout de suite si tendrement l'exemple de la paar de la trautmansdorff
de schafgotss palavicini de l'oija meme vous
doivent bien animer je me flate que mon cher
fils car je le conte pour tel esperant que vous
est sa femme en faira de meme quel bonheur
pour vous et pour moi on dit que j'engraisse
que j'ai le meilleur visage depuis que vous
me rendez si contente si glorieuse par tout
ce qui me revient par tout vous me ferois
vivre ainsi cent ans. il n'y a que la separation
de votre frere et soeur qui vous est actuellement
d'une si grande resource

*...it is up to you to tame the monsters.*

# Jean-Jacques ROUSSEAU

## 1712-1778

Rousseau's letters, which are among the most fascinating of the 18th century, are far less numerous than those of his famous contemporaries, such as Voltaire.

The document reproduced opposite is the original contract fixing Rousseau's fee for *Le Devin du village* (1752). This little comic opera in verse was the author's first major breakthrough; it was performed before the King in October 1752, and produced in Paris in 1753.

From the 1740s onwards, the Marquise de Créquy held a salon at which Rousseau may have met Voltaire. The autograph letter on the right is addressed to her: 'I flattered myself, Madame, that I had a soul that was proof against praise; the letter with which you have honoured me teaches me to have less faith in myself, and if I must see you, that gives me more reasons to have even less faith in myself. Nevertheless, I shall obey, because it is up to you to tame the monsters.' All the same, Rousseau imposed certain conditions before going 'in private' to the salon of Madame de Créquy. 'I shall therefore submit to your command, Madame, on the day that it will please you to set for me. I know that Monsieur d'Alembert has the honour of paying court to you; his presence will not drive me away at all; however, do not think ill of me, I beg you, if any other third party should make me disappear.' The allusion to his liking for d'Alembert (and to himself as a monster) is typical of the 'frankness' that Rousseau always advocated, and it makes this highly ironic letter all the more interesting.

▲ Jean-Jacques Rousseau, 18th-century engraving.
► Jean-Jacques Rousseau, autograph letter signed, 1751.
►► Jean-Jacques Rousseau, document signed, 1753.

Il a été arresté au Bureau de la ville le 23 Juillet 1753 que les honnoraires tant pour les paroles que pour la musique de l'acte du Devin du Village dont le Sr Rousseau est autheur, demeureront fixés à la somme de 1200.# Dont le payement sera ordonné au profit dudit Sr Rousseau

En consequence de l'arresté du Bureau de la ville du vingt trois du present mois de Juillet, Le Sr Deneuville payera au Sr Rousseau la somme de Douze cent Livres pour les causes contenües audit arresté, et rappellées en la notte cy à costé, et en rapportant par ledit Sr Deneuville le present mandement et quittance dudit Sr Rousseau, ladittte somme de Douze cent Livres luy sera passée et allouée dans la depense de ses comptes sans difficulté. fait au Bureau de la ville le 24 Juillet 1753.

De Bernage

pour dejin

Rousseau

*...running round the apartments in Versailles...a certain*
*Milord Gordon...with the taste...for drinking human blood....*

# LOUIS XV *of France* 1710-1774

# *Madame de* POMPADOUR 1721-1764

# *Comtesse du* BARRY 1743-1793

Outside France, it is perhaps for his two famous mistresses that people remember Louis XV. The involvement of Madame de Pompadour (Jeanne-Antoinette Poisson in full) in the artistic and cultural life of her time has gained increasing recognition, and her role in this sphere was recently the subject of major exhibitions in France, the USA and England. The Comtesse du Barry (née Jeanne Bécu), even though she did not have quite the same influence, remains a fascinating character: she seems to have been totally detached from the realities of her time, and her death in the Revolution has made her into a tragic figure.

Like all the kings of France, Louis XV signed vast numbers of documents but wrote relatively few himself. Nevertheless, letters in his handwriting are not as rare as those of Louis XIII and Louis XIV.

The letter reproduced opposite, in the King's own handwriting, is addressed to the Duke of Parma, husband of his daughter Elisabeth. He addresses the duke in the customary manner of sovereigns writing to each other: 'My brother, cousin', and adds his actual relationship: 'and son-in-law'. He goes on: 'desiring above all else your happiness and your repose, loving you truly, and with all my heart, even though I am deprived of the satisfaction of knowing you in person.'

In those days, monarchs rarely travelled, and the princess departed without her father to marry the Duke of Parma. Thus Louis XV missed the chance to meet his son-in-law, who in turn never once went to France.

Madame du Barry wrote the letter above five years after the King died. His former favourite was then living in the house that Louis XV had built for her in Louveciennes. She writes about money, as indeed she did in most of the letters that have come down to us.

▲ Comtesse du Barry, autograph letter signed, 1779.
◄ Louis XV, 18th-century French engraving.
► Louis XV, autograph letter signed, 1752.

LOUIS XV.
*LXV. Roy de France.*

Mon frere, cousin, et Gendre. j'ay vû les copies que m.' de Runal a envoiées a m. de S. contest. je souhaitte de tout mon cœur que vous aies pris le bon parti, et que le roy votre frere approuve vos raisons, desirant pas desus tout votre bonheur, et votre repos vous aimant veritablement, et de tout mon cœur, quoique privé d'la satisfaction devous connoistre personellem.' sur ce je prie dieu qu'il vous aie mon frere, cousin, et Gendre en sa sainte, et digne Garde a Cœy ce .. juin 1752

Votre bon frere, cousin, et beaupere,

Louis

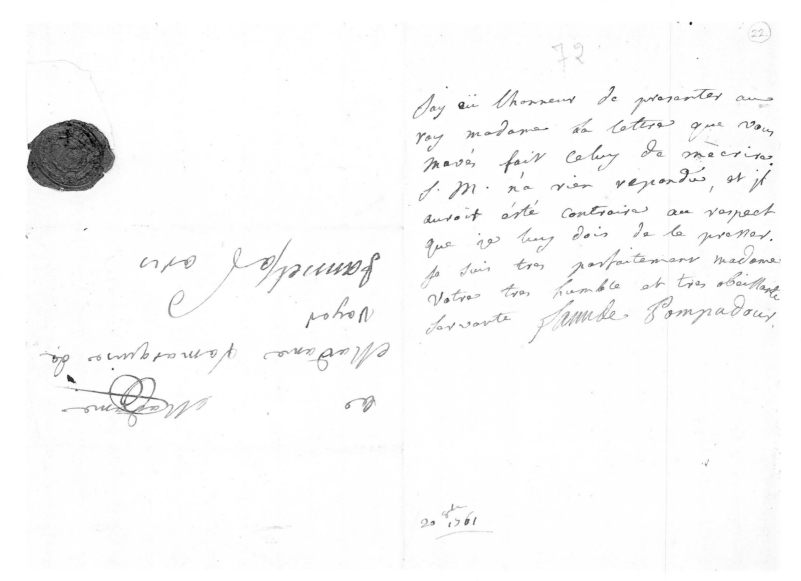

Madame de Pompadour, however, was a talented letter-writer. Despite her sometimes dubious syntax and spelling, her letters have a remarkable delicacy and precision of tone. They have always been quite rare, and for many years have become increasingly sought-after, especially by the great French collectors. Some letters, like the one reproduced above, bear a fine impression in red wax of the famous seal (enlarged on the right), in which one can see the three towers of her coat of arms. This specimen is all the more interesting because the Marquise rarely signed her letters. She deals here rather coldly with a request which the Marquise de Voyer had tried to make to the King: 'I have had the honour, Madame, of presenting to the King the letter that you made me that of writing to me [*sic*]. His Majesty gave no answer, and it would have been against the respect that I owe him for me to insist....'

The content of the second letter seems particularly disturbing. Here Madame de Pompadour is addressing a minister of

the Crown, the Comte d'Argenson, who would at different times be a political ally or adversary of the King's favourite: 'I have the honour of informing you that running round the apartments in Versailles is a certain Milord Gordon who is stark raving mad... there is no sort of lunacy that he has not indulged in here. I do not like to see him close to the King or behind the Dauphin, especially with the taste that he has declared for drinking human blood....'

▲▲ Madame de Pompadour, autograph letter signed, 1761.
▼ Detail of Madame de Pompadour's seal.
▲ Madame de Pompadour, 19th-century French engraving.
► Madame de Pompadour, autograph letter, c. 1760.

A
Monsieur
le
Monsieur de Comte
de Morangiés

je fais tous mes remerciments pour le Conte
et jay l'honneur de luy mander qu'il
court dans les appartements de versaille
un certain Milord gordon qui a
fait qu'il estoit il n'y a pas un mois
il n'est sorte d'extravagances qu'il
nait fait icy je n'aime pas le voir
près du roy et deur le Dauphin sestant
avec le gout qu'il Est de Clovs avois pour faire
du sang humain il est dans le regiment
royal ecossois ainsy je crois prudent a
vur le Conte de le renvoyes au moins à son
regiment

*I have little affairs which keep*
*my memory in a constant state of alertness....*

Giacomo CASANOVA

1725-1798

The eventful life of Giacomo Casanova, the Venetian of humble origin who gave himself the title Chevalier de Seingalt, would in itself be sufficient to justify his reputation as one of the great adventurers of the 18th century. However, it is unquestionably the literary talent manifested in his *Mémoires* – published posthumously and written in French – that made him into a household name and a universal archetype.

Most of the letters and manuscripts that we know of were written in the later years of his life, after he had (at the age of sixty) accepted the post of librarian offered by the Comte de Waldstein. He lived for thirteen years at Dux, in northern Bohemia, where he died on the threshold of a new century to which he could never have adapted. We know that during this time at Dux he corresponded with a dozen friends, and yet scarcely ten items have appeared on the market in the last twenty years, and pieces in his own handwriting date mainly from just before his death.

The letter reproduced here is of special interest: when Casanova was writing it, in August 1766, he was in Dresden and was only forty-one years old. Most of the adventures described later in his *Mémoires* were still ahead of him. The previous month, he had been expelled from Poland, after almost a year's stay, following a duel with a friend of the Polish King.

The letter hints at a mysterious affair which must have led to a misunderstanding involving the Comte de Bellegarde and Casanova's correspondent: 'At the very moment when you perform a generous action on my behalf, for which I thank you, you are pleased to write me a fine and mortifying letter.'

But it is in another sentence that we truly find the Casanova of the *Mémoires*: 'Unfortunately, I have little affairs which keep my memory in a constant state of alertness.' One can conjecture what sort of 'little affairs' might have taken such a hold on his mind.

▼ Giacomo Casanova, 18th-century engraving (frontispiece of his book *Icosaméron ou histoire d'Édouard et d'Élisabeth...*, Prague 1787).
▲ ► Giacomo Casanova, autograph letter signed, 1766.

M. le Co: de Bellegarde, et assez grande pour
moi (deplorez le pauvre genre humain) ne vous
a pas plu, ayez la bonté de la pardonner
à une situation qui ne me laisse pas suivre
les memes sentimens que vous cherissez, et que
dans autres circonstances fussent mes idoles.

J'aurai l'honneur de vous remercier à
diner.

Lisez vous bien ma lettre à M. de Bellegarde,
pensez un peu, et vous verrez que je suis tres
digne d'être honoré de votre estime, et de
me signer avec la plus grande sincerité

Monsieur le Comte              Votre tres humble et tres
                               obeissant serviteur
                               Casanova

*I pray…to Heaven to restore King Louis XVIII to the throne of his ancestors as soon as possible…using…your abilities… for the restoration of your Motherland which so many scoundrels have been devastating for so long….*

# CATHERINE *the Great*

## 1729-1796

As she grew older, Catherine the Great (Catherine II of Russia) grew more and more fearful of the dangers that threatened the order at the very heart of the absolute power of the Russian tsars. Among these dangers were the ideas promulgated by the French Revolution. Although she corresponded with Voltaire and Diderot (from whom she bought the books in his private library), she felt that the thoughts of philosophers and writers should remain the prerogative of an elite few who, in her opinion, should regard them as nothing but an intellectual challenge.

Written just one year before her death, this autograph letter (opposite) reveals the Empress in her most reactionary mood. King Louis XVI (1754–93) had been executed two years earlier, and the old sovereign is telling Marshal de Castries, an aristocrat and a French soldier who had spent some time in Russia, about her repugnance at the events taking place in France: 'I pray as you do to Heaven to restore King Louis XVIII to the throne of his ancestors as soon as possible, and to set you to work, using your brains, your experience and your abilities for the restoration of your Motherland which so many scoundrels have been devastating for so long.'

Catherine never saw the restoration of the Bourbons in France – it did not take place until 1815 – but her descendants continued to rule over Russia for 120 years after her death, until the Revolution of 1917.

The document above, on parchment decorated with an elaborate engraved border, concerns a military promotion. It bears the signature of the Empress in its Russian form (Ekaterina) in Cyrillic script.

▲ Catherine the Great, document signed on parchment, 1781.
◀ Catherine the Great, 19th-century French engraving.
► Catherine the Great, autograph letter signed, 1795.

Monsieur le Marechal de Castres. Je vient de
recevoir Votre lettre en date d'Eisenach du 13. Nov:
Vous ne me devés rien Monsieur le Marechal, je
compte avec le Roy Votre Maitre, je me flate que
Vous me range depuis longtems parmi les amis
les plus constans et les plus inébranlables de Sa
Majesté. Je prie le Ciel avec Vous de retablir
au plutot, le Roy Louis XVIII, sur le Throne
de Ses Ancetres et de Vous mettre a meme
d'employer Vos lumieres Votre experience et
Vos talens a la restauration de Votre Patrie
que tant de Scelerats divers desolent depuis
Si longtems

Catherine

ce 14 Decembre
1795.

*I urge you to arrange a service
which I demand and which I insist that one must hold for him at my
expense in the church where he has been buried.*

# The Marquis de SADE

## 1740-1814

Demonized in his lifetime, imprisoned for nearly thirty years, the 'divine Marquis' (whose full name was Donatien Alphonse François) was always at the centre of countless quarrels and controversies. He spent his life trying to escape from an army of creditors and lawyers.

But Sade was still young and free – thirty-one years old – when he penned the letter reproduced opposite. He had just learnt of the death of Taulier, the steward who looked after the Château de Mazan. Sade wants Taulier's nephew, Ripert, to take over the position, offers him the job, and urges him to arrange a church service for his uncle: 'a service which I demand and which I insist that one must hold for him at my expense in the church where he has been buried.' The Marquis de Sade's insistence on a mass is unexpected, to say the least.

It is certainly less surprising to find him using subtle irony – much more in keeping with the image of the libertine – in the letter reproduced on the right. Addressed to his wife, it is signed: 'the prisoner Sade'. 'You will be pleased, Madame Sade, my wife, on reception of these words, without delay to extract from the funds…the sum of three hundred and thirteen pounds twelve sols…the said payment having two faces… the second [is] settlement for the supply of milk to myself administered by the horned beasts of the government….'

The letter below right comes from 'Madame de Sade' herself, whose mother was the president of Montreuil – a formidable lady who hated her son-in-law (though she was probably in love with him). Despite the private and financial trials and tribulations that punctuated their marriage, the Marquise appears to have remained deeply if not passionately attached to her husband.

▲ The Marquis de Sade, autograph letter signed, c.1800.
◄ Renée Pélagie de Montreuil, the Marquise de Sade, autograph letter signed, 1790.
► The Marquis de Sade, autograph letter signed, 1771.

ce 25 février 1741

Persuadé de votre zele et attachement
à mon interest mon cher monsieur, Je vous
accorde avec plaisir la charge de
mon vizinier et mon procureur à Mazan
qu'occupait votre oncle tautier, dont je
vous avoue que la perte m'a été et ne
sauroit plus sensible. J'espère que vous
voudrez bien le remplacer non seulement
dans ses fonctions, mais même dans son
attachement réel pour ma personne
Je vous exhorte à vous trouver au service
qu'exige et que j'ordonne qu'on fasse
pour lui à ma ... et dépens dans
l'église ou il a été inhumé
Je suis bien parfaitement monsieur votre
très humble et très obéissant serviteur De Sade

*The Queen has very happily just given birth*
*to a boy whom I have named Duke of Normandy.*

# LOUIS XVI *of France* 1754-1793

## Marie ANTOINETTE 1755-1793

### Maximilien de ROBESPIERRE 1758-1794

Few destinies are more fascinating than the fate of this once omnipotent royal couple: a weak king with absolute power, and an imprudent, shallow-minded queen, both of whom met their deaths with the most remarkable dignity.

The document reproduced opposite dates from the last carefree years. The Queen had just given birth to the dauphin, who was to become the sad figure of Louis XVII (1785–95). This letter, handwritten by the King, is quite exceptional: it announces the joyful event to the Emperor Joseph II of Austria (1741–90): 'The Queen has very happily just given birth to a boy whom I have named Duke of Normandy.' Scarcely an hour after the birth of his son, Louis XVI was rushing to inform the sovereign to whom he felt closest, the uncle of the new-born child: 'I know well enough your friendship towards me…to be certain that you will share all my satisfaction.'

The document reproduced on the right, which is just as rare, refers to a very different scene, some eight years later. It concerns 'expenses on behalf of Louis Capet and his family' in the prison du Temple in December 1792. Louis XVI was to be guillotined soon afterwards, on 21 January 1793. This last list of expenses was drawn up by his valet, Cléry, and details some modest purchases which include 'twelve packs of large-sized letter paper, two jars of pomade, half a pound of soap, a portfolio in morocco, and six pounds of fine powder'.

The letters of Marie Antoinette have always been much more sought-after than those of Louis XVI. Throughout the 19th century, there were many high-quality

► Jean-Baptiste Cléry, autograph manuscript, 1793.
►► Louis XVI, autograph letter signed, 1785.

C'est avec le plus grand plaisir mon cher beau Frere que je vous apprends que la Reine vient d'accoucher très heureusement d'un garçon que j'ai nommé le Duc de Normandie. je connois assez votre amitié pour mon cher beau Frere pour être sûr que vous partagerez toute ma satisfaction. j'espère que vous ne douterez jamais de tous mes sentiments et de la tendresse avec laquelle je vous embrasse mon cher beau Frere

Louis

a Versailles le
27 de Mars 1785.
a 8h du soir.

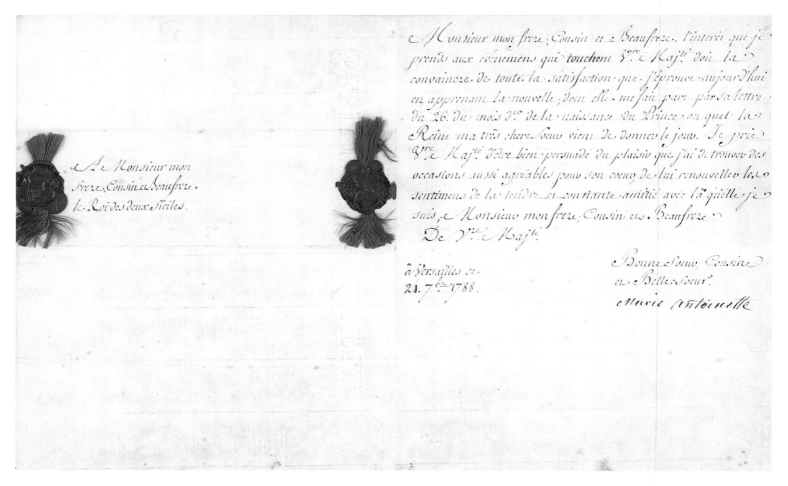

forgeries, some of which even deceived the experts for a long time. The letter reproduced above is particularly well preserved, and still has the ribbons stuck in the wax seals. It was dictated to a calligrapher, and was signed by the Queen herself. She was writing to her sister Marie Caroline's husband, King Ferdinand IV of Naples (1751–1825), sending him a very official expression of her joy on hearing of the birth of their child. The extremely formal tone stands in stark contrast to that of Louis XVI's letter on the previous page, which is much more personal. (The young prince referred to, Carlo Gennaro, was to die six months later.)

The autograph note written by the Queen on the right (below) remains a bit of a mystery. She has not signed it, because she very rarely signed her letters. She is referring to a certain M. d'Agoult, Bishop of Palmiers, probably a relation of her lover, the Comte de Fersen. The note is addressed to the Abbé Poupart and is dated 12 November 1791, eight months before the royal family was imprisoned in the Temple.

The document reproduced opposite emanates from the Committee for Public Safety, which was set up in 1793. Although papers signed by the *Comité* are relatively common, this one is of special note because

it bears the signatures of the revolutionists Robespierre and Louis-Antoine-Léon de Saint-Just (1767–94), who rarely signed jointly, together with those of fellow activists Carnot, Billaud-Varenne, Couthon and various other members of the *Convention*. The fine revolutionary vignette and the actual text are also very interesting: the *Comité* orders two generals of the Rhine Army, Delmas and Laubadère, to be 'arrested and forthwith brought before the *Comité*'. Robespierre's orders were promptly carried out, but his downfall at the Revolution of 9 Thermidor (two months later) saved the two officers. They were discharged after a six-month blockade at Laudun, survived the Terror, and died during the reign of Napoleon.

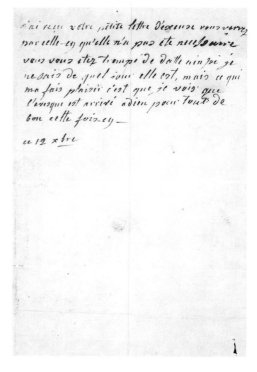

▲ ▲ Marie Antoinette, letter signed, 1788.
▲ Marie Antoinette, autograph letter, 1791.
► Maximilien de Robespierre, Saint-Just, Carnot and others, document signed, 1794.

# EXTRAIT

## DES REGISTRES

## DU COMITÉ DE SALUT PUBLIC

## DE LA CONVENTION NATIONALE,

Du *dix septième* jour de *Prairial* l'an deuxième
de la République française *uue* et indivisible.

———————

Le Comité de salut public arrête que delmar et
Laubadère généraux de division dans l'armée du Rhin
seront arrêtés et conduits au Comité sur le champs. —
michault géné: a *Suchess* de cette armée les Chargé
de l'éxecution du présent decret.

Signés, au Registre billaud varennes, Robespierre
Collotdherbois, S.Just, Couthon carnot et Barere

Pour Extrait

Carnot          Barere          J.Just

          Robespierre,

Collot-dherbois

     Couthon          Billaud Varennes

*I want a precise report on the*
*Muscat wine which is in Adorf....*

## Johann Wolfgang von GOETHE

### 1749-1832

Goethe's long life and his immense output made him the most celebrated German author of his time, and documents in his handwriting are among the most passionately sought-after by German collectors. His letters – and there were vast numbers of them – were jealously guarded by their recipients, but the majority of them are now in various public institutions in Germany, which collected them avidly throughout the 20th century. However, many are still in private hands, and autograph manuscripts of his poems still regularly fetch record-breaking prices at German sales.

Goethe's letters are nearly always fascinating. The one reproduced opposite was dictated to a secretary in 1821 but signed by the author, with an additional note in his own handwriting concerning his duties at Weimar. The letter tells us a little about his personal tastes and his concern with minor, everyday matters: he asks for a 'precise report' on the Muscat wine to be found in Adorf.

Goethe's popularity towards the end of his life was such that he was obliged to sign vast numbers of albums and had to respond to countless requests from female admirers asking for signed copies of his poems. Printed versions such as the one on the right were produced especially on his birthday, and he was happy to sign them. They are now seen as some of the most attractive and therefore most desirable specimens of his autograph.

▲ Goethe, 19th-century German engraving.
► Goethe, printed poem signed, 1826.
►► Goethe, letter signed, with additional autograph lines, 1821.

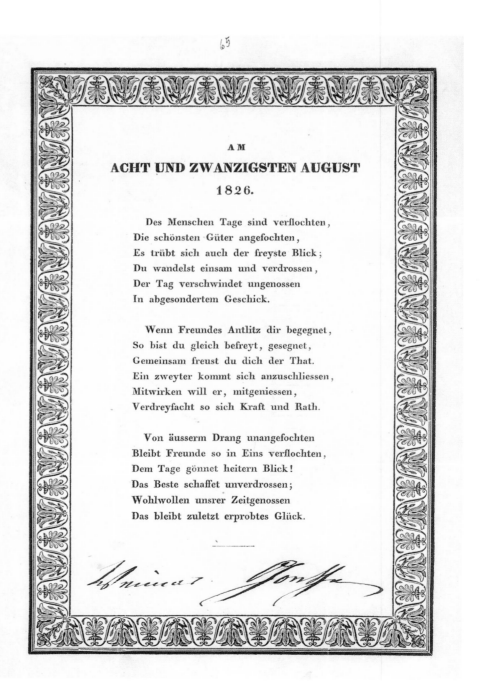

AM
## ACHT UND ZWANZIGSTEN AUGUST
### 1826.

Des Menschen Tage sind verflochten,
Die schönsten Güter angefochten,
Es trübt sich auch der freyste Blick;
Du wandelst einsam und verdrossen,
Der Tag verschwindet ungenossen
In abgesondertem Geschick.

Wenn Freundes Antlitz dir begegnet,
So bist du gleich befreyt, gesegnet,
Gemeinsam freust du dich der That.
Ein zweyter kommt sich anzuschliessen,
Mitwirken will er, mitgeniessen,
Verdreyfacht so sich Kraft und Rath.

Von äusserm Drang unangefochten
Bleibt Freunde so in Eins verflochten,
Dem Tage gönnet heitern Blick!
Das Beste schaffet unverdrossen;
Wohlwollen unsrer Zeitgenossen
Das bleibt zuletzt erprobtes Glück.

Eine löbl. Badesinspection wird ersucht um
mir Anweisung auf ein freyes Badehaus,
welches in Accord liegt.

Mannheim d: 18ten August                 J. W. v. Goethe
                    821.
                         Großherzogl. Sachsen=
                         Weimarischer
                         wirklicher Geheimrath

*To prevent destruction of the town and to
avoid the unnecessary effusion of human blood,
I desire the immediate surrender of your vessel....*

## Lord NELSON 1758-1805

## Lady HAMILTON 1765-1815

The quality of the correspondence between Lord Nelson and Lady Hamilton has fascinated generations of readers for the last two hundred years. Most of the great British and American collectors are constantly on the hunt for the admiral's letters to his mistress, and a simple note addressed to 'Dear Emma' will send the bids soaring. Nelson's autograph missives are in fact more common than those of Lady Hamilton.

When Nelson was writing the letter reproduced opposite, he had not yet lost his right arm – which of course forced him to learn to write with his left hand. In August 1795, he was in command of the *Agamemnon*, which was anchored outside Alassio, and he wrote to the captain of the corvette *Nationale* demanding the immediate surrender of his vessel, which was defending the town. Nelson says that he does not want to attack, as he wishes 'to prevent destruction of the town and to avoid the unnecessary effusion of human blood'. He ends this ultimatum with a warning that is both firm and concise: 'If you do not comply with my desire, the consequences must lay with you and not with your very humble servant....'

The document on the right is an acknowledgment of debt signed by Lady Hamilton on her return to England: she owes her Italian music teacher for fifteen months of lessons. The decease of her husband in 1803, followed not long after by that of Nelson himself, marked the beginnings of the financial problems that beset her during the last years of her life. Her destitute end has undoubtedly contributed to the legend.

▲ Lord Nelson, 19th-century French engraving.
► Emma Hamilton, document signed, 1803.
►► Lord Nelson, autograph letter signed, 1795.

Agamemnon Alassio
August 26th 1795

Sir,

The French having taken possession
of the Town & Coast of Alassio, I cannot but
consider it as an Enemys Coast, therefore
to prevent destruction to the Town and
to avoid the Unnecessary effusion of
Human blood — I desire the immediate
surrender of Your Vessel, If you do not
comply with my desire, the consequences
must lay with You and not with

Your Very Humble Servant

Horatio Nelson

To The
Commander of the
National Corvette (Copy)

*The insults from this wretched queen are getting worse…it is necessary that her reign should come to an end and that I should not hear another word about her….*

# NAPOLEON *Bonaparte* 1769-1821

## *Josephine de* BEAUHARNAIS 1763-1814

Of all the great historical figures, Napoleon I is perhaps the one whose autograph documents are the most popular. It is believed that he may have signed up to half a million letters in the course of his extraordinary career, and yet those that are in circulation outside the public domain cannot satisfy an ever-growing demand, especially for those items whose contents are significant. His letters cover a period of more than thirty years, from the timid writings of Corporal Bonaparte to the rare, nostalgic pieces penned by the fallen Emperor on St Helena.

The spelling in his early letters is somewhat uncertain – in a French that would always be his second language – and his handwriting is among the most illegible of all the great historical figures. Many of the letters he wrote himself are still the subject of much discussion, as the experts cannot agree on the actual content. Later, however, most were dictated to secretaries who had been chosen precisely because of their legible writing. Collectors of these therefore do not have to decipher the incredible jumble of signs that make up his own autograph efforts.

The letter reproduced opposite was dictated to a secretary and addressed to the French statesman Talleyrand (1754–1838) from the palace at Schönbrunn in Austria. The date is 1805. Of all the 'energetic' messages that Napoleon sent around his empire, this is undoubtedly one of the most emphatic. The imperial rage is directed against Queen Marie Caroline of Naples (also the recipient of letters from her mother, Maria Theresa, and her sister, Marie Antoinette – see pages 66–67 and 82). Known for her scheming, her forceful character, and the *de facto* power that she exercised over the kingdom of Naples, Marie Caroline was one of Napoleon's most implacable foes –

a hostility which he returned with interest: 'The insults from this wretched queen are getting worse with every letter…. You know how I have dealt with her. I would be too much of a coward if I forgave inflammatory excesses such as hers against my people. It is necessary that her reign should come to an end and that I should not hear another word about her, absolutely none, no matter what happens….' Talleyrand rarely received an order quite as clear as this from his master. A few months later, Marie Caroline – faithful ally to England and close friend of Nelson and Lady Hamilton – had ceased to reign, and went into exile in Sicily.

This letter is signed with the complete first name, whereas he generally signed with 'N' or 'Nap' in a vigorous scrawl at the bottom of the page. Just above the signature, he has added a note of his own, which not only adds to the interest of the document, but also proves that the Emperor read his own letters carefully before they were sent.

The documents reproduced on the right show the two most common forms of Josephine's signature. During the first years of her marriage, she almost invariably wrote 'Lapagerie Bonaparte', combining her maiden name with that of her husband, as in this letter which she wrote herself and in which, as the wife of General Bonaparte, she is seeking a position for a protégé. Below, in a letter of recommendation dictated to a secretary in 1812, three years after she had ceased to be Empress, she signs only with her first name. By then she had retired to

---

▶ Napoleon, 19th-century French engraving.

◀◀ Josephine de Beauharnais, 19th-century French engraving.

◀ Josephine de Beauharnais, autograph letter signed, c. 1800.

▶ Josephine de Beauharnais, letter signed, 1812.

▶▶ Napoleon, letter signed, with autograph addition, 1805.

Monsieur Talleyrand, je reçois votre lettre du 2 à 5 heures du matin. je vois avec plaisir que vous finirez ; mais je vous recommande expressément de ne point parler de Naples. les outrages de cette misérable reine redoublent à tous les courriers. vous savez comme je me suis conduit avec elle, je serais trop lâche, si je pardonnais des êtres aussi infâmes que les siens envers mon peuple. Il faut qu'elle ait cessé de régner ; que je n'en entends donc point parler. absolument, quoiqu'il arrive, n'en parlez pas, mon ordre est précis. Quant aux Contributions, je vous ai dit mon mot, la moitié &... &. Sa majesté

Schönbrunn le 2 nivôse an 14.
23. Xbre 1805.

Napoléon

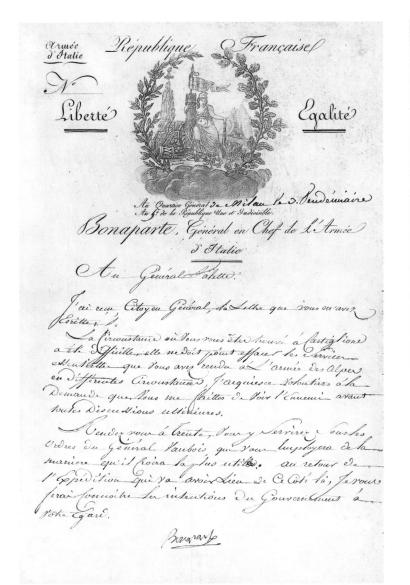

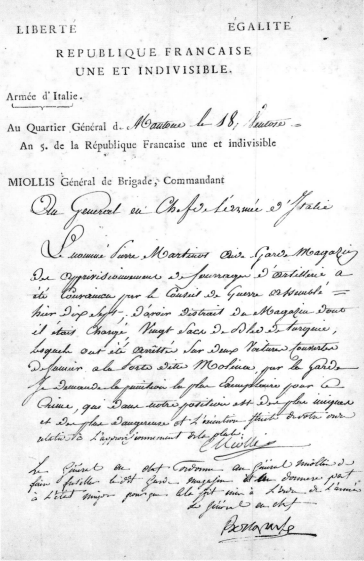

Malmaison, where she was to live for five more years, with a generous allowance from the Emperor.

The two documents reproduced on this page date from the Italian campaign. The one on the left bears a very fine vignette and the heading 'Bonaparte, général en chef de l'armée d'Italie'. The letter, dictated to a secretary, is addressed to General Valette, who had had to evacuate Castiglione. Bonaparte writes: 'The circumstances in which you found yourself in Castiglione were difficult, and should in no way efface the vital services that you have rendered to the Alpine army in different conditions.' In this rare demonstration of tolerance in the face of a setback, Bonaparte adds – with evident sympathy for his correspondent – 'I readily agree to the request you have made of me, to see the enemy before holding any subsequent discussions.' (Valette was discharged, but two years later went back into active service.)

The second document, on the right, is rather sad: it led to the death of a man more than two hundred years ago. The letter was written in Mantua by General Miollis, and informs Bonaparte that an assistant store-keeper named Pierre Martinot has been found guilty of stealing twenty sacks of corn. The future Emperor pronounces sentence at the bottom of the page: he signs the order for the culprit to be shot at once. We know of very few orders for summary execution that were actually written by Napoleon himself, although he was responsible directly or indirectly for hundreds of thousands of deaths.

The document on the opposite page deals with an important event in the early part of Bonaparte's career: the appointment of French soldier Andoche Junot (1771–1813) as his aide de camp in 1794. Napoleon had noticed this twenty-two-year-old officer the year before, during the siege of Toulon. Here he tells him: 'I have chosen you to fill the post of aide de camp to me. If you accept, would you join me as soon as possible.' The somewhat laboured signature (with its Italian spelling of Buonaparte) is that of a twenty-four-year-old man of action who is not yet used to wielding the pen, but who is preparing himself to become one of its greatest utilizers.

The different forms of Napoleon's signature have always aroused much interest. They change from Buonaparte to Bonaparte to Napoleon. The latter was limited to rare documents that required it, or to those moments when he simply felt like using it. As he was always in a hurry, he usually preferred to scrawl an 'N', a 'Nap' or 'Napol' at the bottom of the page, underlined with a flourish that was sometimes so aggressive that the ink splashed all over the paper.

▼ Napoleon (Bonaparte), letter signed, 1797.
▲ Napoleon (Bonaparte), document signed, 1797.
► Napoleon (Buonaparte), letter signed, 1794.

au Cen Junot Lieutenant de Cavalerie.

Je vous préviens Citoyen que Venant d'être
nommé au Grade de Général de Brigade Je
vous ai Choisi pour remplir près de moi les
fonctions d'aide de Camp.

Si vous acceptez, vous voudrez bien Venir
me joindre le plutôt possible, — Dans le
Cas Contraire, m'en donner avis.

Salut & fraternité

Buonaparte

Both of the letters reproduced on this spread were written from the Isle of Elba in September 1814, and were penned fifteen days apart. The one opposite is addressed to General Bertrand, one of the Emperor's most faithful companions. Napoleon has signed it 'Napole' and has added several autograph corrections. He is extremely unhappy about his house: '[The work that] has been done here is like everything else on this island – that is, very bad. The locks on the doors and windows are dreadful. They have to be redone. The [way in which the] house [has been] painted resembles the worst possible cabaret….' Napoleon now has time to devote himself to such details, and worries about all the arrangements he needs to make in order to prepare for the arrival of his mother and sister, who are due shortly: 'What with Madame having a lot of furniture and Princess Pauline expecting several pieces from Paris and Rome, I believe we have enough.' The Emperor proves his extraordinarily precise memory when he asks to be sent 'the bed placed for the Empress above the gallery…my night clock…the small marble-top table…and a billiard table.' Letters that reveal rather intimate aspects of Napoleon's life are scarce, and this one shows his close attention to detail during his stay on the Isle of Elba, when he had to lead a much more modest life than he was used to.

The letter on the left is one of the very rare examples of Napoleon's autograph letters signed from that period. It is part of the limited number that have appeared on the market over the past twenty years. The handwriting is almost illegible, but it is still possible to decipher most of its content: it is addressed to 'my dear Marshall' and asks to 'put these ladies on the brig to Campo from where they will go to Porto Ferraio. I will stay another day. Send a landau or a caleche to Campo for my return.'

The 'ladies' to whom Napoleon refers are undoubtedly Madame Mère and Pauline Borghèse, whose immediate arrival he was expecting, as he reveals in the first letter described on this page.

Monsieur le Comte Bertrand, ce qu'on a fait ici et comme tout ce qu'on a fait dans l'isle, c'est à dire fort mauvais, les fermures des portes et des fenêtres sont horribles, ça sera à refaire, les peintures sont faites comme dans le plus mauvais cabaret possible. = Madame ayant beaucoup de meubles et la Princesse Pauline devant en recevoir de Paris et de Rome, nous en aurons suffisamment. Je vous prie donc de faire venir ici le lit qui était placé pour l'Impératrice dans la pièce au dessus de la galerie, avec les rideaux, la table de nuit, les commodes et généralement tous les meubles qui étaient dans cet appartement. Envoyez aussi 2 lits pour officiers, ma pendule de nuit, le petit guéridon en marbre qui était chez Madame. Comme il y a ici de très grandes pièces, on pourrait y placer un billard = envoyez ici le valet de chambre tapissier pour poser les rideaux; envoyez aussi 2 huissiers 2 frotteurs et le ferblantier. = La Princesse Pauline devant arriver définitivement le 25, je pense qu'il est à propos de préparer son appartement, et les travaux relatifs aux fenêtres d'en bas. = Sur ce je prie Dieu qu'il vous ait en sa sainte garde = Longone le 6 Septembre 1814.

des roses pour mettre dedans, une écritoire en fayence et 6 lampes à huile.

couvert le

désavoyer ? le salon

Napol

*The King – to the Prince Royal his son: I am happier, my dear son, with your handwriting from the day of yesterday.*

# Toussaint LOUVERTURE c. 1743-1803

# Henri CHRISTOPHE 1767-1820

The first independent black republic in the world was Haiti, and at the end of the 18th century it had three military leaders who were born as slaves and became legends in their own right: Toussaint Louverture, Henri Christophe and Jean-Jacques Dessalines (c. 1758–1806). The last two did not hesitate to proclaim themselves king, following the all too tempting example of Napoleon.

Toussaint Louverture, however, remained the perfect example of an idealistic and selfless leader. His anonymous death in a French prison adds a melancholy dimension to a heroic portrait that has required very little retouching from history. The letter reproduced on the right is typical of the man. Writing to Hédouville, a representative of the *Directoire* in Santo Domingo, he declares: 'The position that I occupy obliges me to be truthful.' It is a statement that might be used to describe his whole character.

Historians have been much less favourably disposed towards Henri Christophe, who had crowned himself Henry I in 1811. The bombastic protocol that he imposed on his court in Port-au-Prince has attracted much derision, for in aspiring to ape the customs of Europeans, he merely carried them to absurd extremes.

The letter reproduced opposite does nothing to assuage this image. He writes to his eight-year-old son, encouraging him to improve his handwriting. In a pompous tone, he declares: 'The King – to the Prince Royal his son: I am happier, my dear son, with your handwriting from the day of yesterday [*sic*]. I urge you to persevere. If you continue to give me such subjects of contentment, I for my part will do myself a true pleasure by procuring for you the satisfactions which are dependent upon myself.' The royal

conclusion is delightful: 'I embrace you and am your good papa.' This is the only example known to us of such a correspondence. No other monarch has had recourse to writing an official letter for such a personal matter.

▼ Toussaint Louverture, 19th-century French engraving.
▲ Toussaint Louverture, letter signed, 1800.
► Henri Christophe, letter signed, 1813.

Au Palais de Sans Souci le 18. Juillet. 1813.
l'an dix de l'indépendance.

# LE ROI,
### Au Prince Royal, Son fils.

Je suis plus content, Mon Cher fils, de votre écriture
du jour d'hier; je vous engage de persévérer; Si vous continuez
de me donner des Sujets de Contentement, moi de mon Côté, je
me ferai un vrai plaisir de vous procurer les Satisfactions qui
dépendront de moi.

Je vous embrasse et Suis Votre bon papa

*General Bolívar [offers you] his horse, which served him throughout the Peruvian campaign…. This animal has no distinction other than having borne its master against the enemies of the Motherland….*

# Simon BOLÍVAR

## 1783-1830

General Simon Bolívar fought ceaselessly for twenty years to win independence for his mother country, Venezuela, as well as for Colombia, Peru, Bolivia and Ecuador.

In May 1828, it was a battle-weary man who, after ten years of war, returned to Bogota via Caracas, the city of his birth. He was then the official president of 'Gran Colombia', comprising Colombia (which the Spaniards called New Granada), Ecuador and Venezuela. After several military campaigns which had kept him abroad over a long period, he was finally able to resume contact with the official diplomats who had been sent to negotiate with his government. Of all the envoys from the foreign powers that recognized the independence of these former Spanish colonies in Latin America, the most important was undoubtedly the one from England. Bolívar decided to make him an extraordinary offer: his own horse. The gesture may have been suggested to him by his advisers, or it may have arisen simply out of a personal liking for the Englishman, but whatever the reason, the fact is that he wrote in his own hand (opposite): 'General Bolívar takes the liberty of offering [to Mr Alexander Cockburn] his horse, which served him throughout the Peruvian campaign…. This animal has no distinction other than having borne its master against the enemies of the Motherland….'

This letter, written in the third person, includes his name in his own handwriting twice, which is equivalent to a signature.

On the reverse side of the document (reproduced on the right), the traveller Robert Ker Porter has certified: 'I was present when Bolívar wrote the note' and he states that it was addressed to the British envoy Alexander Cockburn.

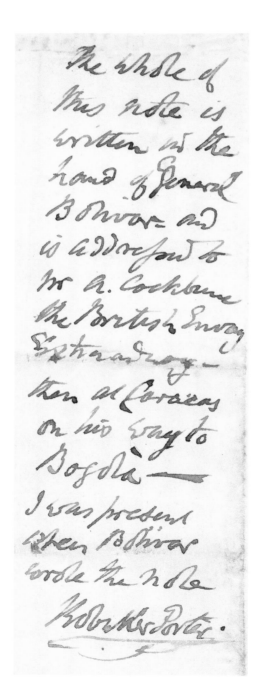

▲ Simon Bolívar, 19th-century English engraving.
◄ Robert Ker Porter, autograph text signed, 1828.
► Simon Bolívar, autograph letter signed, written in the third person, 1828.

El General Bolivar se toma la confianza de ofrecer al Sr. _____ un caballo q.e le ha ser vido durante toda la campaña del Perú. No tiene este animal otra recomendacion q.e el haber llevado á su Dueño contra los enemigos de su patria

El general Bolivar espera ~~el favor~~ del S.r Cockburn el favor de aceptarle este pequeño testimonio de su amistad.

Caracas 6 de Mayo
de 1827.

*Meanwhile, Madame, I take the liberty of informing you that...
I already consider myself to be his tenant....*

## Lord BYRON 1788-1824

## Percy Bysshe SHELLEY 1792-1822

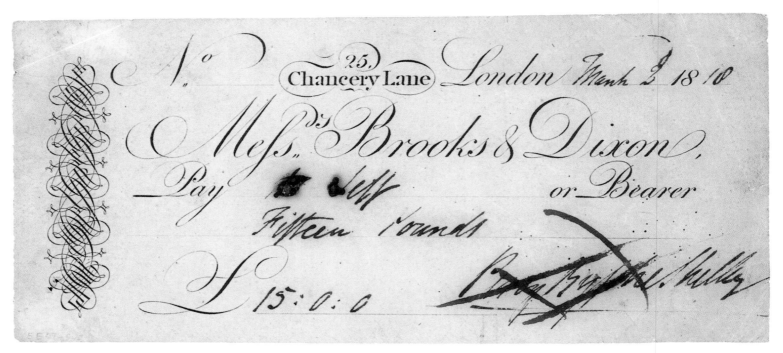

Lord Byron dazzled all his contemporaries. A tireless adventurer, he was the exact opposite of his quiet and reticent friend Shelley, but their names have remained permanently linked to one another. They both epitomized the figure of the romantic poet, and both died young, in their thirties.

Their premature deaths may explain why specimens of their handwriting are so rare, but the fact that the manuscripts of these two literary giants have been snapped up by the cultural institutions of Britain and the USA has also played its part, making their work almost impossible to acquire. Even their letters are uncommon. The only item of Shelley's that may now come on the market is a cheque signed, like the crossed one reproduced above.

The autograph letter from Byron (opposite) is one of the very few that he wrote in French. It is the first that he sent to Mrs Hoppner, wife of the English consul in Venice, to whom he later became very close. In October 1817, Hoppner had just let Byron a villa, and the young poet felt obliged to declare formally to the wife of his new friend that he already considered himself 'to be his tenant'. The villa at Este was to play an important part in the lives of both poets: Byron lent it to Shelley, who spent several months there in 1818 when he lost his young daughter Clara. The letter is remarkably well preserved, and so too is the envelope, marked with Byron's red wax seal (right).

▲▲ Percy Bysshe Shelley, autograph cheque signed, 1818.
▲ Lord Byron, autograph envelope, 1817.
► Lord Byron, autograph letter signed, 1817.

La Mira 8.e 8.re 1817.

Madame

Je viens de recevoir la lettre que vous m'avez fait l'honneur de m'écrire: Rien de plus flatteur pour moi que la permission de faire votre connaissance, dont je profiterai par la première occasion. — En attendant, Madame, je prends la liberté de vous avertir que, selon la proposition qu'a eu la bonté de me faire Mon.r Hoppner, je me considère déjà comme son locataire — et que ma visite — on a côté on a votre maison de Venise, aura pour objet principal vous témoigner combien je me sens touché de la manière très obligeante dont Monsieur votre mari m'a cédé la villa. —

Je vous prie, Madame, d'agréer l'as--surance du respect avec lequel je me souscris votre serviteur,
très dévoué

Byron

*Do eat some of those famous fish soups for me…and pity me.*

# Gioacchino ROSSINI

## 1792-1868

When Stendhal published his biography in 1823, Rossini – then just thirty years old – was the most famous composer of his time. Since the triumph of *The Barber of Seville*, in 1816, he had gone from one success to another, and his operas were performed all over Europe. Having acquired great wealth so early in his career, he became almost as well known for his high living as for his music. In fact, he virtually stopped composing in 1830 and lived on his past glories – which actually remained present glories since his operas were popular right through to the end of his days. He probably succumbed to what we would nowadays call nervous depression because of overwork, and so he composed hardly anything until 1856, with the sole exception of the magnificent *Stabat Mater*, which he finished in 1842. He spent the last twelve years of his life contentedly in Paris, where he composed a few charming trifles, appropriately entitled *Péchés de Vieillesse* [Sins of Old Age].

The letter on the right was probably written in the late 1830s. This is borne out by two clues: the style of Rossini's handwriting, which changed considerably over the years, and the allusion to Olympe Pélissier, with whom he began an affair in 1837. He regrets not being able to take advantage of the hospitality of his 'dear marquis and friend' at Rimini this year – his health obliges him instead to take the waters at a spa, which will deprive him of the famous *brodetti* [fish soups] that he loves so much. The previously unpublished portrait reproduced opposite, signed and dated 1839, comes from an album

► Gioacchino Rossini, autograph letter signed, c. 1838.
►► Tartaglia, portrait of Rossini, watercolour signed by the artist and the composer, 1839.

Napoli Li 3 Sett.e 1839.                    S. Bellini

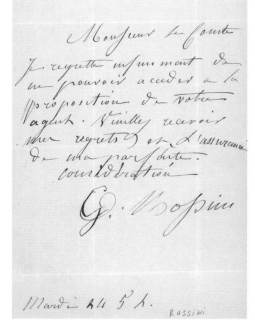

belonging to a family of Neapolitan aristocrats. It is signed by a certain Tartaglia, possibly an amateur artist whose name has been lost in time.

Rossini has a beard, a feature that is only to be seen in two other portraits of him. Such portraits from this time – just before the invention of photography – are in fact very rare, and the recent discovery of this watercolour is a great addition to the composer's iconography. The album also contained a watercolour portrait of Olympe Pélissier (by a different artist), dating from the same stay at the home of the Vicomtes de V. in September 1839. Rossini was married to one of the outstanding singers of his day, Isabella Colbran, whom he left in 1830 during his period of depression. A few years later, he met the former mistress of the painter Horace Vernet, the beautiful Olympe, became her lover in 1837, and when Isabella died in 1845, he married her. It was a happy relationship that lasted until the great composer's death in 1868.

The photograph reproduced opposite was taken by Adrien Tournachon, the brother of Nadar, with whom he collaborated with much success until they quarrelled and parted company. Adrien gave up photography in 1860, and his signed prints of the 1850s are rarities. The original glass negative remained in the Nadar studio. New prints made from the same sitting, dating from the 1880s and signed 'Nadar', show that Félix regarded his brother's photographs as his own property. At the time of this particular portrait, Rossini was seventy years old. He was living a comfortable, upper-class life in Paris, invited and feted everywhere. His stout figure was frequently to be seen in the most fashionable restaurants, where many a fine dish was named after him (e.g. the famous 'tournedos Rossini').

On the far left is a photograph of Rossini taken by Pierson, and in this he seems to be wearing a wig. Next to the photograph is a letter written by Olympe, rejecting a financial proposition.

▼ An anonymous portrait of Olympe Pélissier, signed by her, 1839.
◄ Pierson, portrait of Rossini, c. 1862.
◄ Olympe Pélissier, autograph letter signed, c. 1860.
► Adrien Tournachon, portrait of Rossini signed by the photographer, inscribed and signed by the composer, 1859.

à mon aimable ami John Thomas

G. Rossini

Paris ce 9 avril 1859.

*Chopin and his sister arrive in Paris on the evening of the 28th....*

# Frédéric CHOPIN 1810-1849

# George SAND 1804-1876

The autograph letter and the envelope reproduced opposite recall one of the most famous love stories of the Romantic period. It is a touching memento of the affair that brought together a composer of genius and a great author. The letter was written in 1844 by George Sand (the pen name of Amandine-Aurore-Lucile Dudevant), and the address is in the hand of Frédéric Chopin – thus reflecting the perfect symbiosis between the two lovers. Their relationship, which had by then lasted for six years, was in fact quite stormy. Sand's letter is addressed to Marie de Rozières – '*Chère mignonne*' [Dear darling] – and informs her that 'Chopin and his sister' will be arriving in Paris, where they will be received by the addressee. 'Make sure the keys are there and they can go to bed,' she writes. Chopin's sister, Ludovika, had just come from Poland after the death of their father. George Sand took an instant liking to her, and thought she was 'an angel, just like her brother'. She also talks of the immense weariness she feels after a period of creativity. 'I finished my novel yesterday. I am dead.' (She was referring to *Le Meunier d'Angibault*, which was published in 1845.)

Above right on this page is a reproduction of one of George Sand's famous paintings *à la dendrite* – a watercolour technique with which she worked in the last few years of her life. She would take two sheets of watercolour and press them together, then 'with the aid of the imagination' would elaborate on the patches to make pictures out of them. She used this process to create a large number of almost abstract images which she sold for a good price and which saved her from financial difficulties. In *L'Histoire de ma vie*, she states categorically that her paintings on paper and various small objects (it is believed that there were some 3,000

pieces altogether) guaranteed her a certain income and enabled her to 'create a little business'.

George Sand's handwriting changed a lot after 1850. The example reproduced on the right – a rather formal thank-you letter written in 1856 – is in her more mature style.

At the top of this page is a very fine portrait taken by Nadar and printed in Woodburytype (like that of Baudelaire by Étienne Carjat on page 112). It was published in the *Galerie contemporaine*, one of the most important magazines of the years 1860–80, illustrated with original photographs.

▼ Nadar, portrait of George Sand, Woodburytype, c. 1860.
▲ George Sand, landscape *à la dendrite*, c. 1873.
► George Sand, autograph letter signed, 1856.
►► George Sand and Frédéric Chopin, autograph letter signed by Sand with autograph address page by Chopin, 1844.

## 1

Mademoiselle
Mademoiselle de Rozières
à Paris
Rue St-Lazare N° 48

Cher Mignonne, Chopin
va bien, il m'amène à Paris le
28 au soir, il doit le conduire Dieu
sait, que les clefs y puissent
le suive prendre ... J'ai fait
je ne vous envoie pas ...
nous donnons ... Je suis
... mais je vous ...
je vous aime.

Sand
Lundi.

*And if only one is left, it will be me.*

*Victor* HUGO

1802-1885

The true significance of Victor Hugo to 19th-century French literature has only been fully recognized since the 1970s. His legacy was perhaps too massive for the first half of the 20th century, which felt itself obliged to question his importance so that it could more freely follow the paths of modernity. But once the different movements of the avant-garde had come and gone, this literary giant once more found his rightful place in the pantheon. This was amply borne out by the celebrations that attended the bicentenary of his birth in 2002.

Collectors have never abandoned Hugo, but the abundance of autograph documents and the comparative eclipse of his reputation meant that, fifty years ago, admirers were able to benefit from a far greater selection than exists today. His drawings in particular, which have always exercised a special fascination even during his lifetime, remain in demand, and their value reflects the ever-increasing interest in this side of his work.

The document reproduced opposite is a fragment from the manuscript of *L'Homme qui rit* (1869). It not only reveals the author's working method, but it also has a strange formal beauty of its own. The different paragraphs that he has already worked on have been scratched out with a single stroke of the pen, while the 'blots' – which in fact are quite deliberate – are ethereal, phantom-like figures. The overall impression is of an extraordinary aesthetic power.

The Hugos were passionately interested in photography. Charles, one of Victor's sons, was a gifted practitioner, and photographed his father (above, without a beard) *c.* 1853. Carjat's portrait on the right shows an older Hugo, and an important feature of this is the author's own celebrated comment: 'And if only one is left, it will be me.'

▼ Charles Hugo, portrait of Victor Hugo (without a beard), calotype, c. 1853.
▲ Étienne Carjat, portrait of Victor Hugo, photograph signed with autograph inscription on the mount, c. 1878.
► Victor Hugo, 'Gwynplaine – last phase', autograph manuscript and drawings, c. 1868.

Gwynplaine

—

phase finale

Every day, Hugo would sit down at his desk to deal with his pile of correspondence – a chore which would be the equivalent now of spending hours on the telephone or exchanging emails. His daily dozens of letters involved a vast array of obligations: people asking for books, sending books, requesting theatre seats, offering theatre seats, invitations that he would accept or refuse, appointments to be made or to be granted…. He was the most public of figures for over fifty years, and even in exile (he was banished from France by Napoleon III in 1851) he kept up a huge correspondence. There are probably tens of thousands of notes and short letters, but often he would also send more substantial letters, some of which are magnificent pieces of writing. One remarkable example is a letter to a journalist during his exile (reproduced on the right). 'I have read your last article. No one knows better than you my law which is, for the detail as for the whole, *nothing superfluous*. Everything must serve the purpose…. What you say about Balzac is taken from the very basis of art and of the ideal. I greatly admire your articles, and feel a profound affinity with you. *One admires close to oneself.* I said this in *L'Homme qui rit*. With a deep and intimate satisfaction I observe this kinship of our minds. When I finished reading this last page, so lofty and so noble, written by you about my book, I looked for your hand in order to shake it. Around me I found solitude. Exile sometimes makes one feel its bitter point. I am your friend.'

The drawing above, dated 1847, has recently been authenticated by leading experts as a genuine Hugo. It is very much in the spirit of those dark, almost haunted scenes that he drew between the 1830s and the 1850s.

The fine portrait opposite is by Nadar, who has signed it in orange gouache and marked it 17 September 1862, Brussels. There are not many copies of this photograph, although it is one of the best portraits of Hugo at that time and was used as the basis of an engraving. In the bottom left-hand corner there is a crack from the glass plate, but the picture is so expressive that Nadar did not hesitate to put his name to the print despite this small imperfection.

▲ Victor Hugo, signed pen and ink drawing, 1847.
◄ Victor Hugo, autograph letter signed, 1869.
► Nadar, 'Victor Hugo', original albumen print signed in orange ink, 1862.

*…10,000 florins to the composer*
*Richard Wagner.*

# Richard WAGNER 1813-1883

# LUDWIG II *of Bavaria* 1845-1886

Until he met Ludwig II of Bavaria, who became his patron and benefactor, Richard Wagner seems to have been beset by never-ending financial problems. Both documents reproduced here relate to sums of money that Wagner was desperately hoping to receive. In one he earnestly begs for a loan from a friend, while the other concerns a generous gesture on the part of the patron who was so fascinated by his music.

Wagner's own letter, reproduced opposite, is in German, was written in Paris in 1860, and shows that he was in urgent need of support. He is at pains to explain how desperate his situation is: he needs five hundred francs. Then aged forty-seven, he was soon to return to Germany after having spent twelve years between Zurich and Paris. Napoleon III had just called for a command performance of *Tannhäuser* at the Paris Opera, and Wagner was at work on this massive production, which took place on 6 March 1861. But it was such a disaster that Wagner decided there and then to return to Germany. His balance sheet after a year of hard labour amounted to barely 750 francs – little more than the amount he was requesting from his correspondent.

The document signed by Ludwig II (right) dates from ten years later, a much more prosperous period. The young King, just twenty-four years old, was still keen to finance Wagner, even though this was a very expensive business. However, one can read between the lines that there is a certain reticence connected with this new loan, which was in addition to an advance and to the salary that Ludwig was already paying the composer. 'In addition to his annual salary, my treasurer may also disburse a loan, which will be the last, totalling 10,000 florins to the composer Richard Wagner.'

Repayment was provided for by the deduction of 2,000 florins from Wagner's annual salary, and this bound him for at least five years to the service of the King of Bavaria.

▼ Franz Hanfstaengl, portrait of Richard Wagner, photogravure, c. 1875.
▲ Ludwig II of Bavaria, document signed, 1869.
► Richard Wagner, autograph letter signed, 1860.

Verehrtester Herr!

Ich bin für heute in der grössten Verlegenheit um 500 fl. Könnten Sie mir diese kleine Summe noch einmal anvertrauen, so leisteten Sie mir einen ungemein grossen Dienst. Uebermorgen stelle ich sie Ihnen jedenfalls wieder zu.

Wollten Sie das Geld gefälligst an Conrad dem Bringer dieser Zeilen übergeben.

Ihr
ergebenster

Richard Wagner

Paris,
14 Juni 1860
Nachmittag.

*Je n'oublie rien, et je rêve toujours Wagner et Poe.*

*Charles* BAUDELAIRE

1821-1867

Baudelaire was twelve years old when he wrote the letter reproduced opposite to his brother (the sixth of his known letters, and published in his correspondence). He was writing from the boarding-school to which his mother and stepfather had sent him. Even if he was not yet the genius to whom we are indebted for some of the most startling images of 19th-century French poetry, the text is already remarkably precocious. Baudelaire reveals an intense interest in everything around him, turning a sharp eye on the closed-in world of the boarder.

'Charles the Younger to Alphonse the Elder, hello and Happy New Year. Another year gone, in April I shall be thirteen, and two years will have passed far from my brother, from Madame Tirlet, from Paris. Indeed, from Paris, which I miss so much. How boring it is at school, and especially at the school in Lyons! The walls are so sad, so filthy, so dank, the classrooms so dark, the Lyonnais character so different from the Parisian character!'

The famous portrait of Baudelaire by Carjat (right) was taken in 1857, then printed in Woodburytype in the 1860s and published in the *Galerie contemporaine*, which made it less of a rarity even if it is still much sought-after by all the great poet's admirers.

The remark 'I forget nothing, and I always dream Wagner and Poe', which forms the striking conclusion to an otherwise very ordinary letter written in 1862, reveals two of Baudelaire's main obsessions.

▲ Charles Baudelaire, postscript on autograph letter signed, 1862.
► Étienne Carjat, portrait of Charles Baudelaire, Woodburytype, c. 1865.
►► Charles Baudelaire, autograph letter signed, 1834.

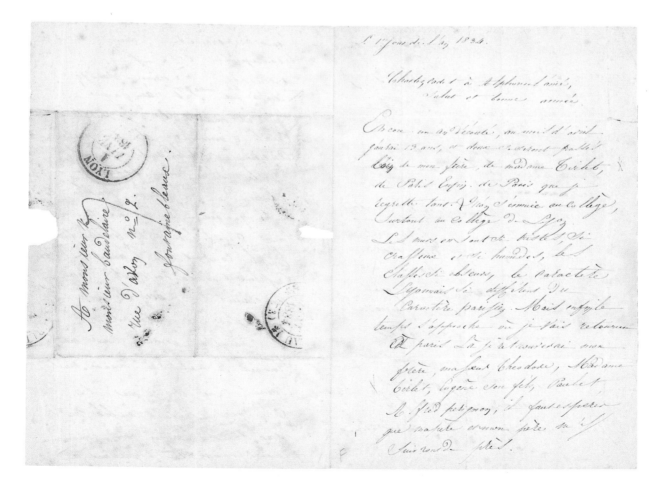

*When you appear, we prostrate ourselves…*

*O Master….*

# Gustave FLAUBERT

## 1821-1880

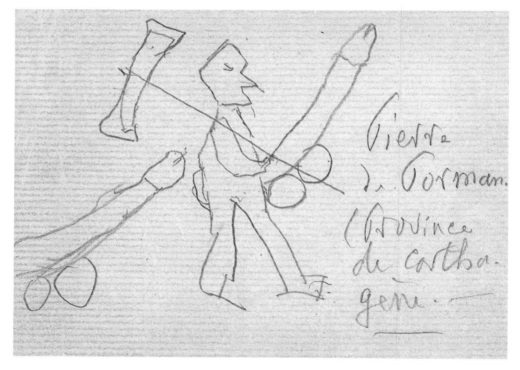

The letter reproduced opposite, addressed to Victor Hugo, is perhaps one of the most remarkable of all that have come down to us. The message from Flaubert (opposite), from one genius to another, certainly reveals the profound reverence which the author of *Madame Bovary* (1857) felt for the older man. Flaubert is filled with sincere admiration for a masterpiece that is not his own, but one can also sense a tinge of irony in the dithyrambic tone: 'Monsieur and dear Master, Only a few days ago I received *L'Homme qui rit*. That is why I have not thanked you earlier. This memento from you has filled me with pride. I will not extend the impertinence so far as to send you tokens of my admiration. When you appear, we

prostrate ourselves. I am, o Master, your very humble, very affectionate and devoted….'

On the reverse side are some words in faint pencil which unfortunately are no longer legible, but they would seem to be Victor Hugo's comment on this extraordinary piece from a rather limited correspondence between the two writers.

The photograph by Nadar (above left) is the best-known portrait of Flaubert, who sometimes amused himself by embellishing the countless notes he made in preparation for his novels with rather crude drawings like the one above on the right. It represents one 'Pierre de Porman from the province of Cartagena', perhaps discovered by Flaubert when he was doing his research for *Salammbô* (1862).

▼ Nadar, portrait of Gustave Flaubert, *c.* 1870.
▲ Gustave Flaubert, autograph drawing, *c.* 1865.
► Gustave Flaubert, autograph letter signed, 1869.

Monsieur & cher Maître

J'ai reçu, il y a quelques jours seulement,
l'Homme qui rit. c'est pourquoi je ne vous en
ai pas remercié plutôt.
Ce souvenir de votre part m'a comblé d'orgueil.

Je ne pourrais par l'insolence jusqu'à
me permettre de vous envoyer les hommages
de mon admiration

Quand vous apparaitez, on se prosterne —

Je suis, ô Maître
Votre très humble, très affectionné & dévoué

GⁱFlauberT

Croisset près Rouen.                    10 Juin 69.

*I am in a position to introduce you…*
*to the best and most intelligent society of Boston,*
*the best in the United States, I think…*

# Mikhail BAKUNIN

## 1814-1876

B orn into an aristocratic family, Bakunin was deported to Siberia after taking part in various revolutionary movements. In 1861, he managed to escape and found asylum in the USA. There he prepared to return to Europe in order to promote his doctrine of militant anarchism. He presented this to the First International in 1868, and it had an immediate and significant impact.

Written in French during the year of his escape, the letter reproduced opposite sounds quite extraordinary coming from the pen of the founder of anarchism. Bakunin announces to a friend: 'I am in a position to introduce you, beginning with Mr Agassiz, to the best and most intelligent society of Boston, the best in the United States, I think….'

One would hardly expect the anarchist to open doors to the very closed society of Boston, but we must perhaps keep in mind that for Bakunin 'best' and 'most intelligent' were complementary terms. He mentions Professor Louis Agassiz (1807–73), a famous naturalist of Swiss origin, whose theories contradicted those of Darwin. His friend was certainly not interested in social advancement but expected to meet the great intellectual figures of New England, who already admired Bakunin for his knowledge and ideas.

The portrait, in the form of a *carte de visite*, was taken by Nadar in Paris during the 1860s – one of several hundred in a collection of miniature portraits of celebrities which the photographer sold and which made his company's fortune.

► Nadar, portrait of Mikhail Bakunin, c.1862.
►► Mikhail Bakunin, autograph letter signed, 1861.

25 Novembre. 1861

Boston — Revere House
Revere House

Mon cher ami — Je ne puis quitter
Boston avant Samedi Soir — Mais
j'espère que sans perdre de temps
Vous vous déciderez à y venir Vous
même. Je serais à même de vous
faire-connaître à commencer par Mde
Agassiz, la meilleure et la plus intelli-
-gente Société de Boston, la meilleure
des États — Unis je pense. En ne le
faisant pas vous perdrez une occasion
unique peut-être — Décidez vous donc cher
ami, le trajet de New-York est de
10 h., le Revere House est un hôtel
excellent et la Société de Boston veut
bien le faire que Vous y veniez — Nous
passerons ensemble quelques journées agréables,
et votre ami en sera fort heureux,
Adieu — Je vous attends
Votre tout dévoué
M. Belloni

*...for what my dear faithful Brown...*
*did for me, no one else can....*

# QUEEN VICTORIA 1819-1901

## Alfred Lord TENNYSON 1809-1892

The picture of Queen Victoria at the age of thirty-six (above) is an original print by the great photographer Roger Fenton (1816–69), and according to an inscription on the back is 'the first that was made of the Queen when the daguerreotype was replaced by the calotype in 1855'.

During the sixty-two years of her reign, Victoria wrote tens of thousands of letters, the majority of which were jealously guarded by her correspondents, members of her family, and the many people who were flattered simply by the fact that Her Majesty had written to them.

The letter on the right, the first and last pages of which are reproduced, is one of the most sincere and revelatory messages that Victoria ever wrote to a particular individual. It was addressed to the Poet Laureate, Alfred Tennyson. The Queen admired his genius and soon afterwards made him a lord. After the death of her husband Prince Albert (1819–61), which plunged her into a profound depression for more than a decade, in 1883 Victoria suffered the loss of her 'best friend', her Scottish servant John Brown, who according to a long-established rumour may even have been her lover. She was then sixty-three years old, and had reigned through four decades. Here with astonishing directness she reveals to the poet just how fragile she is in this time of distress.

She tells him how grateful she is for their last conversation, and says how much she needs his support: 'few have had more trials & none have been or still are in such an exceptionally solitary and difficult position'.

The Queen continues in the same tone: 'It has been my anxious wish to do my duty to my country, though politics never were congenial to me and while my dear Husband lived I left as much as I could to him. Then

when He was taken I had to struggle on alone. And few know what that struggle has been....'

She remembers her dear friend Brown: 'And now again lately, I have lost one who – humble though he was – was the truest & most devoted of all! He had no thought but for me, my welfare, my comfort, my safety, my happiness. Courageous, unselfish, totally disinterested, discreet to the highest degree, speaking frankly the truth fearlessly & telling me what he thought and considered to be "just & right", without flattery & without saying what would be pleasing if he did not think it right. And ever at hand – he was part of my life and quite invaluable! He has been taken & I feel again very desolate, & forlorn – for what my dear faithful Brown – who was in my service for 34 years and for 18 never left me for a single day – did for me, no one else can.

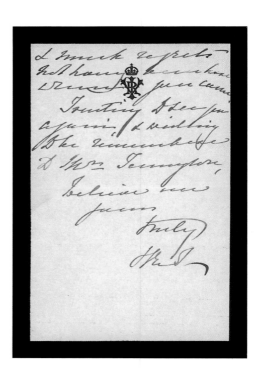

▼ Roger Fenton, portrait of Queen Victoria, calotype, 1855.
▲ Queen Victoria, autograph letter signed, 1883.
► Julia Margaret Cameron, *The Dirty Monk*, photograph signed by Tennyson and the photographer, 1870.

The comfort of my daily life is gone – the void is terrible – the loss irreparable!' Showing particular favour, she says she prefers to write to Tennyson in the first person, 'as the other form is so stiff & it is difficult to express feelings in the third person'.

The portrait of Tennyson opposite bears his signature as well as that of the famous photographer, Julia Margaret Cameron (1815–79), who christened this picture of the poet *The Dirty Monk*.

From life Registered Photograph Copyright Julia Margaret Cameron

A Tennyson

*...show to the porcupine a live snake and observe whether the sight of the snake will make it rattle the quills in the tail, as Mr Bartlett showed me that the porcupine does when angered.*

## Charles DARWIN

### 1809-1882

In 1870, when he wrote the letter reproduced here, Darwin was both a famous and a controversial figure. Despite his age, he continued to be driven by an insatiable curiosity that led to a vast range of reading and experiments. According to his biographers, he wrote ten or more letters every day to correspondents all over the world, trying to obtain or confirm information that might be useful for his research. Here he is asking his son Francis, whom he calls Frank, to persuade a certain Mr Bartlett to carry out a rather strange experiment: to confront a porcupine with a snake, in order 'to...observe whether the sight of the snake will make it rattle the quills in the tail, as Mr. Bartlett showed me that the porcupine does when angered'. At the time, Darwin was working on one of his last books, *The Expression of the Emotions in Man and Animals*, which was published in 1872. In this, he states that: 'Porcupines rattle their quills and vibrate their tails when angered; and one behaved in this manner when a live snake was placed in its compartment. The quills on the tail are very different from those on the body.... Now, when the tail is rapidly shaken, these hollow quills strike against each other and produce, as I heard in the presence of Mr Bartlett, a peculiar continuous sound.' The experiment that Darwin was asking for in this letter was therefore used as evidence for a hypothesis some time before he actually published his conclusions.

The photograph reproduced on the right is one of the best known of Darwin towards the end of his life, and it was taken by his grandson. The great naturalist signed it, rather shakily, less than a year before he died.

► Charles Darwin, signed photograph, 1882.
►► Charles Darwin, autograph letter signed, 1870.

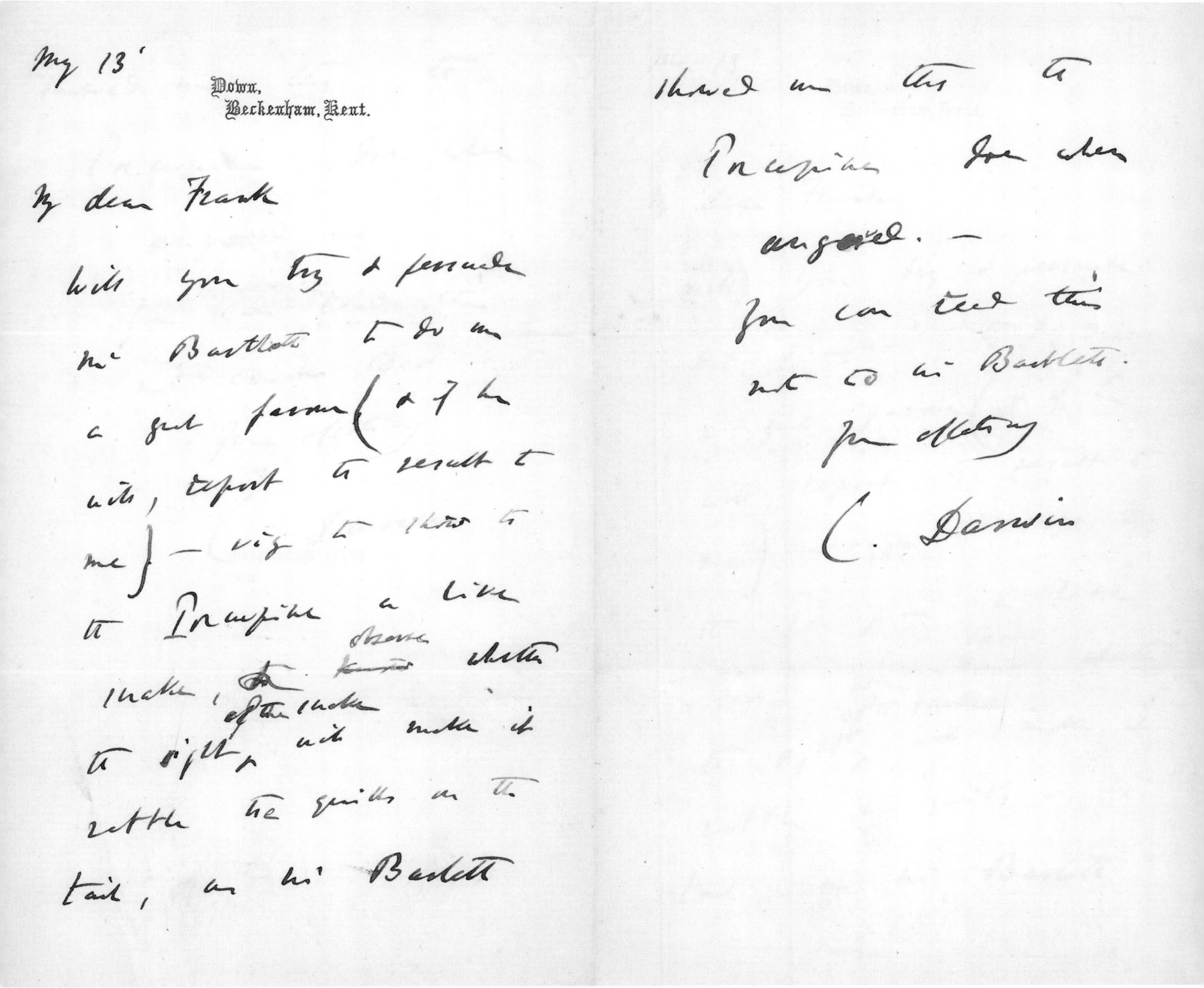

May 13'

Down,
Beckenham, Kent.

My dear Frank

Will you try & persuade
Mr Bartlett to do on
a good person (& if he
will, report the result to
me) — viz to sketch to
the Porcupine a little
snake, to show whether
the sight of the snake
will make it
rattle the quills on the
tail, as Mr Bartlett

shewed me that the
Porcupine does when
angered. —
You can read this
note to Mr Bartlett.
your affectionty
C. Darwin

*…[if you can] find fifty or so
    bottles of Barolo, that is to say good Barolo,
real and authentic, send them to me….*

# Giuseppe VERDI

## 1813–1901

Verdi's reputation really took off with *Nabucco*, which he composed in 1842. The Italian resistance movement against Austrian dominance took the slaves' chorus as its rallying cry, and Verdi became a national hero who symbolized the patriotism of his people. His fame rapidly spread far beyond the borders of Italy. The passionate advocate of liberty and humanism was complemented by the prolific, powerful and highly original composer, whose success was redoubled by the *Risorgimento*.

Verdi was no great lover of the bourgeois way of life, and was certainly no gourmet in the manner of Rossini, who frequented the finest restaurants in Europe. He preferred a relatively simple and quiet life, but all the same he did cultivate certain pleasures.

The letter reproduced here is an eloquent expression of these. Verdi is asking a friend to get him one of Italy's most famous wines. Quite explicitly he sets out the details of his particular liking: 'If you know of a gallant gentleman who might be able to find fifty or so bottles of Barolo, that is to say good Barolo, real and authentic, send them to me. But be very careful. If you are not sure, absolutely sure that it is real and authentic, pure Barolo, don't send it to me. I can do without it. I like Chianti, and if it's not real Barolo, I prefer to do without it.'

The photograph above was taken in Paris by André Adolphe-Eugène Disdéri, the great portraitist of the Second Empire, who generally used the *carte de visite* format.

▲ Eugène Disdéri, portrait of Giuseppe Verdi, albumen print, c. 1858.
►►► Giuseppe Verdi, autograph letter signed, c. 1885.

... le bottiglie di Barolo: una
di buon Barolo, vero e legittimo
Barolo mandatemela. Ma badate
bene, se non vi è la sicurezza
una vera sicurezza che sia
Barolo vero, legittimo, ...
una mandatemelo. Di proposito
farne senza: a me piace il
Chianti, ed a meno non ...
trovi un vero e perfetto Barolo
... far senza di questo
vino.

quindi addio.

Datemi buone notizie,
cioè notizie ...

V.

Verdi

*...to my dear brother....*

## *Fyodor* DOSTOYEVSKY 1821-1881

## *Ivan* TURGENEV 1818-1883

Documents in Dostoyevsky's own handwriting have long been extremely rare in the West. No one knew anything about possible private collections in the Soviet Union, and it was not until the USSR finally broke up that a tiny number of items emerged from these private archives to enrich collections abroad. The magnificent original photograph opposite was taken in 1879, and on the back the Russian novelist has dedicated it to his brother Andrei and has signed it with his own first name. In the last thirty years, only one other signed photograph has appeared on the market. Autograph letters are equally rare – only five or six have been sold in the same period. If there are indeed some manuscripts of great Russian writers hidden away in private collections, they are certainly not being made available to the international market, where there would be enormous interest in such 'unobtainables' as Aleksandr Pushkin (1799–1837), Nikolai Gogol (1809–52) and Mikhail Lermontov (1814–41). Only fellow Russian writer Anton Chekhov, who until a short time ago would also have been classed as one of the rarities, seems to have benefited from the opening up of the Soviet Union. Some twenty signed items have come on the market in the last ten years.

Turgenev manuscripts, however, are more readily available, no doubt because he spent many years abroad – particularly in France. His letters in German and French (addressed, for instance, to Flaubert or to George Sand) are regularly on offer. Far rarer, and indeed almost unique, are photographs such as the one on the right, which he has signed in Russian script.

◄ Ivan Turgenev, signed photograph, *c.* 1875.
► Fyodor Dostoyevsky, photograph inscribed and signed by Dostoyevsky on the back, 1879.

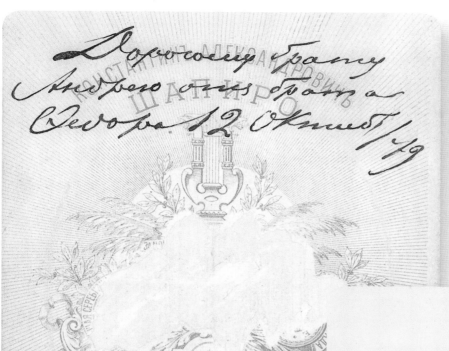

*...I was assailed by such a violent intestinal indisposition...champagne chilled with pieces of ice was the real remedy....*

# Louis PASTEUR

## 1822-1895

One would hardly expect a scientist like Pasteur, suffering from an indisposition 'so violent that you would have said it was cholera', and enduring several days during which his stomach 'could not take a single drop of water', to treat it with a 'real remedy' consisting of 'champagne chilled with pieces of ice'.

This, however, according to his letter, was precisely the self-prescribed treatment chosen by the man who made one of the most crucial medical discoveries of the 19th century (below right and opposite). Texts written by the very serious Louis Pasteur are rarely as surprising as this. His many letters, always greatly sought-after, are generally rather formal and devoid of personal comments. But some are actually moving, especially those written during the most intensive period of his working life, when he was doing research on a vaccine for rabies.

In January 1885, he was coming close to making his discovery. The government had at last allowed him to use the kennels at Meudon, near Paris, for his experiments, and this explains the extraordinary receipt (above right) made out to the owner of a dog that had been bitten by a rabid animal: 'I have received...a dog that has been attacked by one that is rabid. It will not leave my kennels, where I shall attempt to make it resistant to the rabies, despite the probable bite of four days ago.' At this point, he had not yet attempted any experiments on human beings, but he was to do so successfully six months later, on a young man from Alsace named Joseph Meister.

The great scientist was loaded with honours over the last ten years of his life. This was also the time when Paul Nadar took the fine photograph of him at the top of the page.

▶ Paul Nadar, portrait of Louis Pasteur, autograph card signed, c. 1890.
▲ Louis Pasteur, autograph card signed, 1885.
◀ ▶ Louis Pasteur, autograph letter signed, 1879.

Paris, le 22 oct. 1879

Mon cher ami,

Merci de votre aimable souvenir. Je vais mieux. Hier j'ai pu sortir pour aller à l'académie de médecine. A la fin de septembre j'ai été pris à Abbois d'un dérangement intestinal tellement violent qu'on eût dit le choléra. Pendant plusieurs jours mon estomac ne pouvait recevoir une goutte d'eau. Le champagne reposé sur des morceaux de glace a été le vrai remède. Forcés que nous étions de revenir à cause des préparatifs du mariage, fixé au 4 novembre, je me suis mis bravement en route pour Paris à la première marque de convalescence. Nous sommes arrivés le 14 et depuis ce moment je reprends mes forces quoique fort lentement.

Je suis bien charmé d'apprendre que vous vous portez bien et que madame Godin va vous rendre pour une troisième fois avec cette vaillance qui lui est habituelle et qui traduit si bien la beauté vigoureuse de vos chers enfants.

*[Dear] Mallarmé…Madame Manet*
*accepts the invitation to dine at the Degas'*
*and so do I – Renoir.*

## Auguste RENOIR 1841-1919

## Edgar DEGAS 1834-1917

Although invitations are generally of little interest, this one is an exception. The little card (above right) combines four illustrious names: Renoir is telling French poet Stéphane Mallarmé (1842–98) that they will dine together at the Degas', along with Édouard Manet's (1832–83) widow. One can well imagine that such a gathering would have been a memorable occasion. In the collection at the Musée d'Orsay, there is a fine photograph, taken by Degas, of Renoir and Mallarmé together.

Letters by Renoir and Degas are much sought-after, particularly by American and Japanese collectors. But they are far from common, and more often than not the two artists only wrote brief messages anyway. Degas's autograph letter below left (written when the artist was in his eighties) suggests that his eyesight is deteriorating. Degas is urging his correspondent to send him an article that he has heard about concerning the Friends of the Louvre, and he adds: 'I am impatient to read you, or rather to have you read out to me….'

The piece reproduced opposite is of particular interest. It shows the procedure that Renoir used towards the end of his life to authenticate his many works. He had them photographed in small groups, and signed the prints. Then he had his signature certified at the town hall in Cagnes, where he was living at the time. In this manner, he produced a whole collection of 'certificates' which are highly valued today by specialists, especially for compiling catalogues raisonnés. A few have appeared on the market during the last twenty years, much to the delight of collectors.

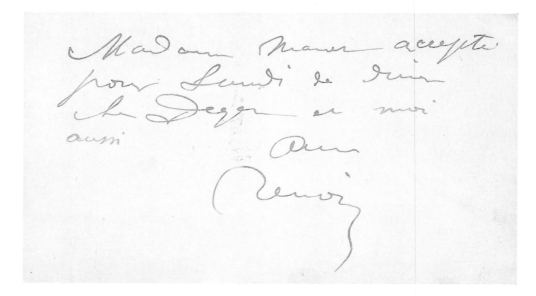

▲ Auguste Renoir, autograph card signed (recto and verso), 1894.
◀ Edgar Degas, autograph letter signed, c. 1914.
▶ Photograph of four works, signed and authenticated by Renoir, 1915.

Vu pour la légalisation de la signature
de Mr Pierre-Auguste Renoir, artiste peintre
apposée ci-contre.
Cagnes, le 21 mars 1915
Le Maire -

Renoir

*...as a loan of the sum of one thousand francs,
which will be repayable on the royalties
from the sale of thirty-five of my paintings....*

# Claude MONET 1840-1926

# Édouard MANET 1832-1883

Today it is difficult to imagine the precarious financial circumstances in which the great Impressionists began their careers. The record prices now fetched by the works of Monet, Renoir, Camille Pissarro (1830–1903) and Alfred Sisley (1839–99) during the 20th century have eclipsed the problems they had in those early days. However, many of these artists only survived by way of mutual help around the 1860s, until the circle of their admirers began to expand.

It is against the background of these difficulties that the letter opposite takes on its full significance. Claude Monet was thirty-five years old when he signed this acknowledgment of his debt to Gustave Manet, Édouard's brother. The latter lent him the fairly modest sum of 1,000 francs (less than 5,000 Euros nowadays) which Monet promised to repay 'on the royalties from the sale of thirty-five of my paintings'. The sale was to take place under the direction of an auctioneer named Oudart. Monet goes on: 'As a guarantee for this loan, on this very day I deposit eight pictures destined for the above-mentioned sale, and the other twenty-seven pictures (including the one representing a lifesize Japanese woman) are to be deposited by me at the same place as and when they are completed.' The *Japonaise* that he mentions is now one of the jewels in the collection of the Museum of Fine Arts, Boston. There could scarcely be a better illustration than this document of how far away the Impressionists were from success.

It was Gustave Manet, Monet's creditor, who together with his brothers Eugène and Édouard signed the document on the right, relating to the purchase of a piece of land. Édouard Manet's letter above it is addressed to his one and only female pupil, the young

Eva Gonzales, with whom he may have flirted. 'Are your two pictures finished? You know that if you need me, I am entirely at your disposal.' Manet kept up a regular and good-natured correspondence with Eva (whose work is now becoming increasingly popular), but it was sold off and is widely scattered. This letter shows Manet's interest in the young girl, and the pleasure he had in their meetings.

▲ Anonymous, portrait of Claude Monet, press photograph, c. 1918.
◄ Édouard Manet, autograph letter signed, 1877.
► Édouard, Eugène and Gustave Manet, document signed, 1881.
►► Claude Monet, document signed, 1875.

Je soussigné Claude Monet reconnais avoir reçu de Mr Gustave Manet à titre de prêt la somme de mille francs, laquelle sera remboursable sur le produit de la vente de trente cinq de mes tableaux qui devra être faite dans le courant de février prochain par le ministère de Me Charles Oudart commissaire priseur

En garantie de ce prêt je dépose aujourd'hui même huit tableaux destinés à la dite vente les autres vingt sept tableaux y compris celui représentant une femme japonaise (grandeur nature) actuellement en cours d'exécution devant être remis par moi au même endroit au fur et à mesure qu'ils seront terminés, le dernier devant être livré au plus tard le premier février prochain

fait à Paris l'an mil huit cent soixante quinze le dix huit octobre
approuvé l'écriture
Claude Monet

chez Me Charles
Oudart /
C. M.

*I don't feel the same passionate appetite for your dog that I felt that evening; it is probably because I have just had my breakfast....*

## Mark TWAIN

### 1835-1910

Mark Twain (the pseudonym adopted by Samuel Langhorne Clemens) was and still is the most popular American author of his generation. Anthologies of his often caustic witticisms still entertain readers all over the world, and Tom Sawyer and Huckleberry Finn are two of the most instantly recognizable characters in American literature.

Mark Twain's letters, always full of ironic humour, were often dictated to a secretary, but were generally signed in his real name. This is the case with the letter reproduced here, which is addressed to a Mrs Ditson in 1906, towards the end of Twain's life. He refers first to a somewhat obscure episode – something that his correspondent had said which 'has moved me, and also modified me, in some degree'. Then comes the main substance of the letter with a flash of typical Twain wit: 'I don't feel the same passionate appetite for your dog that I felt that evening; it is probably because I have just had my breakfast.' He then declares that she must not trust in his good resolutions, because 'for my sake and the dog's, I think it will be better that one of us keep out of the way'.

Above is a postcard photograph, showing Twain the previous year at a time when he was probably the most famous man in America. He has signed it with his pseudonym.

▲ Mark Twain, postcard photograph signed, 1905.
►► Mark Twain, letter signed, 1906.

21 FIFTH AVENUE

March 5. 1906

Dear Mrs Ditson:

I am glad to have that speech; it has moved me, & also modified me, in some degree. I don't feel the same passionate *appetite* for your dog that I felt that evening; it is probably because I have just had my breakfast. I can't really depend on my reforms: They are so likely to be inspirational & temporary; Therefore for my sake &

the dogs, I think it will
be better that one of
us keep out of the
way.

Yours affectionately,

SL. Clemens

*From Guy de Maupassant…*
*on the subject of my tragedy* The Father….

## *Guy de* MAUPASSANT 1850-1893

## *August* STRINDBERG 1849-1912

There are letters which may at first sight seem uninteresting, but which sometimes reveal a dimension that is out of all proportion to their apparent triviality. All the more so when the sender and the recipient are both famous people. This is the case with the note reproduced opposite. The collector who bought it in the 1940s was simply looking for specimens of the handwriting of great authors, and was not at all interested in the content. The French dealer who sold it to him had not taken any notice of what may have seemed to him just a scribble on the back of the sheet, and so he offered it for the modest sum that this text seemed to be worth: 'Dear colleague, I thank you most cordially for your fine drama…it is powerful and profound….'

All well-known writers on being approached by other authors have written such comments. But here we have the only known letter that French writer Maupassant ever wrote to Strindberg. The opinion of the author of *Boule de Suif* (1880) and *Bel-Ami* (1885) on one of the Swedish dramatist's major works certainly gives this piece extra significance. However, what makes it unique is the inscription on the back, because the 'scribble' is in fact in Strindberg's handwriting, and says: 'From Guy de Maupassant…on the subject of my tragedy *Fadren* [The Father, 1887].'

At the top of this page is a photograph of Maupassant by Paul Nadar. On the right, an extraordinary portrait of Strindberg, looking rather dishevelled; it was taken by a remarkable Swedish photographer named Lina Jonn, and is the largest and most striking signed photograph of the playwright to have come on the open market.

▶ Paul Nadar, portrait of Guy de Maupassant, c. 1890.
▲ Lina Jonn, signed photograph of August Strindberg, c. 1900.

▶ Guy de Maupassant, autograph letter signed, with autograph addition by August Strindberg, c. 1890.

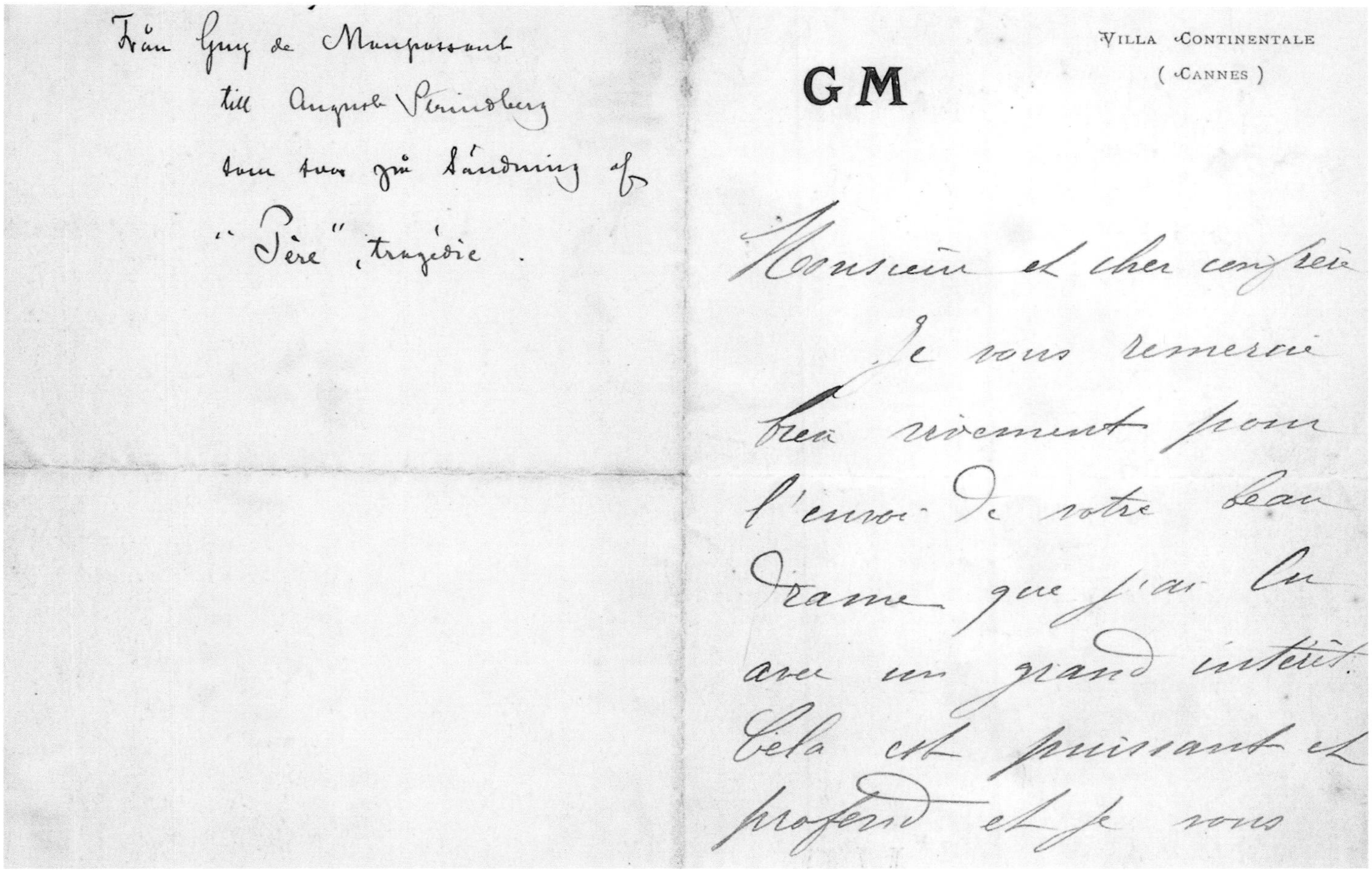

Från Guy de Maupassant
till August Strindberg
som tack för sändning of
" Père ", tragédie .

**GM**

VILLA CONTINENTALE
( CANNES )

Monsieur et cher confrère

Je vous remercie bien vivement pour l'envoi de votre beau drame que j'ai lu avec un grand intérêt. Cela est puissant et profond et je vous

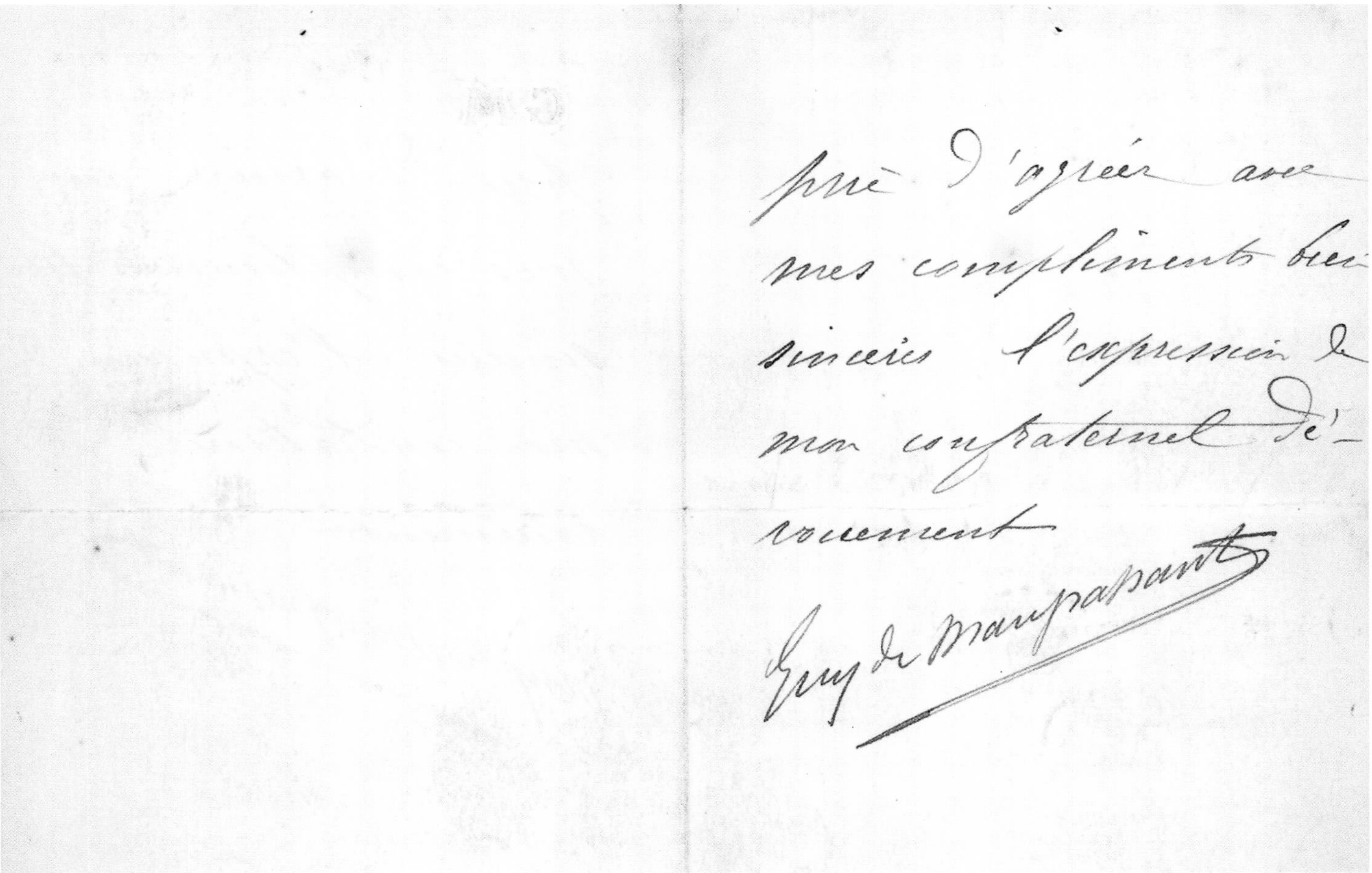

prie d'agréer avec mes compliments bien sincères l'expression de mon confraternel dévouement

Guy de Maupassant

*He proposes...to speak on the scientific basis of Occultism on Palmistry....*

# Oscar WILDE

## 1854-1900

The young Oscar Wilde's triumphant lecture tour of the USA at the age of twenty-five helped to make him famous. Sadly, his fame turned to notoriety as a result of the scandal that was later to turn his world upside down.

In the course of the tour, which lasted 260 days and during which he gave more than 150 lectures, Wilde posed in New York for the photographer Napoleon Sarony, who made what is probably the best-known series of portraits of the great Irish writer. The large-format portrait on the right was taken during this sitting, and shows Wilde dressed in a fur coat, with long hair and pensive expression. The photograph is inscribed to one of his American admirers.

The success of the lectures was such that Wilde maintained special relations with the agencies that had organized them throughout the States. The long letter reproduced opposite is addressed to the Redpath Agency, which had aranged the lectures in Boston. The content is quite unusual: Wilde is recommending a certain Edward Heron-Allen, who proposes to speak on 'the scientific basis of Occultism on Palmistry principally, a subject on which he has written some very remarkable books'. Wilde explains that he is recommending Allen to 'your well known Bureau', because he is convinced that if he 'succeeds in exciting as much interest in the States as he has in London he will have a great success'.

Items signed by Wilde are much sought-after. Important manuscripts have reappeared on the open market over the last twenty years, and have fetched record-breaking prices.

► Napoleon Sarony, portrait of Oscar Wilde, with inscription and signature, 1881.
►► Oscar Wilde, autograph letter signed, c. 1892.

OSCAR WILDE..

NEW YORK.

16. TITE STREET.
CHELSEA. S.W.

Dear Sir.

Will you allow me to introduce to you Mr. Heron Allen who is very anxious to lecture in America

pleasure from his lectures.

He proposes I think, to speak on the scientific basis of Occultism on Palmistry principally, a subject on which he has

16. TITE STREET.
CHELSEA. S.W.

written some very remarkable books, and he will illustrate his lecture by numerous examples, anecdotes, and large Diagrams,

recommend him to your well known Bureau, and hope you will be able to give him the opportunity of speaking under your management

Truly yours

Oscar Wilde

# *Henri de* TOULOUSE-LAUTREC

## 1864-1901

It rarely happens that a collection of a famous person's letters contains both the first and last known items. This, however, is the case with the documents reproduced here, between which there is a gap of thirty years. Opposite is the first letter, sent by Toulouse-Lautrec to his godmother, Louise Tapié de Céleyran, when Henri was seven years old; his mother wrote it, and he signed it with a flourish that one would like to think heralded the artistic talents of the young aristocrat, even though nothing in his environment would have indicated that he would become a painter. The drawing of a postman (above left) comes from a letter to his mother dated 1880, when Toulouse-Lautrec was sixteen years old.

The dramatic nature of his life is well known, as is the importance of the support – albeit intermittent – of his mother. Of all the great painters of the 19th century, he appears to have led the most dissolute life, for which he paid with his early death at the age of thirty-seven.

It was a pitiful Toulouse-Lautrec who, exhausted and desperate, penned the last note that we know of, on the back of a letter from Paul Viaud, dated July 1901 (below right). Viaud was his best friend towards the end of his life, and the artist's last major painting, *L'Amiral Viaud*, shows him from behind dressed in the red uniform worn by admirals in the 18th century. Toulouse-Lautrec's note is succinct: 'Dear mother, we shall be arriving shortly. Viaud will let you know. With love and affection, Henri.' He died six weeks later, three weeks after being paralysed by a stroke.

Toulouse-Lautrec's letters became very rare during the 1970s. A Japanese university and a wealthy American couple set out to purchase several hundred, and almost all the letters that came on the market over a period of thirty years were snapped up. Recently, however, the latter collection has been broken up, and this has helped to normalize what had long been a restricted supply in the face of ever-increasing demand.

▼ Henri de Toulouse-Lautrec, drawing on autograph letter signed, 1890.
▲ Henri de Toulouse-Lautrec, autograph letter signed, 1901.
► Henri de Toulouse-Lautrec, letter signed, 1871.

Château de Céleyran le 28 Avril 71.

Ma chère Marraine

Je vous embrasse ~~ma lettre~~ de
tout mon cœur, et dites-moi si
Mlle Julie va bien, si Amour
Justine et Antoine vont bien.
Je vous embrasse encore une
fois et c'est fini.

henri

*Yesterday…during the* Siegfried Idyll, *I realized that for the
first time in my life I was making music only for money….*

# Gustav MAHLER 1860-1911

# Alma MAHLER-WERFEL 1879-1964

# Oskar KOKOSCHKA 1886-1980

In the dazzling society of Vienna at the beginning of the last century, the young artist Oskar Kokoschka fell in love with Alma Mahler, seven years his senior and only recently widowed, and the affair caused a major scandal. Alma – who went on to marry the American architect Walter Gropius (1883–1969), and then the German novelist Franz Werfel (1890–1945) – remains, next to German writer Lou Andréas Salomé (1861–1937), the most accomplished seductress of the geniuses of her time.

The letter from Gustav Mahler reproduced opposite was written in Moscow, and offers us a striking insight: 'Yesterday…during the *Siegfried Idyll*, I realized that for the first time in my life I was making music only for money….' This is an unexpected confession from one of the most gifted and passionate musicians of his generation.

After her marriage to Werfel in 1929, Alma Mahler-Werfel settled in the USA, where she wrote the thank you letter on the right, addressed to an American musician. Above is a drawing by Kokoschka. A young girl had asked him to sign the programme for an arts festival in Berlin. Kokoschka preferred to do a sketch of her, adding that she was 'the most beautiful girl of the evening'.

▼ Oskar Kokoschka, signed drawing with autograph inscription, 1921.
▲ Alma Mahler-Werfel, autograph letter signed, c. 1943.
► Gustav Mahler, autograph letter signed, 1897.

Liebste Freundin!

Es wäre doch der Gipfel der Undankbarkeit, wenn ich nicht einen dieser Briefe an die echten erwiderte. — Wie lange hätten Sie in meinen Augen vorausgesetzt noch auch erhalten?

Ich habe also nur zuzufügen, daß das Concert gestern vollkommen und das gut ausgefallen ist. — Mitten im Siegfried-Idyll fiel es mir ein, daß ich zum erstenmal in meinem Leben für das liebe Publikum Musik gemacht habe. Auch ein Fortschritt in diesem Jahre! Nun wende ich mich also wieder die bürgerliche Ordnung vorübern!

Mit herzlichsten Grüßen Ihr
Gustav Mahler

# Émile ZOLA 1840-1902

# Alfred DREYFUS 1859-1935

At the end of the 19th century, the Dreyfus affair split France into two camps. Émile Zola's role in defending the accused man probably did as much for his reputation at the time as his novels and his place at the head of the Naturalists.

When papers discovered in a litter bin revealed the treason of a French officer, Jewish Captain Dreyfus seemed to the anti-Semitic army chiefs to be the ideal scapegoat. At the heart of the affair was a document which proved that information had been passed to the German army in Paris. A slight similarity between the captain's very small handwriting and that on the document was enough to have him discharged from the army and deported to Devil's Island in French Guiana.

On 13 January 1895, the eloquent cover of *Le Petit journal* (with a circulation of nearly a million copies in the 1890s) depicted the ceremony at which the condemned man was cashiered. It had a profound effect on public opinion, fuelling the dispute between the pro-Dreyfus and the anti-Dreyfus camps.

The photograph on the right, taken by Gerschel, shows Dreyfus in around 1910. Finally declared innocent, he has the calm air of a man whose honour has been restored. Above is one of his visiting cards, a rare item, which contains a few handwritten words of thanks and indicates the rank he attained at the end of his career.

The principal piece of evidence for the prosecution, the famous document that led to the guilty verdict against Dreyfus, was initially the object of much over-hasty 'expertise',

▲ Alfred Dreyfus, visiting card with autograph addition, c. 1920.
► Gerschel, portrait of Alfred Dreyfus, signed photograph, c. 1905.
►► Cover of *Le Petit journal*, original issue of 13 January 1895, with engraving entitled *The Traitor: Degradation of Alfred Dreyfus*.

GERSCHEL

REPRODUCTION INTERDITE
COPYRIGHT BY GERSCHEL
Gerschel
23, Boul⁴ DES CAPUCINES
PARIS
EN FACE LE GRAND HÔTEL

# Le Petit Journal

**Le Petit Journal**
CHAQUE JOUR 5 CENTIMES
**Le Supplément illustré**
CHAQUE SEMAINE 5 CENTIMES

## SUPPLÉMENT ILLUSTRÉ
### Huit pages : CINQ centimes

**ABONNEMENTS**

|  | TROIS MOIS | SIX MOIS | UN AN |
|---|---|---|---|
| PARIS | 1 fr. | 2 fr. | 3 fr 50 |
| DÉPARTEMENTS | 1 fr. | 2 fr. | 4 fr. |
| ÉTRANGER | 1 50 | 2 50 | 5 fr. |

Sixième année — DIMANCHE 13 JANVIER 1895 — Numéro 217

## LE TRAITRE
### Dégradation d'Alfred Dreyfus

L'affaire Dreyfus.

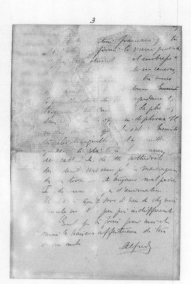

*An autograph letter of Esterhazy\**
\* This identical letter formed part of the evidence laid before the Cour de Cassation.

*An autograph letter of Captain Dreyfus.*

These letters were given me by Madame Dreyfus for the purpose of comparing the pulse tracing in the handwriting of Esterhazy, Captain Dreyfus & the Author of the Bordereau. I discovered that the pulse beat can be found in all handwriting if written slowly, and is characteristic of the writers pulse beat. By this means I discovered that the copy of the Bordereau published in France did not show either Dreyfus' or Esterhazy's pulse, and was undoubtedly a tracing taken by a third party over the original document. The letter of Esterhazy's here shown is an order on his Broker to purchase 5000 Italian Rentes (Consols). The fact that the shares fell in price before Settlement Day landed him in difficulties, and the theory is, that it compelled him to resort to other means to raise the money, by applying to the Secret Service, which resulted in an infamous plot, the consequences of which are felt to this day
G. Lindsay Johnson M.D. FRCS.

but a few years after the trial, suspicion fell on Major Esterhazy (1847–1923). Esterhazy proved to be the real culprit when specimens of his and Dreyfus's handwriting were once more examined by the experts and compared to the chief piece of evidence against Dreyfus. Two of these specimens are to be seen above, mounted by one of the consultants, an Englishman named G. Lindsay Johnson. Esterhazy's letter was presented to the appeal court in 1906, and Johnson states in his own handwritten text that Dreyfus's letter was supplied to him by Mme Dreyfus.

On the right is a fine picture of Dreyfus's defender, taken by Paul Nadar, and signed by Zola himself four years before he died. The pages reproduced opposite are four of the seven that make up the manuscript of the preface to *Une campagne première*, dated 1882. This autograph manuscript contains a number of corrections, though certainly fewer than the first drafts of many of Zola's contemporaries, such as Flaubert. It is nevertheless a fascinating document for the insight it gives into the great novelist's method of working.

▲ Alfred Dreyfus and Ferdinand Esterhazy, autograph letters signed, mounted by G. Lindsay Johnson in 1906.
◄ Paul Nadar, portrait of Émile Zola, signed photograph, 1898.
► Émile Zola, autograph manuscript signed, 1882.

**Préface**

*Une Campagne*

Je réunis dans ce volume les articles que j'ai don-
nés au Figaro, pendant ma campagne d'une année. Pourtant,
on ne les y trouvera pas tous, car j'ai cru devoir mettre
à part les pures fantaisies, les airs de flûte que
je jouais entre deux batailles et que je réserve pour un
autre recueil. J'ai gardé uniquement les articles de polémique.

Aujourd'hui, me voilà dans la retraite. Depuis
quatre mois, j'ai quitté la presse, et je compte bien n'y
point rentrer, sans vouloir toutefois m'y engager par un
serment. C'est un état de bien être profond, ce
désintéressement de l'actualité, cette paix de l'esprit
tout entier à une œuvre unique, surtout au sortir
de seize ans de journalisme militant. Il me
semble déjà qu'un peu de paix se fait sur mes
livres et sur mon nom, un peu de justice aussi.
J'en doute, lorsqu'on ne m'apercevra plus à travers les
colères de la lutte, qu'on verra unique-
ment en moi le travailleur enfermé dans l'effort so-
litaire de son œuvre, la légende imbécile de mon

charivari contemporain, j'ai réussi parfois
à me faire écouter. Refusez-moi tout, dis-
cutez et niez : je n'en ai pas moins rendu à
la littérature le service de la dégager un moment
de ce tas lourd et bête de politique, sous lequel elle
râle, enterrée vivante. Quand je n'aurais servi qu'à
cela, quand je me serais simplement produit pour
allumer des querelles littéraires, pour me faire accabler
d'injures, pour tirer les lettres de leur immobilisme
par ma bataille, eh bien ! j'estime que tous les
écrivains, les jeunes surtout, devraient m'en
garder un peu de reconnaissance. On vit au
moins, lorsqu'on se bat. La passion appelle la passion. Que notre querelle littéraire
disparaisse, et vous verrez la masse informe
de la politique retomber et s'étaler plus odieu-
sement dans les journaux, tout boucher, tout
écraser, au point qu'il faudrait faire
des fouilles, pour retrouver les os
d'un romancier impénitent ou les cheveux du dernier poète !

J'ai un orgueil, je l'avoue : c'est, depuis
ans, d'avoir gardé les mêmes croyances littéraires,
d'être allé tout droit mon chemin, en tâchant simplement de l'élargir sans cesse davantage. Jamais je
ne me suis dérobé, ni à droite, ni à gauche. Je n'ai
pas une ligne à effacer, pas une opinion à regretter,
pas une conclusion à reprendre. On ne trouvera,
dans mes sept volumes de critique, que le dévelop-
pement continu, et seulement de plus en plus appuyé,
de la même idée. L'homme qui l'année dernière, à
quarante ans, publiait les articles d'Une Campagne,
encore étrange, à vingt ans, écrivait
La méthode est restée la même, et le but, et
la foi. Ce n'est pas à moi de décider si j'ai
fait quelque lumière, mais je puis constater que j'ai
toujours voulu la lumière par les mêmes moyens
et dans le même besoin de vérité.

On découvrira cela un jour. Je dors tranquille.
Comme je l'ai déjà dit ailleurs, je n'ai jamais voulu
être que le soldat le plus convaincu du vrai. Sans
doute, on a pu confondre le romancier et le critique,

Donc je me retire égoïstement dans mon
coin, un peu isolé je le confesse, et je n'ai
plus qu'un souhait à faire : c'est qu'il nous
vienne des critiques passionnés, pour qu'on les
injurie et qu'ils nous tiennent en haleine.
Le désir de la
vérité ne suffit pas, dans nos temps troublés ;
il en faut la passion qui exagère parfois, mais
qui s'impose. Allons ! où est le jeune
écrivain qui nous sauvera de cette commère
braillarde de la politique, qui parlera aussi
haut qu'elle, qui plantera dans
les décombres le noble drapeau de la littérature,
si rudement, que la Femme
oubliera au moins pour un jour les tor-
chons sales des partis !

Émile Zola

Médan, 15 janvier 1882.

*Monsieur Rodin has asked me*
*to send you his apologies....*

*Auguste* RODIN 1840-1917

*Camille* CLAUDEL 1864-1943

*Rainer Maria* RILKE 1875-1926

The letter reproduced opposite is not in French sculptor Auguste Rodin's handwriting, and was merely signed by him. Its content is of no great significance, and it would be of little or no interest were it not for the fact that the secretary to whom it was dictated was a man called Rainer Maria Rilke. This very rare piece therefore combines the handwriting of two exceptional talents. The great German poet was in fact Rodin's secretary from 1905 until 1907, when the sculptor – regarded by his contemporaries as the greatest since Michelangelo (1475–1564) – was at the peak of his fame.

Rodin was so much in demand, and was faced with such a vast correspondence, that he took to employing secretaries to deal with most of his mail. He also had to cope with his many female admirers, who in their devotion lavished their attention on him from dawn till dusk. One of his greatest fans was an Italian named Mademoiselle Cimino, whom Rodin often liked and sometimes hated. It was to her that he dedicated the fine photograph on the right, which was left as part of her estate, together with many letters which he wrote to her.

The American Edward Steichen (1879–1973) was responsible for the magnificent photogravure at the top of the page – undoubtedly the finest portrait of the sculptor, taken by one of the greatest photographers of the 20th century.

Overleaf is an inscription written by Rilke a year before his death on one of the works which he had translated into German. When Rodin dictated the letter to Rilke, his famous

▲ Edward Steichen, portrait of Auguste Rodin, photogravure, 1905.
► Auguste Rodin, inscribed and signed photograph, c. 1910.
►► Auguste Rodin and Rainer Maria Rilke, autograph letter by Rilke signed by Rodin, 1908.

*a mon amie M^lle E. Cimino*
*A Rodin.*

19 Févr. 1906

182, RUE DE L'UNIVERSITÉ

Monsieur,

Monsieur Rodin extrèmement
préoccupé et préparant son
voyage à Londres pour demain,
à son grand regret ne peut pas
dans ce moment accorder au-
cune Séance à M. Belleroche.

À son retour de Londres,
au commencement du mois
de Mars, il fera tout son possible
pour vous contenter.

Entretemps M. Rodin vous
présente ses sentiments empressés
et cordials :

J. Rodin

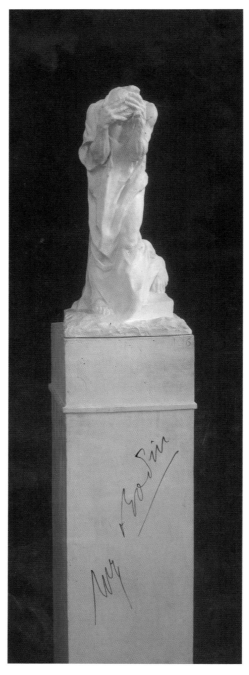

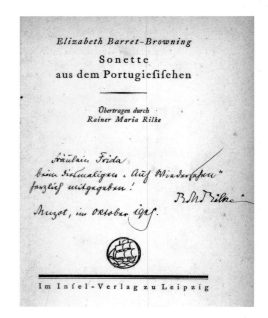

affair with Camille Claudel had long since ended. However, one of her rare autograph letters (above left) shows that she also played the role of secretary during their affair. 'Monsieur Rodin has asked me to send you his apologies….' The young sculptress took advantage of her position to invite the critic and art expert Gustave Geoffroy to come and see her 'waltzers' – probably her best-known work, *La Valse*.

On the visiting card reproduced below left, Rodin writes to one of his pupils ('Dear Mademoiselle Jouvroy'). He wants her to find a way of expressing 'the man holding the keys, who weeps'. Then he adds: 'Make a study for it and show me the model.' This turned out to be one of the figures for *Les Bourgeois de Calais* (1884–86). The note reveals that Rodin's pupils, including Claudel, made a substantial contribution to this work, which is one of his most famous. Mademoiselle Jouvroy had joined the studio at the same time as Claudel, and the end of this message to her – 'yours from the heart and respectfully' – might suggest that she too was very close to Rodin.

Another of the visiting cards (enlarged, opposite) reads 'Auguste Rodin, Sculptor', and is embellished with some drawings that are quite detailed for such a small surface. Rodin also signed large photographs of his works in the early 1900s, one of which is to be seen on the left, in the centre, taken by Reutlinger.

---

▼▶ Camille Claudel, autograph letter signed, c. 1891.
▼ Reutlinger, signed photograph of Rodin sculpture, c. 1910.
◀ Auguste Rodin, autograph visiting card signed, c. 1886.
▲ Rainer Maria Rilke, autograph inscription signed, 1925.
▶ Auguste Rodin, visiting card with autograph drawings, c. 1880.

AUGUSTE RODIN,

STATUAIRE.

*Dear mother, here are six dollars*
*[for your birthday]....*

# Sigmund FREUD

## 1856-1939

It is not surprising that, along with Albert Einstein (1879–1955), Freud is the scientist whose autographs are the most popular. He was a prolific correspondent, and his letters frequently come on to the market, but the dealers and auction houses have no trouble finding buyers since the content is usually of great interest. Freud himself would not have been particularly surprised by this development, for five years before he died he wrote to a close friend: 'I do not in any way share the quasi-fetishistic respect for manuscripts. I am not in the least concerned with my own, and only keep them because I've let myself be convinced that they might one day bring in some pocket money for my grandchildren.'

Private letters are much rarer and therefore all the more coveted by collectors. This is the case with the one reproduced opposite. The founder of psychoanalysis is writing to his mother in 1929 to give her six dollars on the occasion of her ninety-fourth birthday. His 'dear mother' was to die the following year.

Three months after he had sent this letter, he wrote to one of his best friends: 'The loss of a mother must be something very strange, like nothing else, and must give rise to emotions that are difficult to understand. I myself (at the age of sixty-five) still have a mother, and she bars my route to eternal rest, the void to which I aspire because I would never be able to forgive myself if I died before her.'

The photograph on the right, signed in 1922 for a Canadian psychoanalyst, was taken by Freud's nephew, Max Halberstadt, and is still one of the best-known portraits of him.

▶ Max Halberstadt, signed portrait of Sigmund Freud, 1922.
▶▶ Sigmund Freud, autograph letter signed, 1929.

17. 8. 192?

Liebe Mutter

In der beilage habe
ich 6 dollars gut für
nächstes Jahr, das du
in ungestörter freude
mit uns verbringen
sollst. Ich grüße dich
herzlich durch unsern
boten, deine

Sohn

Freud signed in pencil this fine engraved portrait (above left) by Hermann Struck in 1914, when he was fifty-eight years old. In the same year, he wrote to the artist: 'The portrait seems to me to be a charming idealization. That is how I would like to look.'

Centre right is a note written by Freud on the birth of his grandson Gabriel, and it reveals what one might be tempted to call a 'Freudian slip': he has inverted the figures and dated it 1291 instead of 1921.

He died a few months after writing the letter reproduced top right and opposite. In it, he thanks the addressee for sending him his biography of Nietzsche, and tells him which people he should talk to in order to write his biography of the 'father of psychoanalysis' himself. 'Pray excuse my answering you in English which after all is not my native tongue,' he writes to this Frenchman. He recommends that the latter should talk to Marie Bonaparte, who had just rescued him from Hitler's Austria by getting

him to London. But the passage that is most fascinating, and offers a new insight into a relationship which has aroused a good deal of speculation, is the postscript: 'Permit me to correct what I consider to be an error, in the first chapter of your book. You say Lou [Andréas] Salomé is – or rather was – a Jewess. I have known her rather intimately. We were near friends during her last 25 years she practised psychoanalysis as my pupil. I have learned that she was the daughter of a Russian general of French descent but I never heard her mention anything about being Jewish.' Lou Andréas Salomé had just died, and quite touchingly Freud is recalling one of the women to whom he was very close. On the right is a card that Lou herself had written.

▼ Hermann Struck, engraved portrait of Sigmund Freud, signed by the artist and the sitter, 1914.
▲▲▲► Sigmund Freud, autograph letter signed, 1939.
▲▲ Sigmund Freud, autograph note signed, 1921.
▲ Lou Andréas-Salomé, autograph card signed, 1924.

One of them is Mme Marie
Bonaparte (Princess Georges
of Greece) (née Adolphe Joon,
the other Dr Heinz Hartmann
(6 Villa George Sand, XVIe), I
am sure you will get
from them all the help
you want.

Sincerely yours
Sigm. Freud

P.S. Permit me to correct.
what I consider to be an
error, in the first chapter
of your book. You say Lou
Salomé is, or rather was - a Jewess.
I have known her rather intimately. We were near
friends during her last
25 years she practised psychoanalysis as my pupil. I
have learned that she
was the daughter of a
Russian general of French
descent but I never heard
her mention anything
about being Jewish

*...have sent to me the two scores
and orchestral parts of
L'Après midi d'un Faune.*

## Claude DEBUSSY

### 1862-1918

The manuscript reproduced opposite, recto and verso, is one of Debussy's most famous scores: *La Mer*. The composer draws the attention of his addressee, Monsieur Choiseul, to three corrections that he wants incorporated in the score, which is being prepared for publication. The printed version that is still used today reveals that only two of these corrections were actually made – a little puzzle that adds to the interest of this autograph piece.

In the letter reproduced on the right, Debussy sounds rather worried: 'Could you let me know the whereabouts or even have sent to me the two scores and orchestral parts of *L'Après midi d'un faune* (1894). I have urgent need of them, and am very anxious to know whose hands they are in.' Letters alluding to masterpieces by writers, painters and composers are among those that collectors prize above all others, even if – as in this case – they do not describe the work itself.

The photograph of Debussy reproduced above was the favourite of his wife, Emma, who dedicated it to a young pianist fifteen years after her husband had died.

▼ Claude Debussy, photograph inscribed and signed by his widow Emma, c. 1933.
▲ Claude Debussy, autograph letter signed, c. 1906.
► Claude Debussy, autograph score and autograph letter signed, c. 1906.

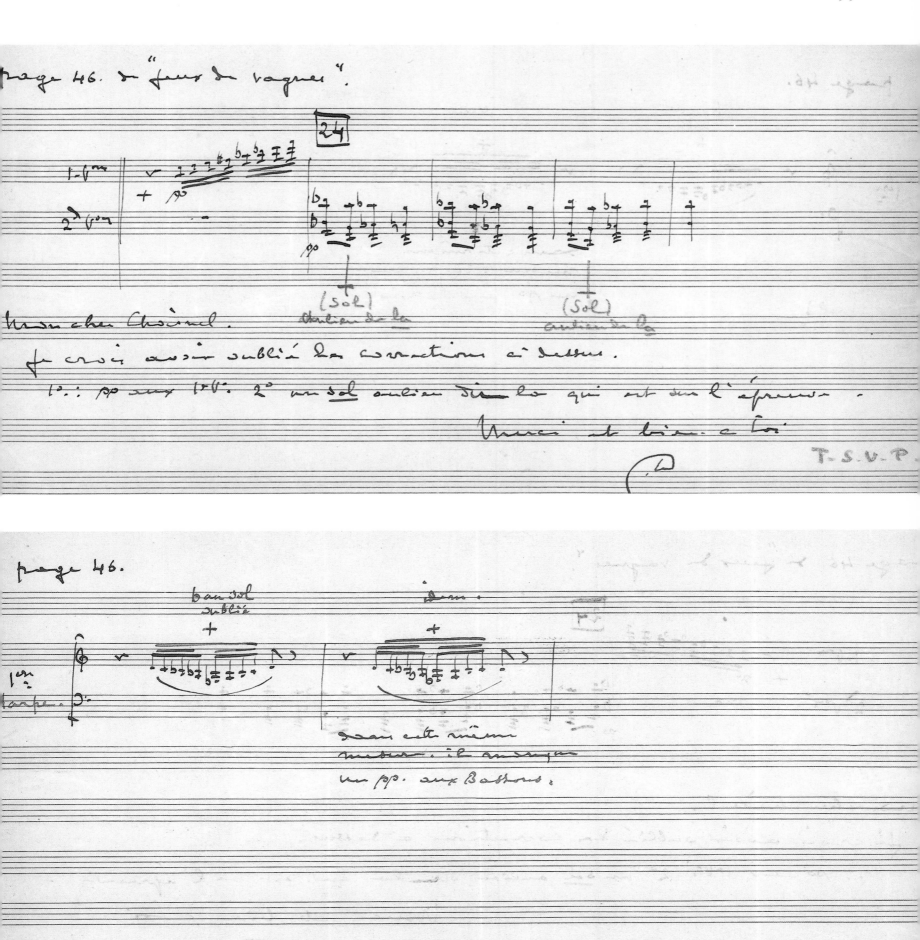

page 46.

## Richard STRAUSS

### 1864-1949

Nowadays regarded as one of the major composers of the 20th century, Richard Strauss conducted his own work in many different countries, and autographs are quite common, such as the extract from *Till Eulenspiegels* reproduced above. The photograph opposite, however, is quite exceptional. This is one of only two known prints made by the great German photographer August Sander in 1925. It also bears Sander's signature in pencil and that of Strauss himself, dated the year of the print itself.

Richard Strauss's reputation suffered a great deal because of his attitude to the Hitler regime. Many criticized him for working too closely with the Nazis. The portrait on the right, signed by the composer three years after the end of the Second World War and just eighteen months before he died, was sent to a Brazilian admirer by his daughter-in-law, who was then living with Strauss. The letter that accompanied it (below) is quite poignant. Writing in English, she talks about the severe shortages in Germany at the time: 'Would it be possible to send us into this dreadful food misery with two boys, the only grandsons of Dr. Strauss some food package, we would be so thankful.'

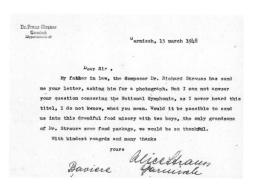

▶ Richard Strauss, autograph musical quotation signed, 1920.
◀ Richard Strauss, signed photograph, 1948.
◀◀ Alice Strauss, typewritten letter signed, 1948.
▶ August Sander, portrait of Richard Strauss, signed in pencil by the composer and the photographer, 1925.

ty. Remwler
Köln 1925

Richard Strauss

13. 6. 25.

*...the fire may quench me, instead of my quenching it.*

## Mahatma GANDHI

### 1869-1948

In the course of his long, non-violent campaigns, Gandhi sent many letters to journalists, writers and European politicians in order to defend and spread his doctrine and his beliefs.

It was, however, a weary Gandhi who, one year before his death, typed a letter (opposite) in response to one from the brother of a friend (whom he had met in his younger days, when he was living in South Africa): 'Of course I knew your brother very well indeed.' This reply might seem somewhat banal, but what follows also has a tragic dimension: 'But I plead with you to spare me at the present moment. I must not divide my attention for things great or small. It will be time for me to consider others if I come out safe from the fire which I am trying to quench. The odds are so great that the fire may quench me instead of my quenching it.' Eleven months after these strangely prescient words, Gandhi fell victim to the bullets fired by a Hindu fanatic.

The photograph on the right, an original by Elliott & Fry – the great studio favoured by the English elite – was taken in 1928. The Mahatma, already famous but described by Winston Churchill as 'a seditious middle temple lawyer, now posing as a fakir... striding half naked up the steps of the viceregal palace', had come to England to plead his cause. Above right, he offers some remarkable reflections on his theory of non-violence in an autograph letter addressed to Ronald Duncan in reply to the pamphlet entitled 'The Complete Pacifist': 'The argument appeared to me to be sound so far as it went. Perhaps there is not sufficient emphasis on personal individual actions irrespective of what society does or does not do. Non-violent action does not depend upon another's cooperation. Violent action is ineffective without the cooperation of others.'

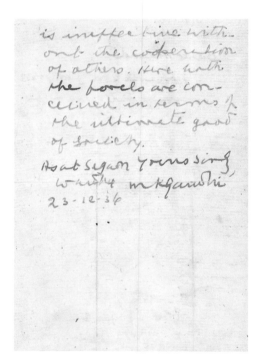

▲ Mahatma Gandhi, autograph letter signed, 1936.
◄ Elliott & Fry, portrait of Mahatma Gandhi, original print, 1928.
► Mahatma Gandhi, typewritten letter signed, with autograph additions, 1947.

Patna.
March 16, 1947

Dear friend,

  Of course I knew your brother very well indeed.  But I plead with you to spare me at the present moment.  I must not divide my attention for things great or small.  It will be time for me to consider others also, if I come out safe from the fire which I am trying to quench.  The odds are so great that the fire may quench me, instead of my quenching the fire.  *if*

       Yours sincerely,

       M.K.Gandhi

Solomon Alexander Esq.
Barrister at Law,
25, Rue Talaat Harb,
Alexandria.
(Egypt)

*No one will ever be submitted*
*[to psychoanalysis] with my consent....*

# Albert EINSTEIN

## 1879-1955

Of all the great figures of the 20th century, Albert Einstein is perhaps the one whose autographs are the most sought-after. The majority of collectors will, of course, have their national preferences. Churchill and Kennedy, for instance, are particularly popular in the UK and the USA respectively, but Einstein's popularity is universal. Fortunately for his admirers, he wrote a large number of letters and signed countless documents during the forty years in which he was world-famous.

There are few letters as illuminating as the one reproduced recto and verso on the opposite page. It is addressed to his ex-wife, and the great physicist is openly discussing the problems of their second son, Eduard, who is suffering from depression. Einstein is convinced that the illness is hereditary, and rejects the suggestion of psychoanalytical treatment: 'I have a very low opinion of psychoanalysis, having seen nothing but bad results among our acquaintances. I consider it to be an extremely dangerous fashion and am totally opposed to it. No one will ever be submitted to this kind of treatment with my consent, and under no circumstances will I encourage it.' Einstein proposes that Eduard should join him in his country home at Caputh, where the peace and quiet and the company of his father should do him good. 'My influence on nervous natures is beneficial, thanks to my calm character.' The letter continues with comments on the situation in Europe: '...this crisis with its terrible unemployment', and he can see no short-term prospects of improvement: 'One can rely on nothing whatever except one's own talents and good health.' His first wife, Mileva, was a Croatian and was herself a brilliant physicist who was capable of following and supporting Einstein's thinking;

her role in the development of the theory of relativity has been increasingly recognized. Despite their separation, the relationship remained close and was by no means limited to matters relating to their children. Einstein tries to comfort Mileva: 'Think of all the tragedies that the world has known, and yet everywhere the flowers go on growing and the birds sing. Nature is not interested in the individual, and man must live out his destiny as best he can.'

This remarkable letter offers us a moment of intimacy and of deep reflection. It also reveals the great physicist's intense dislike of Freud's theories, although Einstein maintained distant but cordial relations with the founder of psychoanalysis.

After their first meeting in 1927, Freud wrote to a friend: 'I spent two hours chatting with Einstein. He is warm, self-confident and likable. He knows as much about psychology as I do about physics, and that is why we got on very well together....'

The signed photograph above dates from Einstein's trip to Rio de Janeiro in 1925. He is surrounded by a group of Brazilian scientists at a reception that was being held for him.

Most of Einstein's known letters were typewritten and date from the last fifteen years of his life, when he was living in the USA. The content is sometimes very interesting, like the one reproduced overleaf. Here he is congratulating the Austrian novelist Hermann Broch (1886–1951) on the quality of the manuscript that he had sent – it was Broch's masterpiece *The Death of Virgil* (1945).

Einstein's comments – one of the very rare occasions on which he expressed his views on a literary subject – offer warm praise of one of the great fictional works of the 20th century.

▲ ▲ Albert Einstein, signed photograph, 1925.
▲ ► Albert Einstein, autograph letter signed, 1932.

Pasadena 29. II. 32.

Liebe Mileva!

Ich dachte mir schon, dass mit Tete nicht alles in Ordnung sei, weil er so lange nicht schrieb. Auch mahnte manches in seinen Briefen. Wir müssen uns damit abfinden, dass eine krankhafte Erbanlage vorliegt und müssen es eben hinnehmen, wie es kommt. Auf Psychoanalyse halte ich gar nichts und habe in meinem Bekanntenkreise nur schlechte Erfahrungen damit beobachtet. Ich halte es für eine überaus gefährliche Mode und bin unbedingt dagegen. Mit meiner Einwilligung unterwirft sich niemand einer derartigen Behandlung, auf keinen Fall begünstige ich es.

Ich glaube es wäre für Tete gut, wenn er zu mir nach Caputh käme, vorausgesetzt, dass er nicht immer nach Berlin fährt. Das Leben dort ist still und beschaulich, und mein Einfluss ist auf alle nervösen Naturen günstig durch meine ruhige den 25.Februar 1942

Lieber Herr Broch:

Ich habe Ihr Manuskript mit grossem
Interesse durchgelesen und glaube wirklich, dass Ihre
Methode den wichtigen Gegenstand dem Verständnis näher-
bringt. Es wird mich freuen, wenn mir Gelegenheit ge-
boten wird, Ihrer Arbeit durch mein Urteil nützen zu
können.

                    Mit freundlichen Grüssen

                              Ihr

                              A. Einstein.


Herrn Hermann Broch
35 West 75 Str.
New York City

---

l'affaire Sacco et Vansetti; nous savons assez combien le sentiments de l'équité est
profond chez le peuple américain pour espérer qu'il ne laissera pas s'accomplir un nouveau
déni de justice. Voudrait-il,pour de nombreuses années à venir,porter le même fardeau
d'angoisse et de remords qui a pesé sur la France à la suite de l'affaire Dreyfus ?

          Nous espérons de toute notre âme que le verdict de Charlotte ne sera
pas confirmé.

          Veuillez croire à mes meilleurs sentiments

J.HADAMARD,Professeur au Collège de France,Membre de l'Académie des Sciences;
          25 Rue Jean Dolent,Paris XIV⁰

Above is an unpublished poem that Einstein wrote on the back of his visiting card. He composed it while on the trip to Brazil in 1925, in homage to Rosalina Lisboa, a poetess less famous for her poetry than for her beauty, to which Einstein was apparently far from indifferent (he even mentions it in his published journal).

The signed portrait reproduced opposite is by the young Lotte Jacobi, who was then working in the family studio in Berlin. It is one of the finest known portraits of Einstein but has seldom been reproduced. Lotte Jacobi was able to photograph him again during the 1940s at Princeton.

The document on the left gives us insight into another aspect of Einstein's character, for he enthusiastically embraced a large number of good causes. Here we have the end of a letter signed by several petitioners challenging the 'Charlotte verdict' – comparing it to the Sacco and Vanzetti affair (American political radicals who were executed in 1927 on charges of murder and theft, despite widespread belief in their innocence) and the Dreyfus affair. This protest was initiated by the great French mathematician Jacques Hadamard (1865–1963), and was also signed by Einstein and the philosophers Lucien Lévy-Bruhl (1857–1939) and Léon Brunschvicg (1869–1944).

---

▲▲ Albert Einstein, typewritten letter signed, 1942.
▲ Albert Einstein, Jacques Hadamard, Lucien Lévy-Bruhl and Léon Brunschvicg, fragment of typewritten letter signed, c.1950.

◀ Albert Einstein, autograph manuscript signed, 1925.
▶ Lotte Jacobi, portrait of Albert Einstein, signed by the sitter, 1930.

*Albert Einstein 10. X. 35.*

*Thank you for sending me*
*your libretto….*

## Enrico CARUSO 1873-1921

## Giacomo PUCCINI 1858-1924

Some of Caruso's greatest triumphs were achieved in roles created by Puccini. Considered the greatest tenor of his time, Caruso was swamped with demands for autographs, and he was usually happy to comply. He loved cartoons, and often drew sketches of his own. The self-portrait opposite, drawn in Montevideo, is one of his most accomplished, and is the only known example of a Caruso with three heads.

The sketch above shows him smiling, and was drawn during a trip to Rio de Janeiro in 1917; it is typical of his art, which was generally practised on the pages of albums.

Puccini too was immensely popular, and signed countless pieces for his admirers – printed scores, postcards, programmes. His manuscript scores, however, are extremely rare, whereas his letters are numerous and interesting enough to satisfy the needs of most collectors. The one on the right is written completely in his own hand, and is addressed to a Brazilian author who had offered him what was no doubt a somewhat mediocre libretto: 'I have acquainted myself with your literary, theatrical work and have registered the good intentions and the quality….' Puccini, who was in Buenos Aires at the time, politely rejects the subject, however, explaining that he is already fully occupied with various other projects, and 'I absolutely cannot devote myself to anything else' – one of those projects being a opera based on Marie Antoinette, which was never to see the light of day.

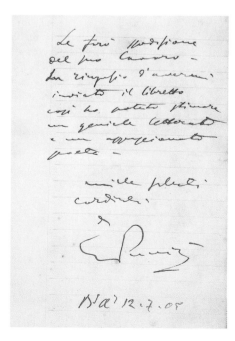

▾ Enrico Caruso, self-caricature, 1917.
◂ Giacomo Puccini, autograph letter signed, 1905.
▴ Giacomo Puccini, postcard photograph signed, c. 1900.
▸ Enrico Caruso, signed self-caricature, 1903.

# *Grigori* RASPUTIN 1872-1916

# NICHOLAS II *of Russia* 1868-1918

# ALEXANDRA *of Russia* 1872-1918

The monk Rasputin exercised an extraordinary influence over the imperial Russian family, and over the Empress Alexandra in particular. He was believed to possess strange powers, especially when it came to easing the terrible suffering of the haemophiliac crown prince Alexis. The latter had inherited the disease through Queen Victoria, his great-grandmother, and it had a profound effect on his parents. The Tsar feared that his son's illness would place the succession in jeopardy, and so it was kept secret, and this subsequently rendered the imperial family's intimacy with Rasputin even more inexplicable in the eyes of the Russian people. The monk's hypnotic gaze fascinated and also disturbed most of the courtiers, but he had the favour of the Tsarina and of a small group of important people who had fallen under his spell. He was eventually assassinated by Prince Félix Yusupov, of whom a portrait – signed twenty years later – is reproduced above. This came as a great relief to many people, but the fall of the empire was already inevitable. Rasputin autographs are extremely rare, and there is virtually no known photograph apart from the one opposite, which was presented to one of his female admirers (many of whom also became his mistresses). Rasputin has signed it 'Grigori' and has added a somewhat obscure phrase: 'Eternal peace is not an isolated glimmer of hope but comes from the shining light of heaven.' The official document on the right is signed by Nicholas II and confers an important honour on French general Georges Picquart (1854–1914), who had denounced the conspiracy against Dreyfus.

Overleaf are two superb photographs signed by the imperial couple, of a quality reserved only for the elite, and magnificently framed by the goldsmith Fabergé.

▼ Félix Yusupov, signed photograph, 1949.
▲ Nicholas II, document signed, 1908.

► Grigori Rasputin, inscribed and signed photograph, c. 1915.
OVERLEAF Alexandra and Nicholas II, signed photographs, 1904.

Григорій

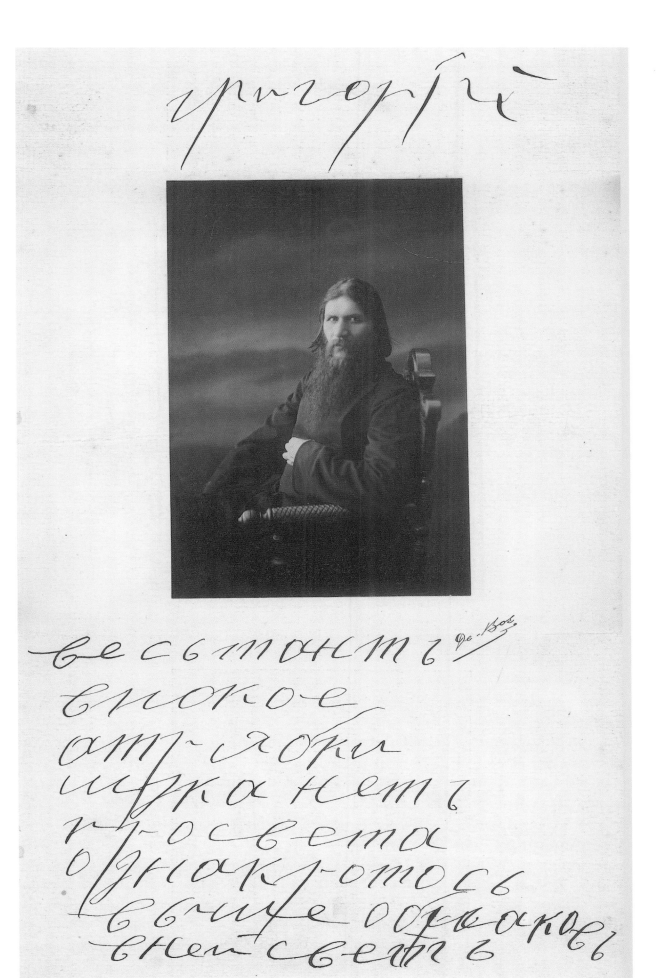

Весьма нить Dе Вог

спокое

от любви

ирка нетъ

г—о свѣта

однако—то съ

свыше облаковъ

снеи свѣтъ

*Nicolas*

1904.

*So you can write to me there, but still*
                 *only as Lady MacLeod.*
*I have not spoken of Mata Hari.*

# MATA HARI

## 1876-1917

If Mata Hari is now a mythical figure, this is certainly in spite of herself. Margarete Gertrude Zelle, otherwise known as Mata Hari, became a legend after being found guilty of espionage and then shot. With a little more luck and a little less absent-mindedness, her story might well have had a completely different ending. Which would she have preferred: to live a few more years in mediocre obscurity, or to die world-famous, with her career re-enacted in the cinema by Greta Garbo less than twenty years after her death? From what we know of her, the answer is that she would have preferred to live, with or without a future.

When she wrote the letter reproduced on the right and opposite, Mata Hari was still a dancer with a dubious reputation: there were postcards in circulation that showed her in highly suggestive poses such as the one illustrated above. This was perhaps the reason why she preferred to retain the name of her first husband (sticking 'Lady' on the front of MacLeod) when identifying herself to a concierge. Writing to a lover, whom she addresses both as 'tu' and as 'vous', she informs him that she has been delayed. 'I have not had time to pack my suitcases.' Then she goes into details about how she has paid the rent, the concierge and various expenses for the apartment. 'And so you can write to me there, but still only as Lady MacLeod. I have not spoken of Mata Hari.'

The first page contains the mysterious comment '*Saisie de lettres*' [seizure of letters] in thick blue pencil. One is tempted to assume that this letter was seized along with other pieces of evidence for her trial.

▲ Mata Hari, postcard, c. 1910.
►►► Mata Hari, autograph letter signed, c. 1910.

GRAND HÔTEL
12 Boulevard des Capucines
PARIS

Adresse Télégraphique
GRANOTEL-PARIS

Teleph Central 35-48
35 49 35-50

Spedit smot.

Toutes mes
gentillesses. votre

Mata Hari

J'ai payé le loyer
de la concierge et.
Vous pourrez donc
si écrire là
mais seulement
encore comme
Lady Mac Leod.
Je n'ai pas parlé de
Mata Hari . . . .

*I need to inform you that the sum*
*I am asking [for your installation*
*in my State] is fifty thousand dollars....*

# Pancho VILLA 1878-1923

# Emiliano ZAPATA 1879-1919

Two names immediately spring to mind when one mentions the Mexican Revolution of 1910: Francisco (known as Pancho) Villa and Emiliano Zapata. The picture above is one of the rare occasions on which they were photographed together. It was taken on 6 December 1914 by the great Mexican photographer Agustín Casasola. Pancho Villa is seated in the presidential chair which Zapata, looking slightly ill at ease by comparison with a smiling Villa, had refused to sit in even for the sake of a photograph.

Their characters were in fact totally different: Villa was outgoing and effusive, whereas Zapata was reserved almost to the point of taciturnity. The ideals of Zapata, who had no doubts about the role he should play on behalf of the peasants, were perfectly summed up by his motto 'Land and Liberty'.

Both men suffered tragic deaths after the revolution, but that of Villa was less heroic: he was ambushed by a group of bandits in the town of Parral, which he had taken over by force. His final years were none too glorious either. The autograph letter on the right, of which the second page is reproduced, was written three years before his death, and shows him in the role of extortionist. He was writing in 1920 to the president of an American mining company which had set up operations in the region controlled by the former revolutionary leader. Villa makes himself very clear: 'The Potosi Mining Co. – of which you are president – is a business of very great importance for this State, and if you are working without any problems this is due to the guarantees given to you by my forces. I could still prove to you that other factions are not in a position to guarantee you the same protection. It is therefore right that you should help me, on the understanding

that I will provide you with safe-conduct. To this effect, I have authorized W. S. Harrison to arrange this matter with you. I need to inform you that the sum I am asking you for is 50,000 (fifty thousand) dollars.' This enormous sum undoubtedly confirmed Villa's power in the region, but it also earned him the increasing hatred of his enemies.

The letter from Zapata (opposite) is very different. It finishes with the rallying cry 'Reform, Liberty, Justice and Law'. Typed on a poor-quality typewriter and corrected here and there in Zapata's own handwriting, it is a modest document bearing in mind the stature of this military leader; it is also a

moving reminder of the most turbulent period in the recent history of Mexico. It reveals a Zapata anxious to suppress the disorder that was increasing three years after the beginning of the revolution. He lists the individuals that the people of Ocotopec were accusing of causing damage and possibly also the death of a man, and he demands a return to order, 'because such abuses are not to be tolerated'.

Letters written by the main protagonists in the Mexican revolution are rare. Many collectors have been pursuing them for years, and record prices have been fetched at public sales, particularly for those of Zapata.

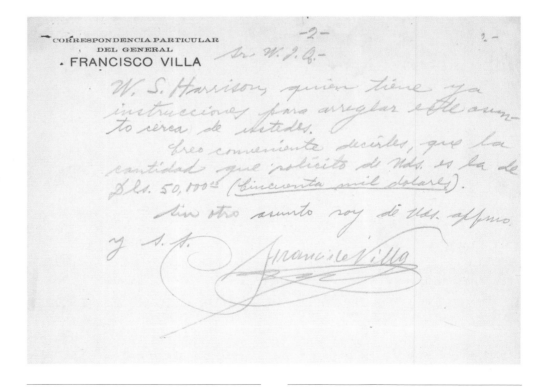

▼ Agustin Casasola, Pancho Villa and Emiliano Zapata in the Presidential Palace, original print of 1914.

▲ Pancho Villa, autograph letter signed, 1920.
► Emiliano Zapata, typewritten letter signed, with autograph additions, 1913.

REPUBLICA MEXICANA.

EJERCITO LIBERTADOR DEL SUR Y CENTRO.

Al General Genoveve de la O.

Su Campamento:

El Pueblo de Ocotepec se queja de que los indivi-
duos Juan Cervantes, Atilano García, Lorenzo Balderas, Leandro Gár-
cía y Manuel Paredes, *cometieron algunas depredaciones* quienes aparecen responsables de la muer =
te de Paulino López, que fué vecino del referido Pueblo y como
han cometido varios abusos que no deben tolerarse, mucho le re =
comiendo llame al orden á estos individuos y proceda en contra
de ellos por las responsabilidades que sobre ellos aparezcan.

Lo que comunico á usted para su inteligencia y
fines consiguientes.

Reforma, Libertad, Justicia y Ley,

Campamento Revolucionario en Morelos, abril 1
de 1913.

El General en Jefe del Ejército del Sur y Centro.

Emiliano Zapata.

*The bearer is a member of the*
*Social Democratic Workers' party of Russia....*

# LENIN 1870-1924

## *Joseph* STALIN 1879-1953

These two leaders of the Russian Revolution presided over the destiny of the Soviet Union during its first thirty-five years, the one succeeding the other. Their relationship was not without its problems.

Lenin (originally called Vladimir Ulianov), brother of a revolutionary who had been executed at the end of the 19th century, was exiled for a while in Switzerland, where in 1912 he wrote the letter reproduced opposite. His letters have always been rarities, and for more than forty years, from the 1940s onwards, the majority of those that came up for sale were acquired by an American millionaire, Armand Hammer. He had close business relations with the USSR and liked to offer original documents to dignitaries at the Kremlin. This particular letter came back on the market after his death, and it was put up for sale by the descendants of its Swiss addressee, Dr Huber. It has a double signature, which is the dream of all collectors: Vladimir Ulianov Lenin. The concise content and the stamp of the 'Central Committee of the Social Democratic Workers' Party of Russia' add to the value of this letter of recommendation, even though the content itself may seem of no great importance.

Autograph documents of Joseph Stalin were also virtually unobtainable in the West for many years. Just occasionally one would find signatures given to American or British officials, for instance at the Yalta conference in 1945. However, we can be quite certain that Stalin must have signed a vast number of documents during his thirty-year rule, and some of these have now surfaced since the break-up of the Soviet Union. The military orders reproduced on the right contain some autograph additions and Stalin's signature in red pencil.

▲ Joseph Stalin, document signed, with autograph additions, 1942.

► Lenin, autograph letter signed, 1912.

An Rechtsanwalt
Dr. Huber
Kirchstr. 17. Rorschach
(Kt. St.-Gallen).

Werter Genosse!

Gestatten Sie mir Ihnen den Ueberbringer dieses, Genossen Bagotzky bestens zu empfehlen und Sie zu bitten ihm mit Rath zu helfen. Genosse Bagotzky ist seit langem Mitglied der Soz. Dem. ArbeiterPartei Russlands.

Im Auftrage des Zentralkomitees der Soz. Dem. ArbeiterPartei Russlands N. Lenin
Wl. Ulianow
in Sörenberg (Kt. Luzern)

ЦЕНТРАЛЬНЫЙ КОМИТЕТЪ
Р. С.-Д. Р. П.
Comité Central du Parti Social-Démocrate ouvrier de Russie

Mit Parteigruss Wl. Ulianow

*You replied that you wanted
[my book] to be published by you. And so that is agreed,
at least for the first edition....*

# Marcel PROUST

## 1871-1922

Collectors drool over autographs by French novelist Marcel Proust. Even though there are vast quantities of letters, there can never be enough to satisfy a demand that has grown massively over the last twenty years. Certain institutions profited from the fact that in the 1960s prices were still very affordable, and they managed to build up excellent collections – for instance, the University of Illinois has over a thousand autograph letters. Its collection was assembled and arranged by Philip Kolb, an indefatigable researcher who published Proust's complete correspondence in twenty-one volumes, comprising more than five thousand letters (although we can be quite sure that the future will uncover many more unpublished ones).

In 1918, the proofs of *À l'ombre des jeunes filles en fleurs*, with a large number of handwritten corrections by the author, were divided up and attached to the first fifty copies of the original edition. These proofs now give Proust-lovers the chance to possess a manuscript fragment of perhaps the greatest masterpiece of 20th-century literature.

The manuscript reproduced opposite is one of these fragments, and corresponds to page 378 of the first edition of *Jeunes filles*. By comparison with the printed text, it still contains several variations, because much to the exasperation of the typographers, Proust insisted on a number of corrections even to the final proofs. This manuscript is in three sections, reproduced here at twice their original size, and we can see a number of tiny corrections to the last lines. The passage describes a meeting that is important to the narrator: 'Shortly after the party, one morning when it was almost cold and it had been raining, I was accosted on the "front" by a girl in red wearing a close-fitting toque and carrying a fur muff, completely different from

the girl I had met at Elstir's party – one would have said this was a sketch in which it was impossible to recognize her as the same person....'

The photograph on the right, in the *carte de visite* format, was taken by Hermann *c.* 1882. Proust (seated) is eleven years old, and Robert – his only brother, who became a doctor – is ten. They seem like good little upper-middle-class boys, but their poses reveal very different characters: there is a certain affectation in the thoughtful attitude of young Marcel, in contrast to the relaxed naturalness of his more robust younger brother.

Overleaf are two pages (out of eight in the collection) from the proofs of *Du côté de chez Swann* (1913), with Proust's handwritten corrections. These proofs, from the estate of Dr Robert Proust, constitute the only part of the first volume of *À la recherche du temps perdu* to be listed in a private collection. The proofs are relatively 'clean' by Proust's standards, since most others are full of corrections, deletions, insertions and additions. At this time the novel was called *Les Intermittences du coeur*, as can be seen from the title written at the top of the page on the left. This extract introduces a character that is very important in *Swann*, the author Bergotte, who undoubtedly bears certain similarities to Anatole France. The most significant autograph correction concerns a passage in which the young narrator reveals his total admiration for Bergotte: 'I should have liked to have his opinion on all things, but especially on those that I would have had the opportunity to see for myself.'

Proust's drawings are rare and for many years have been much sought-after. About a hundred have been listed, illustrating virtually all the letters he wrote to the

HERMANN & Cᵉ                    20.Chaussée d'Antin.

Venezuelan composer Reynaldo Hahn (1875–1947), who was perhaps his closest friend. They used to give each other various affectionate nicknames, the most common being Proust's invention: 'my little Binibus'.

The drawing reproduced on page 180 on the right is part of a six-page autograph letter to 'dear Monsieur de Binibus', dated 1904. The text is full of gossip and anecdotes about the literary world and the smart Parisian set with which the two young men liked to mingle.

▲ Hermann & Co., portrait of Marcel and Robert Proust, *c.* 1882.
► Marcel Proust, autograph manuscript, *c.* 1915.
OVERLEAF Marcel Proust, corrected proofs of *Du côté de chez Swann*, 1913.

me fit les rencontrer. Mais cela arrivait
il tous les jours, il était fort à craindre qu'
elle se contentât de répondre de loin à
mon salut. De sorte que cela
durerait ainsi toute la saison sans que
je fusse plus avancé.
Quelques jours après la matinée, un matin

Quelques
jours après la matinée, un matin où il faisait
presque froid et où il avait plu, je fus abordé
sur la digue par une jeune fille en toque rouge avec
un toquet en nageoire de fourrure, absolument diffé-
rente de celle que j'avais vue à la matinée d'
Elstir, et en croquis sur — on dit où
il était impossible de reconnaître que c'
était la même personne, si bien qu'elle s'écriât
                                                        opération que
j'ai vous répondre à jamais pas après ter reprendre ou
depuis que je crois ne lui échappe pas. A quel
temps me dit-elle. Alors vous ne faites rien ici !
bals de
on ne vous voit jamais en golf, aux casinos ; vous ne montez pas
à cheval non plus. Comme vous devez vous ennuyer
mais vous que vous croire qu'êtes pas comme moi j'adore
tous les sports !

liste qui avait déjà été, sans que je m'en rendisse
compte, la cause du plaisir que je prenais à lire Bergotte, je n'eus plus l'impression d'être en présence
d'un morceau particulier d'un certain livre de lui,
traçant à la surface de ma pensée une figure pure-
ment linéaire, mais plutôt en ~~quelque sorte~~ du « morceau idéal » de Bergotte, commun à tous ses livres
et auquel tous les passages analogues qui ~~seraient~~
~~se rapporter à~~ lui, donneraient une sorte d'épaisseur,
de volume, dont mon esprit, ~~pour le contenir,~~ sem-
blait agrandi.

*) confondre avec*

*) idéale*

  Je n'étais pas tout à fait le seul admirateur de Bergotte ; il était aussi l'écrivain préféré d'une amie de
ma mère qui était très lettrée. Pour lire son dernier
livre paru, le Dr du Boulbon faisait attendre ses ma-
lades ; et ce fut de son cabinet de consultation, et d'un
parc voisin de Combray, que s'envolèrent quelques-
unes des premières graines de cette prédilection pour
Bergotte, espèce si rare alors, aujourd'hui universel-
lement répandue, et dont on trouve partout en Europe,
en Amérique, jusque dans le moindre village. jusque
dans les champs, la fleur ~~charmante~~ et commune. Ce
que l'amie de ma mère, et paraît-il le Dr du Boulbon
aimaient surtout dans les livres de Bergotte c'était
comme moi, ce même flux mélodique, ces expressions
anciennes, quelques autres très simples et connues,
mais pour lesquelles la place où il les mettait en lumière semblaient révéler ~~chez lui~~ un goût particulier ;
enfin, dans les passages tristes, une certaine brusque-
rie, un accent presque rauque. Et sans doute lui-même
devait sentir que là étaient ses plus grands charmes.
Car dans les livres qui suivirent, s'il avait rencontré
quelque grande vérité, où le nom d'une célèbre cathé-
drale, il interrompait son récit et dans un einvocation,
une apostrophe, une longue prière il donnait un libre
cours à ces effluves qui dans ses premiers ouvrages
restaient intérieures à sa prose et ~~n'étaient~~ décélés

*) de sa part*

dans les bras d'un père retrouvé. Chaque fois qu'il
parlait d'une chose dont jusque-là la beauté m'était
voilée, vague, presque sans charme, des sapins, de la
grêle, de Notre-Dame avec une image, il ~~en~~
faisait exploser cette beauté ~~qui s'approchait de moi,~~
~~était claire, m'enchantait.~~ Aussi sentant combien il y
avait de parties de l'univers que ma perception ~~infime~~
~~ne dénicherait~~ jamais s'il ne me les décrivait pas, j'aurais voulu avoir ~~sa description, son opinion de toutes~~
~~choses, surtout de celles que j'avais l'occasion de voir,~~
~~plus que toutes de celles dont un mot de ses livres~~
~~m'avait fait penser qu'il les aimait particulièrement,~~
~~donc qu'elles étaient certainement riches de beauté,~~
~~la vieille architecture de France, les paysages marins.~~
J'imaginais Bergotte comme un vieillard faible et ~~dé-~~
~~sillusionné~~ qui avait perdu des enfants et ne s'était
jamais consolé. Aussi je le lisais, je chantais intérieu-
rement sa prose, plus « dolce », plus lentement peut-
être qu'elle n'était écrite, et la phrase la plus simple
s'adressait à moi avec une intonation attendrie. Plus
que tout j'aimais sa philosophie, je m'étais donné à
elle pour toujours. Elle me faisait rêver du temps où
je serais au collège dans la classe appelée Philosophie.
Mais je ne voulais pas qu'on y fît autre chose que
vivre uniquement par la pensée de Bergotte, et si l'on
m'avait dit que les métaphysiciens auxquels je m'at-
tacherais alors ne ressembleraient en rien à lui, j'aurais ressenti le désespoir d'un amoureux qui veut aimer
pour la vie et à qui on parle des autres amours qu'il
aura plus tard.

   Un jour, pendant ma lecture au jardin, je fus dé-
rangé par Swann qui venait voir mes parents.

   — Qu'est-ce que vous lisez, on peut regarder ? Tiens
du Bergotte ? Qui donc vous a indiqué ses ouvrages ?
Je lui dis que c'était Bloch.

   — Ah ! oui, ce garçon que j'ai vu une fois ici, qui
ressemble tellement au portrait de Mahomet II par

Proust quotes Robert de Montesquiou, and the book that he has just finished, divided into two parts: '1) the beauty that does not allow its noble old age to be seen: the Comtesse de Castiglione, and 2) the ugliness that exhibits its decrepitude: old P....' (The book was published the following year under the title *Professionnelles beautés*.) Then he turns his mockery on Arthur Meyer, the founder of the journal *Le Gaulois*, who was such a snob that he 'announced his marriage to all the sovereigns or at least the dukes. He met [French writer and politician Maurice] Barrès and told him: I am leaving for Versailles, so would you like me to give your regards to my cousin Louis XIV?' Proust continues to recount 'other idiocies' of the journalist, whom he compares to Monsieur Jourdain ('another *bourgeois gentilhomme*'). His unremitting attack on Meyer's snobbery, particularly over the Dreyfus affair, may perhaps be explained by Meyer's surprising support of the anti-Dreyfus faction, bearing in mind that the journalist was himself a Jew; so great was his desire to be accepted by the high society that he admired so much, he actually went so far as to embrace their prejudices even if they should have been offensive to him.

The letter reproduced opposite was for a long time a missing link in Proust's correspondence. It concerns a key moment in his literary career: the first publication of *Du côté de chez Swann*. The circumstances are well known: Proust had been rejected by all the publishers, including – to his great disappointment – the *Nouvelle revue française*. He therefore proposed to young Bernard Grasset that he should publish the book at Proust's own expense. Grasset had nothing to lose, accepted the offer, and published the work in 1913. Jean Schlumberger read it, was enthusiastic, and gave it to André Gide, who was at the NRF and had already rejected it. Gide read the printed edition at a single sitting, realized that he had made a monumental blunder ('the most humiliating mistake of my life,' he later wrote to Proust), and proposed to the author whom he had just rejected that he should publish the subsequent volumes of *À la recherche du temps perdu*. Proust, charmed by this '*mea culpa*', found himself confronted by a dilemma which today we would call 'Proustian': should he publish the rest of his work with the publisher of his dreams and abandon the new firm that had given him a start, or should he remain loyal to Grasset (who had been more receptive to Proust's money than to his talent)?

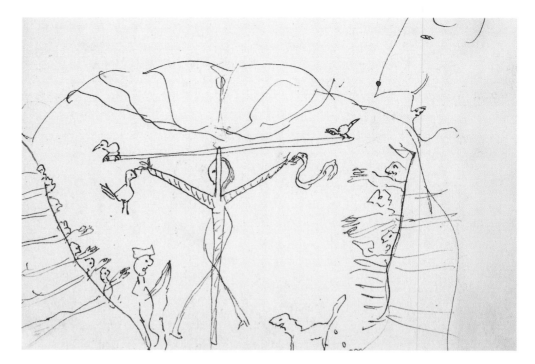

Through an intermediary, as was his custom, Proust first approached Grasset. The latter's response was disappointing, for he referred back to their earlier and rather weak contract. When Proust reacted unfavourably, Grasset realized that he had made a mistake and that he risked losing this unexpectedly successful author. He therefore sent him a very different message, releasing him from all obligations. This was the right tactic. Proust wrote at once to Gide, informing him that Grasset had used the one weapon against which he had 'no defence': kindness. It is to this disarming letter from Grasset that Proust replied with the letter reproduced opposite. His mode of address is very carefully chosen: 'Dear friend' says a lot about his new state of mind. The opening words are quite explicit: 'Your second letter (charming, and I thank you for it a thousand times) correcting what was certainly the erroneous interpretation I had made of your first....' He hides the indignation that he had felt when faced with Grasset's first reaction, but quickly gets to the point: 'I asked you whether I would be acting against your wishes (to which I already bowed in advance) if I put publication of the 2nd and 3rd parts in the hands of the NRF. You replied…that you wanted them to be published by you. And so that is agreed, at least for the 1st edition.' Then Proust neatly confirms their 'reconciliation': 'Who wrote that charming doggerel about a word having caused and a word having calmed the storm, and one always ends up more affectionate than ever. Allow me to hope that these lines may apply to our relationship as well.' But Proust stresses

the fact that the agreement applies only to the first edition: 'As regards the terms under which later editions might be put in the hands of the NRF, you will let me know your feelings.' One can already sense the precedence he would give to the NRF once Grasset had been mobilized and he felt free from his obligations. Nor does he hesitate to rebuke his publisher for an error of judgment: 'What you say about not printing any more since December upsets and above all astonishes me. It was precisely then that the word, I might even say the sensation, began to spread.'

This fascinating letter must have been acquired very early on by a private American collector to have escaped from the clutches of Philip Kolb. It reappeared in 1978 in the USA, and was acquired for this collection. The text was published in France during the 1990s.

Most of the manuscripts passed down to the Proust family were sold to the Bibliothèque Nationale de France. Nevertheless, during the last thirty years a larger number of important Proust autographs have been found than perhaps of any other major 20th-century writer, even though the truly essential items have since been acquired by institutions and will not be seen again on the open market.

▲ Marcel Proust, drawing inserted into autograph letter, 1904.
► Marcel Proust, autograph letter signed, 1914.

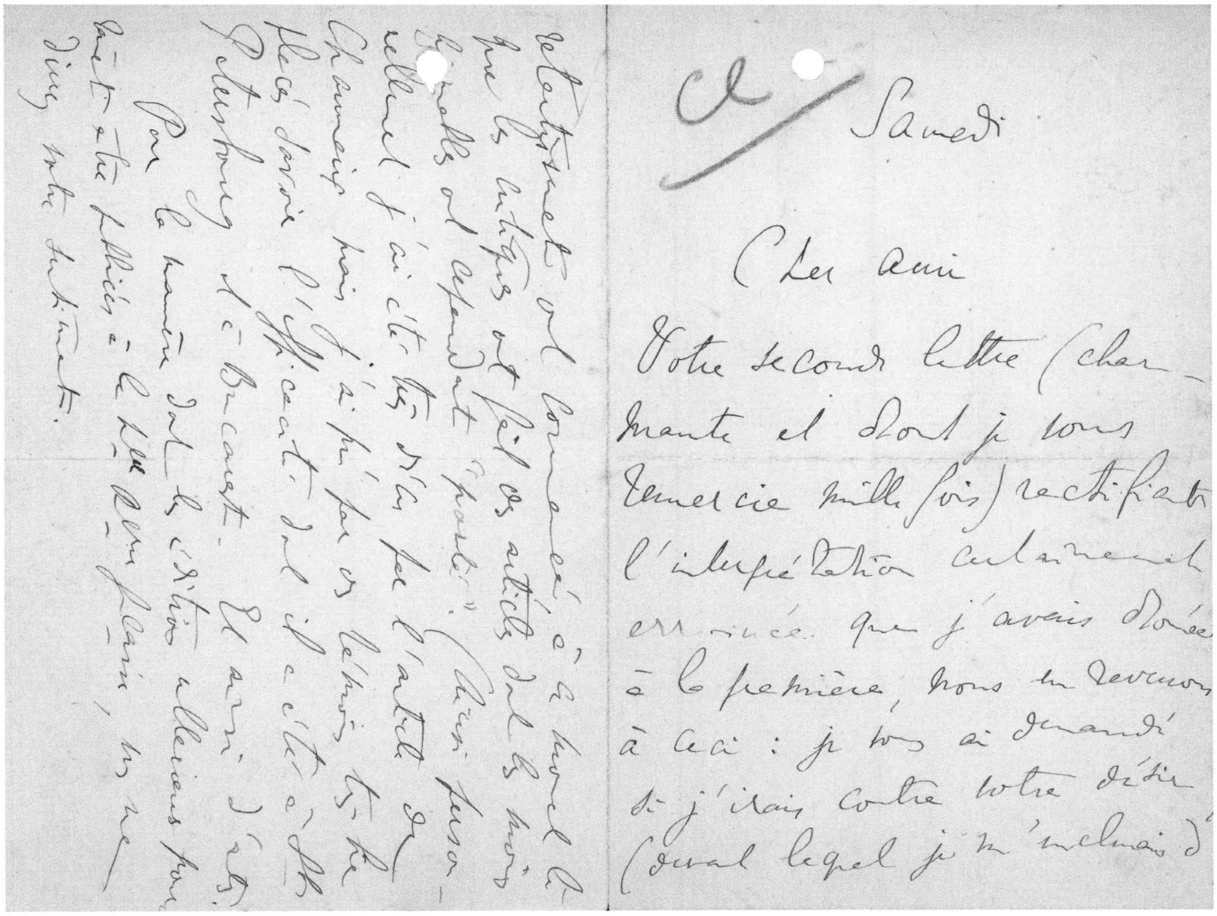

Samedi

Cher ami

Votre seconde lettre (charmante et dont je vous
remercie mille fois) rectifie
l'interprétation certainement
erronée que j'avais donnée
à la première, nous en devenons
à ceci : je vous ai demandé
si j'irais contre votre désir
(duquel lequel je m'inclinais d'

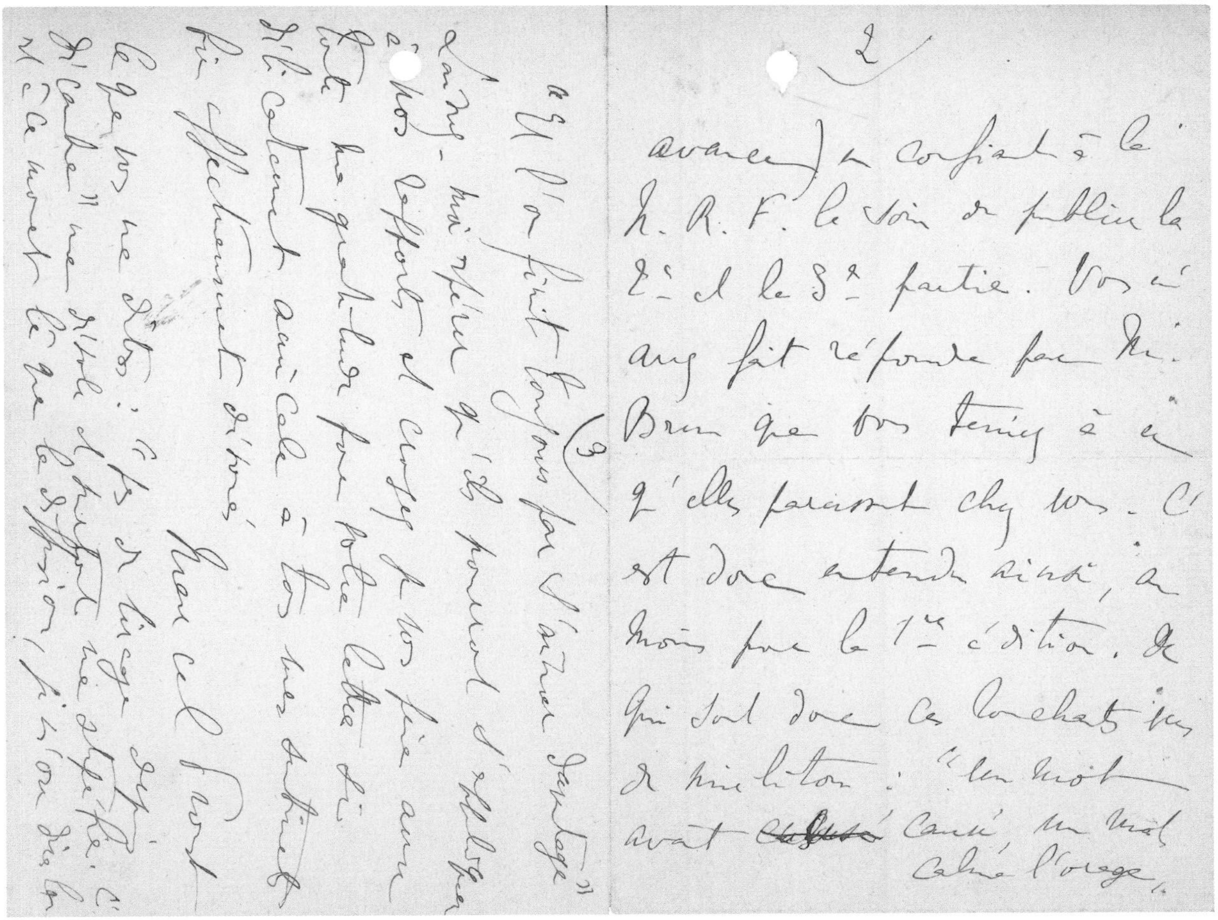

2

avance) en consistant à la
N. R. F. le soin de publier la
2e et le 3e partie. Vous me
avez fait répondre par Mi.
Brun que vous teniez à ce
qu'elles parussent chez vous. C'
est donc entendu ainsi, à
moins pour la 1re édition. De
qui sont donc ces touchants vers
de midi lit... : "Un mot
avant ~~...~~ Cancé, un mot
calme l'orage."

3

"Il l'a fait toujours par l'avenir partagé"
dans... lui répère qu'il [...] pouvant s'expliquer
à vos rapports et certes je les prie avec
toute la gratitude pour votre lettre si
si cohérent aussi cela à très bien distinct
si effectivement d'une

Pour ce font
le plus ne dites : "[...]
il cache" ne s'étale [...]
M. [...] le me le suffirait, je [...]

# Henri MATISSE

## 1869-1954

Matisse and Picasso are often grouped together. These two pioneering painters of the early 20th century had great admiration for each other, and their relationship has been the subject of many studies and exhibitions. Although he was famous from the beginning of the century onwards, Matisse preferred to stay away from the bright lights of Paris. In his art he searched for the purity of basic forms and colours, a quest which led this uniquely audacious colourist to work with *gouaches découpées*, the most famous of which are the *Nus bleus* [Blue Nudes].

The three sheets reproduced opposite, attached to a notebook, were part of an order Matisse placed for materials. He drew the shape of the knives, brushes and jars, and indicated the exact mixtures of oils and pigments he required. He is equally precise in describing the colours: 'ordinary and burnt Siena, vermilion, dark ultramarine blue, emerald green, red ochre....'

Signed photographs of Matisse are very rare (much more so than those of Picasso), but towards the end of his life he sometimes entered into the photographic spirit, and we see him here in front of some preparatory sketches for the *Way of the Cross*, on which he was working for the Chapel of the Rosary at Vence.

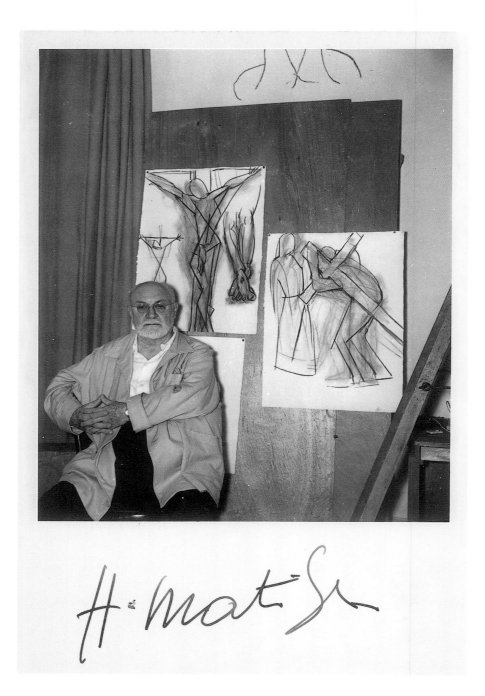

► Henri Matisse, signed photograph, *c*. 1952.
►► Henri Matisse, drawings and autograph manuscript signed, *c*. 1940.

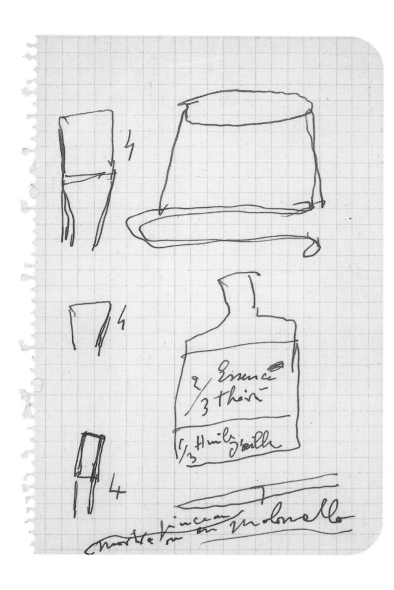

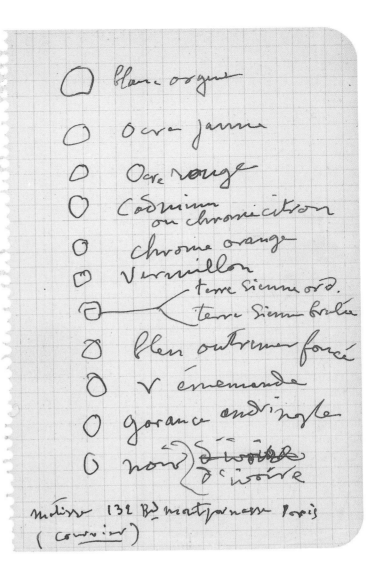

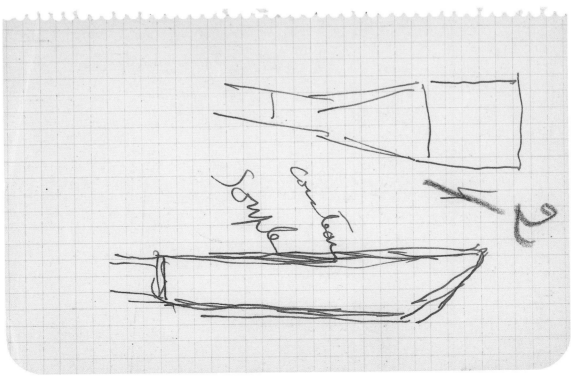

*Some unauthorized paragraphs have been circulated in the press, but I do not propose to send any notice elsewhere.*

# Winston CHURCHILL 1874-1965

# William Somerset MAUGHAM 1874-1965

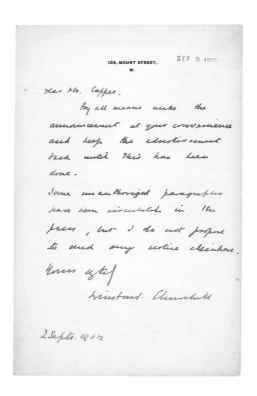

By a strange coincidence, Winston Churchill and the writer William Somerset Maugham were born in the same year and died in the same year. The two men were close enough friends in later life for Churchill to spend part of the summer of 1959 at the Villa Mauresque, Maugham's splendid home on the Côte d'Azur.

Above, on the right, is a rare photograph – part of the Maugham estate – signed by the two octogenarians. They are sitting in the gardens of the villa, six years before they died.

More than half a century separates this photograph from the portrait at the top of the page: here we have Somerset Maugham at the age of twenty-five, and the picture is dedicated to a friend, and signed 'Bill'.

Churchill was twenty-eight when he wrote the letter on the left. He had been an MP for two years, and was already a successful author. He was probably writing to his publisher to complain about extracts from his last book being published without his permission: 'By all means make the announcement at your convenience and keep the advertisement back until this has been done. Some unauthorized paragraphs have been circulated in the press, but I do not propose to send any notice elsewhere.'

Opposite is a photograph by Walter Stoneman, which is one of the best-known portraits of Churchill. It was taken at the height of the war, when he was a universally admired statesman. It remained his favourite,

and he signed this copy in 1949, a few years after the war had ended. Two years later, he became Prime Minister once more.

Although Churchill autographs are available in large quantities, they remain so popular among British and American collectors that they fetch prices that are rare for 20th-century politicians.

---

▶▶ William Somerset Maugham, signed photograph, c. 1899.
▶ Winston Churchill, autograph letter signed, 1902.
▲ Winston Churchill and William Somerset Maugham, signed photograph, 1959.
▶ Walter Stoneman, portrait of Winston Churchill, photograph signed by Churchill, 1949.

1949     Winston S. Churchill

*Marie is finishing a picture that is admirable
in tone and composition....*

# Guillaume APOLLINAIRE 1880-1918

# Marie LAURENCIN 1885-1956

The affair between Guillaume Apollinaire and the young Marie Laurencin, whose gifts were recognized very early on, lasted from 1907 until 1913. They were one of the most celebrated couples at a time when Montmartre contained an extraordinary constellation of artists from all corners. Marie Laurencin did this pencil portrait of Apollinaire (right) during their relationship, but no one knew of its existence until it surfaced during the 1990s in the estate of the poet's widow. As for the letter reproduced above, Marie wrote it much later, in 1956 – the year she died.

Opposite is a long autograph letter from Apollinaire in which he says that Marie 'is finishing a picture that is admirable in tone and composition'. This would certainly have been the famous *Apollinaire and his Friends* (1909), her best-known work during this period. She depicts the poet among his friends, who included Max Jacob (1876–1944) and Pablo Picasso (1881–1973). Apollinaire had just moved to Passy, and the mythical

Bohemian life of Montmartre was fading, as he states quite explicitly: 'Max Jacob seems to have renounced my friendship, and Passy seems to him to be too far away. For my part, I find that there is no comparison between Montmartre and my new environment, which wins from every angle.'

▼ Marie Laurencin, autograph letter signed, 1956.
▲ Marie Laurencin, drawing of Guillaume Apollinaire, c. 1909.
► Guillaume Apollinaire, autograph letter signed, 1909.

**Messidor**

JOURNAL QUOTIDIEN

TÉLÉPHONES { 280.19 286.76

50, Rue Notre Dame des Victoires

Paris, le _____ 190_

Cher ami

Je suis malade et n'ai été incapable
d'écrire ce mois ci ma chronique
des Romans. Le mois prochain
vous aurez votre été aussi fouillé
aussi complète qu'il me sera
possible. Votre livre est très
beau. Il est puissant, attachant
et lyrique. J'admire votre
imagination où tout est grâce
et tendresse, votre culture
si raffinée et votre esprit si dé-
licieux. J'aime beaucoup
l'Arlequin, idée charmante
et je regrette de ne point
pouvoir goûter de cette
ligueur. Mon éditeur a agi
très bêtement avec vous,
car je lui avais montré
votre lettre pour l'adresse,
spécifiant toutefois que
le livre serait porté à mon
compte. Nous l'a envoyé

contre remboursement. Je vous
enverrai à ma première sortie
les 3 frs de l'Arlequin et vous me
rendez quittes et vous me
pardonnerez. Si votre ami a laissé
prévoir une nouvelle édition,
prévenez-moi je connais quelques
amateurs de lettres qui réduits
par la liste de la fin souscriraient
je pense volontiers.
Marie a des névralgies qui ne
veulent céder à aucun remède.
Elle travaille beaucoup et
termine un grand tableau
admirable de ton et de
composition.
Vous m'avez offert de me
faire connaître quelques
personnalités influentes
dans les salles de rédaction
et chez les éditeurs. Faites
-le, cher ami, vous me rendrez
service. Retiré à Parroy
je travaille beaucoup, ne
voyant fort peu de monde.
Max Jacob semble avoir

renoncé à mon amitié
et Parroy lui semble trop
lointain. Pour ma part
je trouve qu'il n'y a pas
à hésiter entre Montmorency
et mon nouveau
quartier qu'il l'emporte
de toutes les façons.

Je suis votre ami très
dévoué

Guillaume Apollinaire

# *Vaslav* NIJINSKY 1890-1950

# *Isadora* DUNCAN 1878-1927

# *Anna* PAVLOVA 1882-1931

These three names evoke a golden age of ballet that lit up the beginning of the 20th century. From 1910, the explosive impact of Russian ballet revolutionized choreography and conquered Paris. Russian art critic and impresario Sergei Diaghilev (1872–1929), the founding father, had a genius for combining the talents of dancers, musicians, choreographers and designers. Together with his American composer Igor Stravinsky (1882–1971), he premiered two of the most sensational artistic events of the century: *Petrushka* and *The Rite of Spring*.

The young Russian ballerina Vaslav Nijinsky was the undoubted star. His athleticism, musical sense and natural grace made him the most admired dancer of his time. Autographs are very rare, because he was struck down by mental illness and after the 1920s never danced again. His letters are practically unobtainable, and even signed albums and photographs are extremely difficult to find. The autograph quotation reproduced opposite is one of only two or three known specimens.

Anna Pavlova, who was also Russian, was one of Nijinsky's co-stars, and her perfect technique, figure and beauty won her ovations all over the world. She is still regarded as the ballet dancer *par excellence* of her generation.

The signed photograph on the right shows her in her late thirties. The picture openly exploits the parallel between the graceful elegance of the dancer's body and the long neck of the swan – an image which inspired many photographs after the success of *Swan Lake* at the end of the 19th century,

► Anna Pavlova, signed photograph, c. 1920.
►► Vaslav Nijinsky, autograph musical quotation inscribed and signed, 1917.

3187/1  Portrait by Lafayette, London.

Anna Pavlova

„Ross" Verlag

notation de la danse

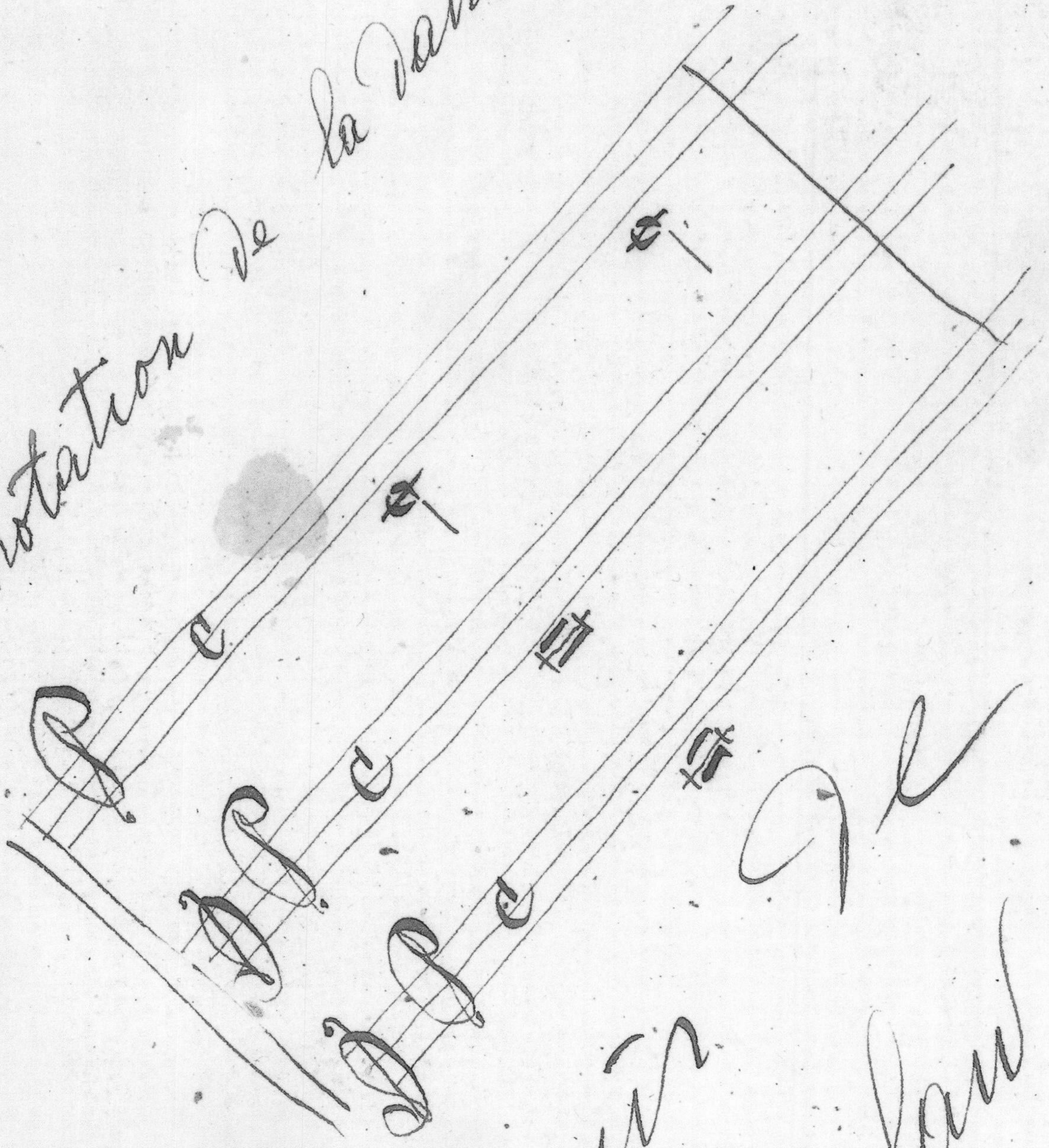

Souvenir de Waslaw Nijinsky

24.8.17

Rio

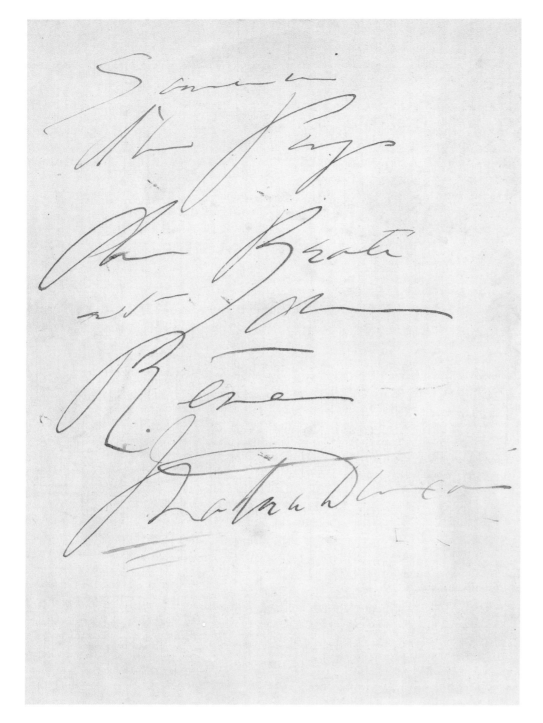

but which had already begun to seem a little outmoded at the time when this picture was taken. Nevertheless, there is no doubt that *Swan Lake* was one of Anna Pavlova's finest roles.

Isadora Duncan was at the forefront of those dancers who revolutionized the ballet at the beginning of the 20th century. She liberated the body and its language from all conventional, academic restraints. Her accidental and extraordinary death – she was strangled by her long scarf, which got caught on the axle of a car she was travelling in – was somehow a fitting conclusion to the life of a character who defied all the norms of her era.

Worshipped in her lifetime, Duncan inspired many artists, such as the painter and sculptor Antoine Bourdelle (1861–1929). It is to him that we owe the magnificent watercolour portrait reproduced opposite, which is somewhat reminiscent of the drawings by another sculptor, Rodin. Despite her immense popularity, autographs of Duncan are far from common, and signed photos of her are even rarer. The two pictures above right offer two very different images. The one at the top shows her on her best behaviour, in her thirties and in full bloom, and it is signed with her full name. The second photograph, taken about ten years

later, portrays her in more relaxed mood. She has dedicated it simply to someone called Billy.

It was during a trip to Brazil that she wrote the note reproduced above, on the left, in the form of a declaration of love: 'Souvenir of a Country of Beauty and Dreams'.

▼ Isadora Duncan, autograph note signed, c. 1915.
▲▲ Isadora Duncan, signed photograph, 1914.
▲ Isadora Duncan, signed photograph, c. 1924.
► Antoine Bourdelle, *Isadora*, signed watercolour, c. 1917.

Isadora

Ant BOURDELLE

affectueusement
à Miss Mac Neal

## Igor STRAVINSKY 1882-1971

## Maurice RAVEL 1875-1937

Scores inscribed by one great composer to another are very rare and much coveted by collectors. The one below, signed in 1919, is particularly interesting: it is an original edition of the score for *Renard*, and it unites two of the most influential composers on the French musical scene during the period between 1910 and 1920. Stravinsky, who had burst onto the world stage with the Russian ballet and, especially, with *The Rite of Spring* a few years earlier, has inscribed this major work to Maurice Ravel. On the right is a photograph signed in 1936 in Argentina, where Stravinsky is posing with his son Soulima, and below is a postcard of the municipal theatre in Rio de Janeiro on which Stravinsky has written an extract from *Persephone*. The portrait of Ravel (opposite) is dedicated to Brazilian pianist Souza-Lima.

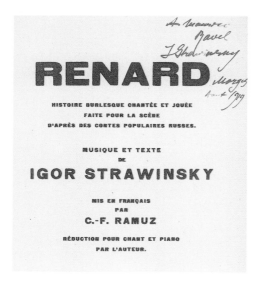

▲ Igor Stravinsky, printed score inscribed and signed, 1919.
◀ Igor and Soulima Stravinsky, inscribed and signed photograph, 1936.
▶ Igor Stravinsky, autograph musical quotation signed, 1936.
▶ Lipnitzki, portrait of Maurice Ravel, inscribed and signed, 1930.

à Souza-Lima

sympathique souvenir

Maurice Ravel

14/5/30

*What pleasure I take in a writer*
*who penetrates the femininity of men.*

# COLETTE

## 1873-1954

Undoubtedly it was Colette's personality as much as her work that brought her an international reputation enjoyed by few other 20th-century French writers. The English-speaking world in particular has taken a great interest in her, thanks to the numerous biographies inspired by her life.

A prolific author, she tackled a wide variety of subjects. The sheet of manuscript reproduced opposite is the last page of a text she wrote on the secrets of beauty, commissioned by the women's magazine *Marianne*. It contains some advice that is both useful and peculiar: 'It is in order to "have it", the sought-after bosom, that mad women have invented slimming. But they did not realize that there is no such thing as a pretty bosom on a thin body.'

The portrait on the right, inscribed to the actress Suzanne Després, is rare in that it shows a young and elegant Colette. It was taken at the 'Nadar-Marseille' studio. The famous photographer, having given his Parisian studio to his son Paul, had settled in the south, where he had allowed his successors to use his name.

At the top of the page is a photograph of a much older Colette, sitting in her apartment at the Palais-Royal. The message written on a blue card is addressed to French journalist and writer Joseph Kessel (1898–1979), who had become a close friend and whose powerful writing was much admired by Colette: 'What pleasure I take in a writer who penetrates the femininity of men.' Colette autographs are far from rare, but they remain popular with collectors all over the world, notably those with a special interest in outstanding women – a branch that has blossomed in recent years.

▼ Sidonie-Gabrielle Colette, signed photo, c. 1950.
◀ Nadar-Marseille, portrait of Sidonie-Gabrielle Colette, inscribed and signed photograph, c. 1900.
▲ Sidonie-Gabrielle Colette, autograph letter signed, c. 1940.
▶ Sidonie-Gabrielle Colette, autograph manuscript signed, c. 1930.

naissent, à ces deux mots, sur les traits
e mes ~~des~~ lectrices...

~~naissent~~ ... Plats, quadrangulaires, pliés,
vidés, anéantis, voire amputés, reviendrez-vous
comme des exilés fiers, au prochain
changement de régime, vous qui fûtes
la fleur, le fruit, la cime visitée
par l'aurore, vous,

    " Seins élastiques et légers,
    Seins de la belle sans rivale..."

                Colette

    S. H. — Oui, mes lectrices peuvent
m'écrire à " Marianne ".

# Pablo PICASSO

## 1881-1973

Already much admired by the time he was barely thirty, Picasso had become a monumental figure by the 1940s. During the last thirty years of his life, he was often given the title – sometimes difficult to bear – of 'the greatest living painter'.

Although nowadays everyone agrees that he was the giant of 20th-century art, his work caused a great deal of controversy during his lifetime. Paradoxically, the controversy also contributed to his universal fame. He himself had a somewhat ambiguous attitude towards this, very rarely giving in to the constant assault by his admirers, but in the course of his long life, there were many who did manage to get close to him. Such meetings were often concluded by inscriptions or sketches in his books (for important collectors), or a plain signature on reproductions of his work, on an exhibition programme, or even on a paper napkin from a restaurant table (for strangers).

Picasso was perhaps the only modern artist who, like a present-day Midas, could in one way or another transform everything he touched into gold. A simple sketch produced in a few seconds would be accepted anywhere and everywhere in exchange for services or goods, and it appears that he was not averse to making use of this method of payment.

Picasso is also one of the most popular targets of the forgers, who of course have imitated not just his works but also his autographs. There are many forgeries in circulation, and sometimes they are good enough to deceive respectable dealers, who in all good faith reproduce these works in their catalogues. Indeed a veritable industry of forged autographs and inscribed drawings seems to have sprung up in the last twenty years, and the provenance now plays a vital part in establishing the authenticity of any work apparently signed by the artist.

The superb signed portrait opposite comes from the estate of one of Picasso's greatest collectors, Douglas Cooper. Picasso has embellished the inscription with the head of a bull. On the right is a delightful drawing of two hearts pierced by an arrow, next to a *découpé* photograph signed by Picasso and his last wife, Jacqueline, and this too formed part of the Cooper collection. Above is a photograph of Picasso with the great American pianist Arthur Rubinstein (1887–1982), to whom the picture is inscribed. It symbolizes the friendship that bound together these two major figures of 20th-century culture.

▲ ▲ Pablo Picasso and Arthur Rubinstein, photograph inscribed to Rubinstein and signed by Picasso, 1971.
▲ Pablo Picasso and his wife Jacqueline Roque, signed drawing (also signed by Jacqueline Roque), c. 1960.
▶ Pablo Picasso, photograph (by Joel Mariaud) inscribed and signed, with drawing, 1961.

Pour mon cher ami Douglas
Cooper
29.10.61.
Picasso

This magnificent photo by Herbert List, *Picasso with Owl*, is one of the best-known portraits of the artist. It was in the library of Douglas Cooper, to whom it was given in 1963, and is perhaps the finest signed portrait of Picasso to have appeared on the market in the last twenty years.

The autograph letter opposite, and its envelope (right), was addressed to a ceramics collector, M. Ascher. Picasso was trying to persuade him to lend some of his pieces for a planned exhibition at Vallauris ('you will be the kind friend that you are'). And if Picasso wanted something, he knew how to play the seducer: he made his request as attractive as he possibly could by using nine different coloured pencils.

▲ Herbert List, portrait of Pablo Picasso, signed by the artist, 1963.
► Pablo Picasso, autograph letter signed and autograph envelope, c. 1953.

Vallauris le 6 juin 1953
A.M

Mon cher Archox

Voici Monsieur Georges Ramié
qui vient de ma part
pour te parler du sujet
de l'Exposition de Vallauris

Tu vas être le petit
que tu es.

J'espère te voir bientôt
ici ou à PARIS

bien à toi
picasso

*I admit…contempt for pretended leaders who refuse to look facts in the eye….*

## *Ezra* POUND 1885-1972

## *William Butler* YEATS 1865-1939

The American Ezra Pound and the Irishman W. B. Yeats were two of the giants of 20th-century poetry in the English language. The link between them here is the fact that for a short time in 1913 Pound was Yeats's secretary. It was during this period that the young American poet stayed at Stone Cottage, Yeats's rented home in Sussex, and wrote the letter reproduced below right in the name of his employer. Their handwriting and signatures were very different, and the dealer who owned this letter assumed that it was not by Yeats and therefore sold it for very little, as being 'written by a secretary'. He was not actually wrong, but he had not checked a scribble under the signature: 'pp.E.P.', which Ezra Pound had taken the trouble to append.

The typewritten letter reproduced opposite contains several handwritten corrections by Pound. The headed notepaper adds interest, with the fine portrait of Pound in profile that was executed by his friend the sculptor Henri Gaudier-Brzeska (1891–1915). Pound is writing to the editor of the English magazine *Everyman*. He is giving vent (as he often did in his letters) to some strong opinions: 'I shd. be deeply interested in learning from you…where there is any trace of *personal* antipathy in my "ABC of Economics"…. An antipathy to men who advocate starvation and sabotage has no need of being personal.'

Above right is a document that Yeats signed when he was thirty-five. It is part of a publisher's contract for his dramatic poem *The Shadowy Waters* (1900), which was actually not published until five years later. His brother, the great Irish painter Jack Butler Yeats (1871–1957) – whose work has been increasingly recognized as an important contribution to 20th-century art – has signed

the contract on the left as a witness. Their two signatures together are quite a rarity and add an extra dimension to this item.

▲ W. B. Yeats, typewritten document signed, 1900.
► Ezra Pound, autograph letter signed with his initials, 1913.
►► Ezra Pound, typewritten letter signed, with autograph additions, 1939.

13 April

**E. POUND** **RAPALLO**

VIA MARSALA 12-5

Edtr/ Everyman                    ( " trusting you may find space for " )

   I shd. be deeply interested in learning
from you or your reviewer where there is any trace of
<u>per</u>sonal antipathy in my "ABC of Economics." And I defy
*either of you* ~~him~~ to name a single line in which any such trace
of personal feeling is present.

   I admit a thoroughly impersonal feeling not only of
antipathy but of contempt for pretended leaders who
refuse to look facts in the eye , and who suppress for ~~decade~~
               the
decade after decade the discussion of ~~fundamentals~~ of
economics.

   Can you indicate to me any *single* ~~city~~ British daily
paper which has openly stated the cause of recurrent
crisis ?

   Or which has admitted that every factory
creates prices faster than it distributes the power to
buy ?

   An antipathy to *men* ~~men~~ who advocate starvation and sabotage
~~can~~ has no need of being personal.


   yrs. very truly

          Ezra Pound

*How could you have done that without talking to me about it first? It makes me sick. Ah, I can tell you, I could have done without that....*

## James JOYCE 1882-1941

## Samuel BECKETT 1906-1989

Of all the talented young writers that were disciples and friends of James Joyce, only Samuel Beckett attained a stature comparable to that of the master. For many, Joyce shares with Proust the accolade of being the greatest writer of the first half of the 20th century. Beckett, along with Jorge Luis Borges (1899–1986) and one or two other notables, must be a serious candidate for the second half. Of course it is too soon to say how posterity will view the last century, and no one can tell whether the judgments of twenty years ago will still apply in twenty years' time.

Whatever the future may hold, Joyce's letters have always remained highly desirable and, for the last ten years, extremely rare – even those whose content is unexceptional. Signed photos of Joyce are also highly sought-after, but only a handful have come on the market over the same period. The beautiful photograph opposite was taken by photographer Ruth Asch during a trip to Berlin in 1930. Joyce signed it for an acquaintance the following year in Paris.

Beckett's reticence was legendary. His social life was restricted to a small circle of close friends, he avoided photographers, and never granted interviews. By contrast, however, he was a prolific and entertaining letter-writer, and never left a letter unanswered. Notes written on cards bearing his name are very common, signed photos (like the one above) are less so, and significant manuscripts and letters are rare. The autograph letter signed (right) is therefore all the more special. It reveals a Beckett disappointed by and furious at the treachery of a friend, Nino Frank, who had been introduced to him by Joyce in 1928. Thirty-seven years later, in 1965, Frank had published a private conversation with him

in the form of an interview: 'I never give interviews, but never. I thought we were simply having a chat, as friend to friend. How could you have done that without talking to me about it first? It makes me sick. Ah, I can tell you, I could have done without that.'

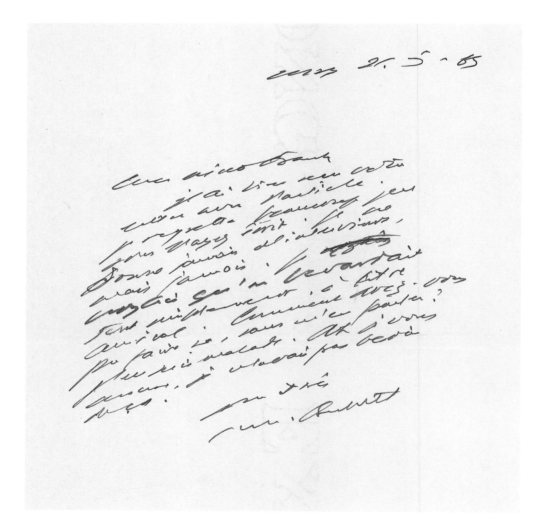

▶ Samuel Beckett, photograph inscribed and signed on the back, 1969.
▲ Samuel Beckett, autograph letter signed, 1965.
▶ James Joyce, signed photograph, 1931.

James Joyce
Paris : 18 . IV . 95

*I asked God to give me Lucie Valore*
*as my wife, and He answered my prayer.*

# Maurice UTRILLO

## 1883-1955

For much of his life, Maurice Utrillo was afflicted with poverty and physical degeneration. His mother was Suzanne Valadon, a model and also mistress to some of the greatest painters of the time, while she herself was a painter of talent – as her son was later to become. But even though his views of Montmartre are now world-famous, he suffered for many years from extreme poverty and an alcoholism that earned him the reputation of a man accursed. It was only after he met Lucie Valore that his life attained some kind of balance, although his enemies accused Lucie of completely dominating her artist husband. Nevertheless, their marriage lasted for twenty years, until Utrillo died in 1955. Lucie herself also tried her hand at painting, albeit without showing much talent of her own.

The drawing opposite has long been regarded as a self-portrait. The signed inscription on the right is in Utrillo's handwriting: 'I asked God to give me Lucie Valore as my wife, and He answered my prayer.' Some people have since argued that the portrait might have been drawn by Lucie, but as it was first done in pencil and then finished in Indian ink, like the autograph inscription, it is more than likely that the work is Utrillo's. If so, it is a very rare self-portrait by an artist who otherwise never did such things, and there is an added poignancy in the fact that it dates from just a few weeks before his death.

The photograph on the right shows him at roughly the same time, looking very fragile, arm in arm with his wife. They have both dedicated it to a *commissaire de police* who specialized in tracking down forged pictures in Paris. The forgers produced so many 'Utrillos' that Commissaire Isnard had become a personal friend of the couple.

▲ Maurice Utrillo and Lucie Valore, photograph signed by both, 1954.
► Maurice Utrillo, self-portrait with autograph inscription signed, 1955.

Je demandai à Dieu
Lucie Valore pour femme
et il m'exauça,

Maurice, Utrillo, V,

28-8-1955

*What a to-do about*

*a wretched book!*

# T. E. LAWRENCE

## 1888-1935

The saga of Lawrence of Arabia (Thomas Edward Lawrence, later changed to Shaw) has become one of the best-known adventure stories of the 20th century, thanks in part to David Lean's epic film. But if the rest of the world only discovered Lawrence after the huge success of the 1962 film, English readers had for some thirty years already admired this Anglo-Irish soldier and writer whose career had been non-conformist in the extreme. He was the author of the monumental *The Seven Pillars of Wisdom* (1926), an account of the Arab Revolt of 1916, which many considered to be a masterpiece. Among his greatest admirers was Winston Churchill. His premature death at the age of forty-seven in a motorcycle accident somehow helped to foster his legend. A passionate advocate of Arab independence, he helped the English to win major victories against the Turks during the First World War, and was then bitterly disappointed when the Anglo-Arab pact was broken by the Treaty of Versailles, which shattered hopes of independence for the Arab regions under European control. He felt that his own compatriots had betrayed his Arab friends. He resigned, and in search of anonymity changed his name first to Ross and then to Shaw. He actually lost the manuscript of his account, which he had written in Versailles, and so he rewrote *The Seven Pillars of Wisdom* from memory. This book won him a reputation which he himself considered to be out of all proportion. The autograph letter reproduced opposite (and signed T. E. Shaw) is dated 1932, and reveals precisely this attitude. Lawrence writes to his correspondent, who had asked for a copy of the book: 'What a to-do about a wretched book! I assure you, solemnly, that it is not worth any trouble at all.'

Letters by Lawrence about his masterpiece are very rare, and such self-critical comments are even rarer. Most of his abundant correspondence has been published, but the enthusiasm of the collectors (particularly English and American) remains unabated.

The portrait above, by Augustus John, is certainly the best known of Lawrence. It was reproduced in the first edition of *The Seven Pillars of Wisdom*, which was published with a print run of just 170 copies.

▲ Augustus John, portrait of T. E. Lawrence, photogravure, 1926.
► T. E. Lawrence, autograph letter signed (T. E. Shaw), 1932.

Plymouth

12 · X · 32

Dear Benham

I have both your letters, and no Seven
Pillars. Group Captain Nichol, who said he was
sending It back at once, has let me down. It
shall follow this letter as soon as it arrives.

What a to-do about a wretched book!
I assure you, solemnly, that it is not worth any
trouble at all —

Yours ever

R Shaw

*She seems to be distinguishing herself
as a good actress, letting the glamour girl slide.
And I am glad of that.*

## Frank Lloyd WRIGHT 1867-1959

## LE CORBUSIER 1887-1965

Along with Ludwig Mies van der Rohe (1886–1969) and perhaps also Walter Gropius, Le Corbusier and Frank Lloyd Wright were the leading lights of 20th-century architecture. Wright was twenty years older than Le Corbusier, and began his revolutionary career around 1905, reaching the peak of his international fame in the 1930s.

The letter reproduced opposite offers an important insight into the private life of this American architect, whose marital problems separated him from his children. His granddaughter Anne Baxter became a famous Hollywood actress (she won an Oscar in 1947 at the age of twenty-four). In 1944, when her relations with her grandfather were still rather vague, she decided to write her first letter to him. His reply bears the red logo of Taliesin, his famous home and workplace: her letter was 'The first to grandfather. And this is the first to granddaughter. She seems to be distinguishing herself as a good actress, letting the glamour girl slide. And I am glad of that.' The signed photograph shows Anne Baxter in one of the romantic roles that she was famous for at the beginning of her career.

The part played by Le Corbusier in the history of architecture is well known, but fewer people know of his work as an artist. His drawings, however, can be extremely interesting, like the one on the right, which was done on the back of a duplicated circular.

Above left is an inscription to a Brazilian friend, dated 1929 and written in his book *L'Art décoratif d'aujourd'hui*. The text gives some idea of the great Swiss architect's intentions at the time: 'America claims that I make philosophical comments. Well, perhaps in this book there really is a little glance in the direction of wisdom.'

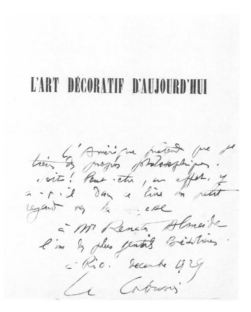

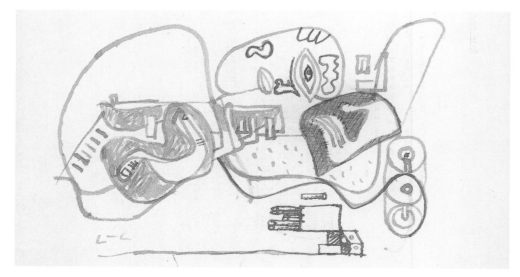

▼ Le Corbusier, autograph inscription signed, 1929.
▲▲ Anne Baxter, signed photograph, 1940.
▲ Le Corbusier, signed drawing, c. 1945.
► Frank Lloyd Wright, typewritten letter with autograph addition, signed 'Grandfather', 1944.

Dear Anne:    Such a nice little letter.

The first to grandfather. And this is the first to
grandaughter. She seems to be distinguishing herself
as a good actress, letting the glamour girl slide. And
I am glad of that.

We will be seeing you soon in L.A. of all places. I
hope that we can see something of you and go places
together a little.

We are quite well and hopeful as usual but trying
to keep off the war, etc.

Give my love to your mother (Taffy at the studio door,
etc.) with all —

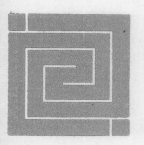

Affection from   And now we've lost your address and must send
Grandfather/     this care of Hay?.
Frank Lloyd Wright                          March 21st, 1944

# D. W. GRIFFITH 1875-1948

## *Sergei* EISENSTEIN 1898-1948

D. W. Griffith and Sergei Eisenstein are generally recognized as two of the giants of silent cinema. American-born Griffith was self-taught and created the monumental *Birth of a Nation*, filmed in 1915. Eisenstein was a Russian film director who considered himself to be a disciple of Griffith, and who created several masterpieces, including *The Battleship Potemkin* (1925).

Their autographs are rare and much sought-after, and signed photographs are even rarer. That of Griffith (opposite) is certainly the biggest and finest to have appeared on the market. It shows him around 1920, at the age of forty-five, at a time when his career was about to fall into terminal decline with the advent of talkies in 1931.

During the 1930s, Eisenstein left Russia, and his journey to Mexico resulted in the extraordinary *Que viva Mexico!* He continued his travels, and his critical work – which was to have enormous influence on the aesthetics of the cinema – went on developing through the years that he spent outside the Soviet Union. Nevertheless, Eisenstein made two more great historical films in his home country: *Alexander Nevski* in 1939 and, above all, *Ivan the Terrible* in 1945–46, which he completed two years before his death.

In 1927, such was the impact of *The Battleship Potemkin* that the American magazine *Vanity Fair* devoted several pages to its director, including the photograph on the right. The inscription on the back in red ink was to a female colleague. The pencilled notes served for classification and also add to the impressiveness of the document.

▶ Sergei Eisenstein, photograph inscribed and signed on the back, 1927.
▶▶ D. W. Griffith, inscribed and signed photograph, c. 1920.

To John L. E. Pell
from his friend
D.W. Griffith

## Leon TROTSKY 1879-1940

## Frida KAHLO 1907-1954

Diego Rivera (1886–1957) and his wife Frida Kahlo were militant members of the Mexican Communist Party, and they remained faithful admirers of Leon Trotsky even when Joseph Stalin condemned him to death *in absentia* in 1936. They played a crucial part in Trotsky's decision the following year to go into exile in Mexico together with his wife. The famous Mexican artists found them a house close to their own, where the ageing Russian revolutionary continued indefatigably to denounce Stalin's dictatorship.

Their close proximity soon led to an affair between Frida Kahlo and Trotsky in 1937. It was at this time that Trotsky – who communicated with his mistress in French or a sort of English – wrote Frida the autograph letter reproduced opposite. He cautiously advises her to send her written messages 'thruw two or three intermodiarys' because 'nothing is sure'. The tone of the letter is otherwise quite inoffensive: Trotsky asks for news of Frida's sister Cristina, sends his regards to D. D. (Don Diego Rivera), and observes that 'It rains. It rains'.

The break-up of the Soviet Union has brought to the West a number of administrative documents that Trotsky signed during the Russian Revolution. Autograph letters, however, remain scarce, especially those written during his exile in Mexico. Frida Kahlo autographs are even rarer. This fine photograph showing one of her numerous self-portraits is especially interesting, as Frida coloured and inscribed it.

▲ Leon Trotsky, autograph envelope, 1937.
▶ Frida Kahlo, hand-coloured photograph, inscribed and signed, c. 1945.
▶▶ Leon Trotsky, autograph letter signed, 1937.

Dear "Sra" Frida, When [...] it seems to me that you ded'nt receive my cards*); it is the only one reason why I permited me to cable yesterday.

Cann you bes so kind and send the card to D. Hidalgo? I dont have his adres (☰) (la dirección*).

It rains. It rains. and —————→

My besh thanks and greetings to D. D. and to yourself

Yurs L. T.

P. S. Do you see Natalia? What about Cristina? ————— you

L. T.

*) every thing must be send throw two or three intermediarys ... nothing is sure (excuse my english, please)

(excuse the two inks.)

"Nací para cantar
a Stalingrado

Pablo
Neruda

## Diego RIVERA 1886-1957

## Pablo NERUDA 1904-1973

The political commitment and powerful lyricism of the Chilean poet Pablo Neruda brought him worldwide recognition and earned him the Nobel Prize for Literature in 1971. His death, twelve days after the ousting of President Allende (1908–73) by General Pinochet, spared him the pain of seeing his country suffer under a long and tyrannical dictatorship.

Neruda was elected to the Senate at the age of thirty-nine, but was driven into exile for having supported the Communist Party during the 1940s. After his return to Chile in 1950, he published his famous *Canto general*, a poetic masterpiece in praise of Latin America as it had once been, and condemning the exploitation of his people. The manuscript reproduced opposite is an extract from one of the best-known poems in the collection, which Neruda had copied out by hand. These are the first two couplets of the poem *America*: 'America, I do not invoke your name in vain….'

It was the famous Mexican painter Diego Rivera who illustrated this poem with a drawing of a spotted jaguar. In 1953, Neruda and Rivera were both in Santiago, Chile, for a peace conference organized by the Communist Party. Neruda asked the painter – who was as politically committed as himself – to illustrate the manuscripts which he intended to put up for sale in order to raise funds. In the end, only a few were illustrated, including this one, which was bought from the poet by a Brazilian militant who took it back to his own country.

Neruda himself could also draw when he wanted to. The branch on the right was a memento left in the album of a friend he visited in Rio in 1956. On another album page, reproduced above, Neruda wrote: 'I was born to sing of Stalingrad.'

Pablo Neruda
1956 Rio

17.11.56

▼ Pablo Neruda, autograph quotation signed, c. 1955.
▲ Pablo Neruda, signed drawing, 1956.
► Pablo Neruda and Diego Rivera, autograph manuscript signed by Neruda, drawing signed by Rivera, 1953.

America, no invoco tu nombre
en vano.
Cuando sujeto al corazón la espa-
da,
cuando aguanto en el alma la
gotera,
cuando por las ventanas
un nuevo día tuyo me penetra,
soy y estoy en la luz que me produce,
vivo en la sombra que me determina,
duermo y despierto en tu esencial
aurora:
dulce como las uvas, y terrible,
conductor del azúcar y el castigo,
empapado en esperma de tu especie,
amamantado en sangre de tu herencia.

Pablo
Neruda

Santiago de Chile 1953

Diego Rivera

*An abject and miserable individual
named Fernando Pessoa....*

# Fernando PESSOA

## 1888-1935

Fernando Pessoa was the greatest
20th-century poet of the Portuguese
language, but when he died in 1935
at the age of forty-seven, he was virtually
unknown. During the decades that followed,
his work – for the most part unpublished –
began to find its way into print, and to be
appreciated by an ever-increasing number
of readers in Portugal. Since the 1980s, his
fame has spread even further afield, and
his name now figures prominently in world
literature. The profound originality of his
work has a lot to do with the fact that he
signed his texts under several different names,
each one corresponding to a very distinct
literary style. He used four principal
identities, which he called 'heteronyms'.

Unfortunately for his admiring
collectors, Pessoa autographs are
extremely rare. He left his family a trunk
of manuscripts which is still yielding up
unpublished works, and which since 1975
has belonged to the National Library of
Lisbon. Most people he corresponded with
had nothing to do with the world of literature,
and so they saw no reason to keep the letters
of an unknown; hence only about 250 letters
are known to have survived.

The most important collection is that
of forty-nine love letters addressed to the only
woman in whom he seems to have had an
interest, his 'fiancée' Ophelia Queiroz. The
letters remained unpublished until 1978,
when they caused a sensation in Portugal.
This complete and immensely important
correspondence now forms part of the
collection on which this book is based. The
exchange of letters with Ophelia took place
in two phases: 1920 and 1928, with eight years
of silence in between. The letter reproduced
here, on the right, belongs to the second
phase. It is the only one signed with a

◄ ► Fernando Pessoa,
autograph letter signed
(Alvaro de Campos), 1929.

'heteronym' – perhaps the most famous:
Alvaro de Campos.

Under cover of this identity,
Pessoa/Campos accuses the 'abject and
miserable individual named Fernando Pessoa'
of having deliberately deceived Ophelia as
regards his intentions, and he forbids her '1) to
weigh fewer grams. 2) to eat little. 3) to sleep
little. 4) to have a fever. 5) to think about the
individual in question.'

Exma. Senhora D. Ophelia Queiroz:

Um abjecto e miseravel individuo chamado Fernando Pessoa, meu particular e querido amigo, encarregou-me de communicar a V.Ex.ª — considerando que o estado mental d'elle o impede de communicar qualquer coisa, mesmo a uma ervilha secca (exemplo da obediencia e da disciplina) — que I. Ex.ª está prohibida de:

(1) pesar menos grammas,

(2) comer pouco,

(3) não dormir nada,

(4) ter febre,

(5) pensar no individuo em questão.

Pela minha parte, e como

1918

# *Jean* COCTEAU

## 1889-1963

If the work of Jean Cocteau, in all its diversity, had come down to us under different identities, each would certainly have been considered a master in his particular field. We would have had at least one great poet, one remarkable novelist, one admirable designer, one inspired playwright and one outstanding film director. To this list may be added Cocteau's indisputable role as the greatest cultural agitator in France during the first half of the 20th century. However, it is precisely this vast range of talents embodied in one man that his contemporaries and immediate posterity have found so difficult to come to terms with. Cocteau was therefore branded with a reputation for superficiality in all his different fields. The general agreement was that the term 'genius' could only be applied through the expression – always bracketed with his name – '*touche-à-tout de génie*' [jack-of-all-trades genius], as if a multitalented person could only produce minor works in each of his domains.

There are signs, however, that people are beginning to give Cocteau his rightful place in the various arts in which he excelled. Of these, drawing was not the least, as can be seen from the works reproduced here, including the head of an Adonis that embellishes the inscription on the right, the hand holding a scarf (above), and the pictures overleaf.

The manuscript reproduced opposite is fascinating for more than one reason. First of all, it is evidence of the friendship between Cocteau and Giorgio de Chirico (1888–1978) – the Italian painter illustrated one of Cocteau's books of poetry. It also – and more

▲ Jean Cocteau, signed drawing, 1928.
▶ Jean Cocteau, autograph inscription signed, with drawing, 1925.
▶▶ Jean Cocteau, autograph manuscript, c. 1930.

à mon cher Florent de tout cœur

PORTRAITS-SOUVENIR

Jean

Sa figure chevaline, son masque
~~peint~~ de plâtre aux ~~dents~~ dents d'or,                    ~~de sa présence chevaline,~~
            ~~mystifie~~          Son accent                      ~~pâle aux dents d'or,~~
                              bourru, bref

La personnalité, l'envergure, le grand format et
~~votre~~ ~~jambe~~
de Chirico ! — ~~de~~ sa ~~pâle~~ ~~aux dents d'or~~ présence réelle, en chair et en os, ~~sa~~
                                              "C'est ce ~~grand format~~"
présence ~~dans~~ ~~tableaux~~ peinte ou écrite, rapetissent
                                              meurt peint, de
tout ce que ~~qu'on~~ ~~on~~ peut lui opposer de plus neuf, de
        ~~dégou~~ ~~oppressif,~~ d'exaltant ou ~~inquiétant~~ violent
plus ~~oup~~, de ~~plus sérieux~~, de ~~plus grand~~, de plus riche ~~intègre~~
~~déconte~~                 tout fait                    d'une attitude qui
en ~~énigmes~~, et ~~fait~~ ~~de déroute~~ ~~on il~~ déroute et
révolte si fort le zèle excessif de ses anciens adeptes,
d'une ~~direction~~ attitude
~~dans~~ ~~notre~~ singulière qu'il a prise, quelque chose
      nouvelle
de vénérable et d'intriguant, au même titre, dans
   ~~de singulier~~
une sphère somme toute moins séduisante, que
                                  mythes sa mythologie
ses architecture mystérieuse, ~~ses~~ ~~passages~~, ~~ses ana logies~~
~~mariés~~
~~les~~ ~~mobilières~~ et ~~ses rencontres d'objets~~.
            Ses rencontres d'objets..            la sorcellerie
      ~~fétiches~~                                        de ses
      ~~les accessoires familiers.~~                      premiers
                                                         tableaux.

octobre
1921

à
Maurice martin du gard
Son ami
Jean Cocteau

. L'Égoïsme .

▲ Jean Cocteau, inscribed and signed photograph, c. 1921.
◄ Jean Cocteau, autograph manuscript, c. 1910.
► Jean Cocteau, drawing, c. 1925.
►► Jean Cocteau, self-portrait, 1924.

importantly – demonstrates the reception at that time of the Italian artist's radical change of style. After the hallucinatory compositions of his youth, which had enormous influence on early 20th-century art, he suddenly decided to revert to a classicism which in all respects he considered superior to his previous style, although this caused great consternation to Cocteau as well as to most of his other admirers.

When De Chirico asked Cocteau to write a text to accompany one of his exhibitions, Cocteau naturally forced himself to omit his reservations about this new phase in De Chirico's work. But the large number of corrections to the manuscript show how difficult it was for him to convey a message in which he did not believe. One can read his misgivings between the lines and in his many deletions. In his embarrassment, he tries to get round the problem by emphasizing the 'personality' of the painter, who 'makes small everything that one can set against him that is better painted, more original, more solid, more haunted, more violent, more integral'. One can clearly sense the hard labour involved in this manuscript, which has been corrected in two stages (the last in pencil) and which reveals the creative mechanism of one of the 20th century's great stylists.

The manuscript reproduced top right dates from the beginning of Cocteau's literary career, when his admiration for Anna de Noailles led him to imitate not only her style but also her handwriting. It appears also to have been corrected at a later date, but this is still a minor piece of juvenilia.

The erotic drawing above dates from the 1920s, and is of very fine quality. Another version that is more explicit was exhibited in Paris: in this, one can see the lower half of the bodies coming together. It would appear that either Cocteau himself decided to draw a less intimate version, or someone else was only interested in the top half.

The photograph top left shows Cocteau c. 1915, but he only dedicated it six years later – to the brother of the winner of the Nobel Prize for Literature, Roger Martin du Gard.

The magnificent self-portrait opposite was discovered a few years ago in an American collection that was assembled during the 1930s. It was done at Villefranche in 1924, at a time when Cocteau was creating some of his most famous drawings, depicting himself in the midst of texts written in his own hand. This portrait, however, is one of the very few from that period that he did not incorporate into such a setting.

For the last twenty years or so, an extraordinary number of Cocteau forgeries have flooded the French market, but those that have been unmasked would only appear to be the tip of the iceberg. Some have even found their way into major exhibitions. If the experts do not take the trouble to identify the many fakes, soon the forgeries will outnumber even the copious genuine articles.

# *Charlie* CHAPLIN 1889-1977

# *Alfred* HITCHCOCK 1899-1980

Charlie Chaplin and Alfred Hitchcock had a number of things in common: their English origin, their enormously successful careers in Hollywood, and a worldwide popularity matched by few other film-makers.

Chaplin's career was perhaps the most complete all-round success in the history of the cinema, not only for its longevity but above all for his dual role as director and actor. The character of Charlie remains in a class of its own as a universal symbol unique to the cinematic medium. The signed photograph opposite shows a dignified and elegant Chaplin, very different from the figure of the Little Tramp. Wealthy and adored by his millions of fans, at the peak of his fame, he is looking down at the photographer from his chair. At the time when he dedicated this photograph, in 1941, he was producing his own films and had long been one of the most powerful men in Hollywood, despite the slanderous campaigns mounted against him by puritanical adversaries who were outraged by his many divorces. Ten years later, he became a victim of McCarthyism, and although then a naturalized American, he was forced to leave the USA (1952). He spent the last twenty-five years of his long life in Switzerland, and it was there that in 1966 he drew the Little Tramp character (above right) on an album belonging to the photographer Alfred Eisenstaedt.

On the right (below) is Hitchcock's own sketch of his famous profile, which was used to introduce his many TV series that were broadcast all over the world.

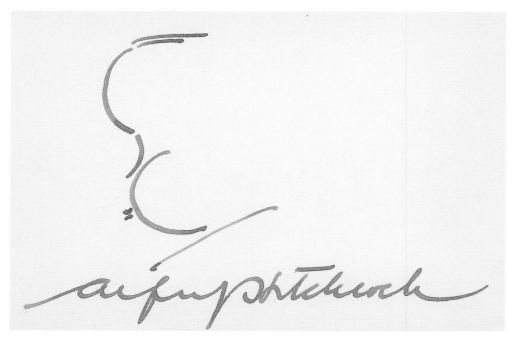

◄ Charlie Chaplin, signed self-portrait, 1966.
► Alfred Hitchcock, signed self-portrait, c. 1970.
►► Charlie Chaplin, signed photograph, 1941.

To Norman.
Thanks and best wishes
Charlie Chaplin
14-41

*I spend whole hours*
*working on a poem, only to leave it*
*as it wishes itself to be....*

Federico García LORCA

1898-1936

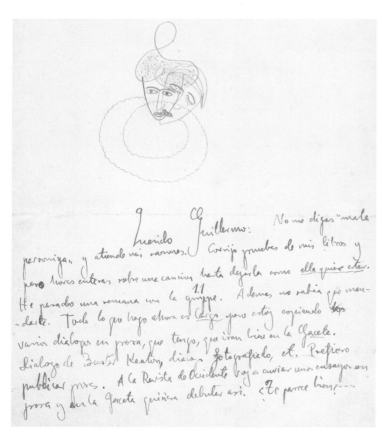

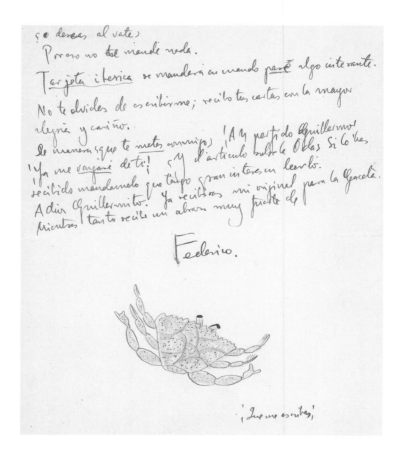

Poet and playwright García Lorca was already in his own lifetime the greatest Spanish representative of modernism. His execution at the beginning of the Spanish Civil War aroused the wrath of intellectuals the world over, but at the same time it cemented the legendary status of the writer. His dazzling career had taken him at an early age to North and South America, for triumphant lecture tours and public readings of his works.

Lorca was a close friend of Salvador Dalí, and was himself a remarkable artist, influenced by Surrealism. During his stay in Buenos Aires, he also became friends with Guillermo de Torre, a Spanish writer, and his painter wife Norah Borges, sister of Jorge Luis Borges. Torre is the addressee of the autograph letter reproduced above and decorated with two drawings in coloured crayon, one of which is his famous 'falling mask'. In the letter, Lorca talks about his latest works, and offers some prose dialogues for a review in Madrid, including a 'Buster Keaton Dialogue'. He is correcting proofs and works tirelessly on a poem, only to 'leave it as it wishes itself to be'. A few years later, he illustrated a slim volume by the Argentine writer Ricardo Molinari with several fine drawings such as the one reproduced at the top of this page.

Opposite is an autograph inscription which Lorca also wrote in Buenos Aires two years before his death. It was written on one of his best-known works, *Romancero gitano*, and contains another fascinating illustration.

▼ Federico Garcia Lorca, drawing, 1934.
▲ Federico Garcia Lorca, autograph letter signed, 1927.
► Federico Garcia Lorca, autograph inscription signed, with drawing, 1934.

Para Rudy

Con un abrazo de

Federico García Lorca

—Buenos Aires—1934—

# KING EDWARD VIII 1894-1972

## *The Duchess of* WINDSOR 1896-1986

There has been endless speculation about the true nature of the relationship between the Duke and Duchess of Windsor. Theirs was the love story that brought about the almost unimaginable abdication of a King of England, and it became the media sensation of the 1930s, with a hugely controversial impact on public opinion all over the world.

From a dynastic point of view, Wallis Warfield Simpson, an American who had been divorced twice and was no longer in the first flush of youth, could scarcely claim to be the ideal fiancée for King Edward VIII. He had succeeded his father in 1936, and ascended the throne of the most powerful empire on the planet. In order to marry Wallis, after a reign of barely ten months he turned his back on a task which he found impossible 'without the help and support of the woman I love'.

The romantic nature of this renunciation fired many imaginations. However, the ex-king – who was then given the title Duke of Windsor – found himself cast off with no sense of purpose throughout the next thirty-five years of his life. Apart from the reverberations of a hectic social life, he seemed to parade his boredom through all the capitals of the world except that of his home country, where he was *persona non grata*. Even his desire to have his elegant wife addressed and treated as a 'Royal Highness' was thwarted by his brother George VI (1895–1952).

The photograph opposite, signed by both the Duke and Duchess, also bears the signature of a well-known American fashion photographer, Toni Frissell. She shows the luxurious, meticulously arranged surroundings which the Duchess designed for her husband, and in which one can see

the attention to detail, the painstaking quest for perfect harmony. More natural, even if it is deliberately staged, is the rare print above, which Edward signed in the course of his very short reign.

The greetings card on the right is the last the couple ever sent to their friends. It is dated 1972, the year the Duke of Windsor died.

▼ Duke and Duchess of Windsor, card signed by both, *c.*1970.
▲▲ Duke of Windsor (as Edward VIII), signed photo, 1936.
▲ Duke and Duchess of Windsor, greetings card signed by both, 1972.
► Toni Frissell, portrait of the Duke and Duchess of Windsor, photograph signed by the photographer, and inscribed and signed by the Duke and Duchess, 1967.

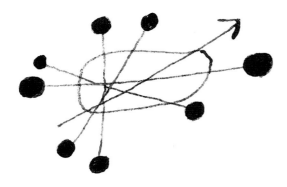

# Joan MIRÓ

## 1893-1983

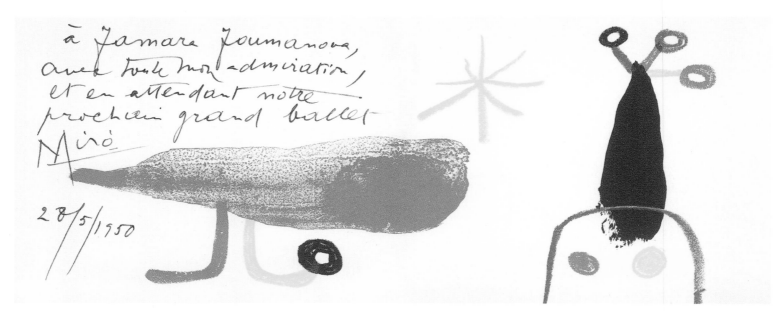

Like Salvador Dalí and René Magritte (1898–1967), Joan Miró was a shining light in the world of the Surrealists. Having settled quite early in Paris, the young Catalan was already well known in artistic circles when he posed in 1936 for the British photographer Peter Rose Pulham. The resultant double portrait (opposite) is completely in the spirit of the Surrealist movement that inspired Miró. The photograph is inscribed to Douglas Cooper, the great English collector of Cubist art and one of Picasso's friends. Miró seems to have made a mistake with the first name of the dedicatee, as he wrote David instead of Douglas. To correct the error, he improvised a charming drawing. Inexplicably, this extraordinary portrait – remarkable both for its subject and for its photographic skill – is not very well known.

During the 1950s, the artist had acquired an international reputation, and although

he led a relatively quiet life, he met a number of fellow artists and creative people, some of whom became personal friends. One of these was the dancer Tamara Toumanova. Too young to have fully taken in the era of the Ballets Russes in Paris, Tamara was engaged by American choreographer George Balanchine (1904–83) at the age of thirteen, and she enjoyed a dazzling career until the end of the 1950s. Miró sent her an invitation to his next exhibition on a card decorated with a coloured engraving of one of his works (above).

The autograph letter signed, on the right, is addressed to a poet friend in 1956, and refers to an exhibition in Switzerland.

▲ Joan Miró, original engraving on card, inscribed and signed, 1950.
► Joan Miró, autograph letter signed, 1956.
►► Peter Rose Pulham, double portrait of Joan Miró, with drawing and inscription signed by the artist, 1936.

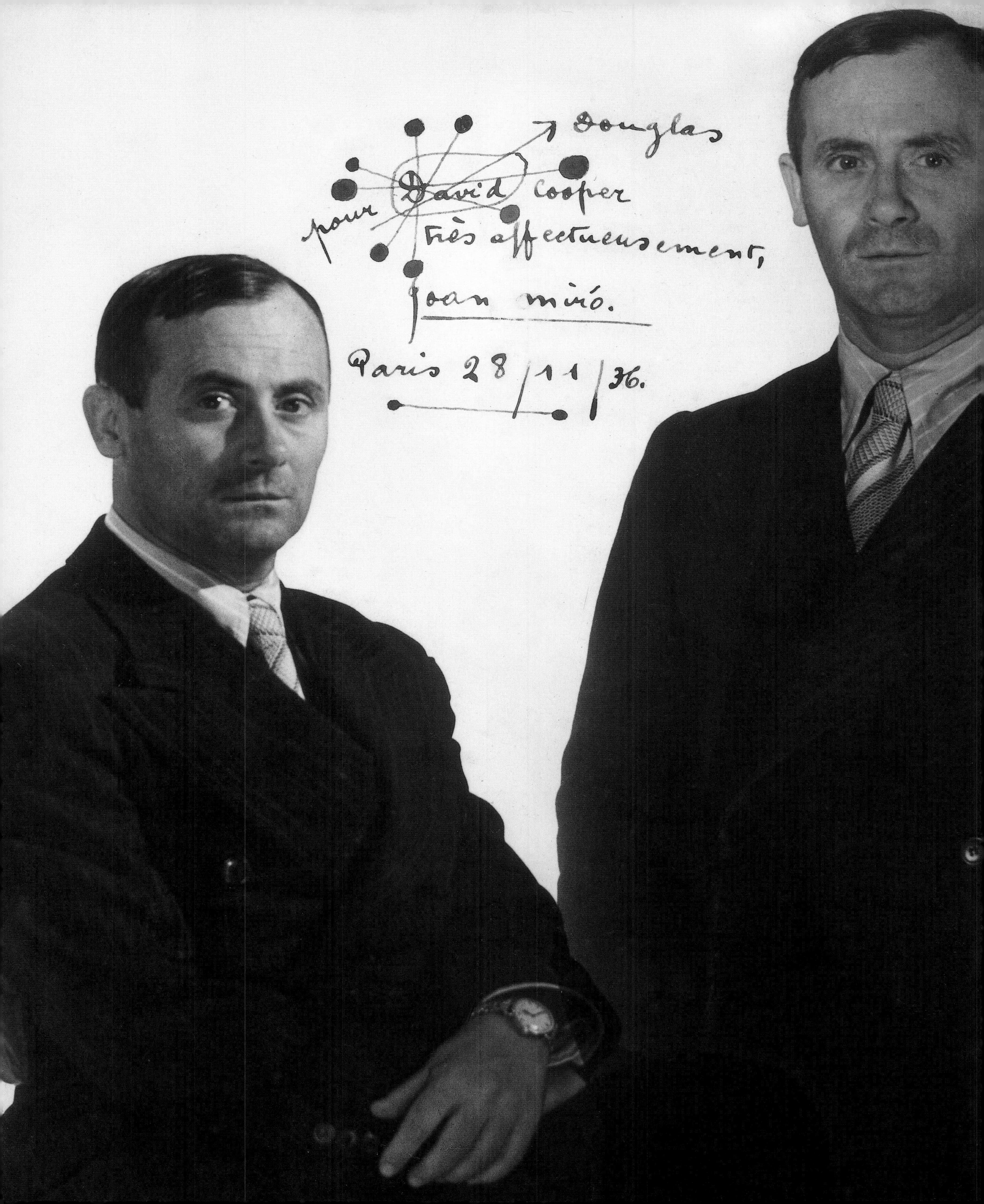
Douglas
pour David Cooper
très affectueusement,
joan miró.
Paris 28/11/36.

# Antoine de SAINT-EXUPÉRY

## 1900-1944

As the author of one of the best-loved tales of modern times, *The Little Prince* (1943), Antoine de Saint-Exupéry enjoyed a degree of international fame attained by very few French writers. In France itself, his portrait adorned a banknote for some time, and his novels such as *Night Flight* (1931) and *Wind, Sand and Stars* (1939) are still on the school syllabus. His career as an airman, his heroism during the Second World War, and his mysterious death during a reconnaissance mission have all added to the legend and helped to make him the model novelist-cum-hero. Only his friend Mermoz can perhaps match the reputation as a knight of the air that has grown up around him since his death.

Despite his shyness, Saint-Exupéry's friendly nature was well known. A page from the proofs of *Flight to Arras*, the American edition of *Pilote de guerre*, reproduced opposite, is a fine example. With his illustrator, Bernard Lamotte, he covered this page with drawings and gave it to a friend one year before his death. The two men amused themselves by reversing their signatures, each attributing their own drawings to the other. That of a small boy top right, closely resembling the preliminary sketches for *The Little Prince*, was certainly done by the author himself. Lamotte also drew the hitherto unpublished portrait of Saint-Exupéry at the top of this page.

The photograph showing the author at the age of thirty-five – one of the finest portraits he ever posed for – is a rare original print signed by Roger Parry from around 1936.

Above it is an autograph letter to René Char, whom Saint-Exupéry knew briefly during the 1930s. This document is perhaps the only evidence of the friendship between the two writers.

Saint-Exupéry autographs have always been quite rare, but when his wife Consuelo died, his love letters were auctioned off in the 1980s along with a number of his drawings, including some from *The Little Prince*. This was the best ever opportunity for collectors to acquire some fascinating letters and masterly drawings, but very few of these have reappeared on the market, and so once again they have become rare.

▼ Bernard Lamotte, portrait of Saint-Exupéry, signed drawing, 1942.
▲ Antoine de Saint-Exupéry, autograph letter signed, c. 1935.
► Roger Parry, portrait of Saint-Exupéry, signed by the photographer, c. 1936.
►► Antoine de Saint-Exupéry and Bernard Lamotte, proof with drawings and autograph inscriptions, 1942.

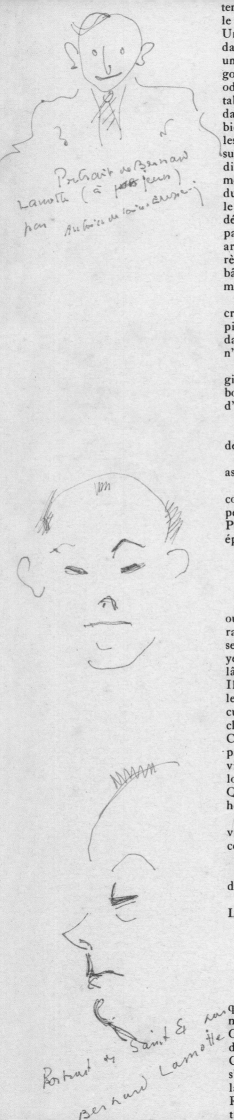

temps à autre je m'enfonce plus loin dans le rêve et jette un coup d'œil par la fenêtre. Une branche d'arbre y balance doucement dans le soleil. Je regarde longtemps. Je suis un élève dissipé... J'éprouve du plaisir à goûter ce soleil, comme à savourer cette odeur enfantine de pupitre, de craie, de tableau noir. Je m'enferme avec tant de joie dans cette enfance bien protégée ! Je le sais bien : il y a d'abord l'enfance, le collège, les camarades, puis vient le jour où l'on subit des examens. Où l'on reçoit quelque diplôme. Où l'on franchit, avec un serrement de cœur, un certain porche, au delà duquel, d'emblée, on est un homme. Alors le pas pèse plus lourd sur la terre. On fait déjà son chemin dans la vie. Les premiers pas de son chemin. On essaiera enfin ses armes sur de véritables adversaires. La règle, l'équerre, le compas, on en usera pour bâtir le monde, ou pour triompher des ennemis. Finis, les jeux !

Je sais que d'ordinaire un collégien ne craint pas d'affronter la vie. Un collégien piétine d'impatience. Les tourments, les dangers, les amertumes d'une vie d'homme n'intimident pas un collégien.

Mais voici que je suis un drôle de collégien. Je suis un collégien qui connaît son bonheur, et qui n'est pas tellement pressé d'affronter la vie...

Dutertre passe. Je l'invite :

— Assieds-toi là, je vais te faire un tour de cartes...

Et je suis bien heureux de lui trouver son as de pique.

En face de moi, sur un bureau noir comme le mien, Dutertre est assis, les jambes pendantes. Il rit. Je souris avec modestie. Pénicot nous rejoint et pose un bras sur mon épaule :

— Alors, vieux camarade ?

Mon Dieu que tout cela est tendre !

Un surveillant (est-ce un surveillant ?...) ouvre la porte pour convoquer deux camarades. Ils lâchent leur règle, leur compas, se lèvent et sortent. Nous les suivons des yeux. Le collège est fini pour eux. On les lâche dans la vie. Leur science va servir. Ils vont, comme des hommes, essayer sur leurs adversaires les recettes de leurs calculs. Drôle de collège, d'où l'on s'en va chacun son tour. Et sans grands adieux. Ces deux camarades là ne nous ont même pas regardés. Cependant les hasards de la vie, peut-être bien, les emporteront plus loin qu'en Chine. Tellement plus loin ! Quand la vie, après le collège, disperse les hommes, peuvent-ils jurer de se revoir ?

Nous courbons la tête, nous autres qui vivons encore dans la chaude paix de la couveuse...

— Ecoute, Dutertre, ce soir...

Mais la même porte une seconde fois d'ouvre. Et j'entends comme un verdict :

— Le Capitaine de Saint Exupéry et le Lieutenant Dutertre chez le Commandant.

Fini le collège. C'est la vie.

— Tu savais, toi, que c'était notre tour ?

— Pénicot a volé ce matin.

Nous partons sans doute en mission, puisque l'on nous convoque. Nous sommes fin mai, en pleine retraite, en plein désastre. On sacrifie les équipages comme on jetterait des verres d'eau dans un incendie de forêt. Comment pèserait-on les risques quand tout s'écroule ? Nous sommes encore, pour toute la France, cinquante équipages de Grande Reconnaissance. Cinquante équipages de trois hommes, dont vingt-trois chez nous,

Portrait de Bernard Lamotte (à ??? jeune) par Antoine de Saint-Exupéry

Portrait de Saint Ex par Bernard Lamotte

Portrait de pilote par Bernard Lamotte

Portrait de Pilote par Antoine de Saint Exupéry

# *Greta* GARBO 1905-1990

# *Rudolph* VALENTINO 1895-1926

Hollywood's golden age brought to a few dozen actors and actresses the sort of worldwide adulation that is difficult to imagine even today, and which only the cinema could have engendered during the first half of the 20th century. They were all blessed with a degree of talent and good looks, but it took special circumstances to endow a handful of them with mythical status in the eyes of a public that was avid for images of perfection. The cinema was the miraculous medium that gave these gods an almost palpable physical presence.

Rudolph Valentino during the 1920s, and Greta Garbo during the decade that followed, were perhaps the brightest stars of all in a new form of popularity that verged on idolatry. Valentino's death in 1926, at the age of thirty-one, provoked a wave of emotion that was unprecedented; countless 'widows' all over the world dressed themselves in black. Signed photographs of Valentino are very rare, and the large-format one opposite is regarded as one of the finest known portraits of him.

Of all the Hollywood stars, Greta Garbo was certainly the most reticent when it came to autographs, and she systematically refused to sign photographs or albums for her unknown fans. Her friends steered well clear of making requests for such things, even after her premature (and self-imposed) retirement. All the photographs signed in her name were actually the work of secretaries, except for more recent forgeries. A few contracts and cheques signed 'Greta Garbo' have been put on sale during the last forty years, but they are virtually the only known autographs, along with two or three private correspondences that have been dispersed since her death.

The publication rights to Greta Garbo's letters are fiercely guarded by her nieces,

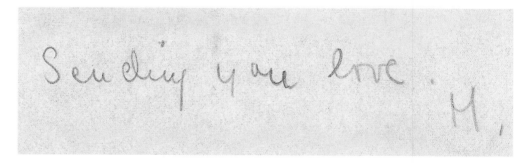

and no letter has been published since her death. For this reason, the autograph letter in this collection cannot, unfortunately, be reproduced or transcribed in its entirety.

Only a few words of the content are permitted, which is why the greeting and signature are reproduced above. In this case, Garbo chose to sign with the initials of Harriet Brown – a pseudonym she invented in the late 1930s, in the hope that her letters might be sent more discreetly.

The letter in pencil dates from November 1956 and is addressed to her great friend, the English photographer Cecil Beaton. She asks him to buy her woolly clothing in London. While the tone is friendly, the former actress says that she has no news of friends because she sees no one and goes nowhere. This admission sums up Garbo's existence in last four decades of her life.

▲ Greta Garbo, autograph letter signed 'H', 1956.
► Rudolph Valentino, signed photograph, c. 1924.

*I imagine that the book will please you.*
*It will be historical….*
*The hero is the 'Prince of Salina'….*

# Giuseppe Tomasi di LAMPEDUSA

## 1896-1957

Giuseppe Tomasi, Prince of Lampedusa, was the author of a single novel, *Il Gattopardo* [*The Leopard*], which was published a year after his death in 1958, and caused a sensation in Italy. A few years later, Italian director Luchino Visconti's (1906–76) extraordinary film gave it the status of a classic, and made it into the most famous Italian novel of the post-war era.

The person who would have been most surprised by this success was Lampedusa himself, for despite his noble birth he lived modestly in his hometown of Palermo, and never published anything in his lifetime. During the First World War, he was based with the Italian troops in Piedmont. A big, shy young man, passionately fond of literature, he became great friends with Guido Lajolo, who was from Turin, and the photograph of him on the right in uniform is inscribed on the back to Lajolo ('G[iuseppe] T[omasi] to his only friend') – eloquent testimony to his affection.

After the war they separated, and Lajolo emigrated to Brazil. The two friends lost touch for more than thirty years, but chance eventually reunited them in the 1950s, shortly before Lampedusa died. He then wrote Lajolo three long letters recounting the story of the last thirty years. The one reproduced opposite is the most remarkable, as it reveals the genesis of *The Leopard*: 'I imagine that the book will please you. It will be historical, and will reveal nothing sensational, but rather the emotional and political reactions of a Sicilian nobleman…at the fall of the Bourbons. The hero is the "Prince of Salina" – a thin disguise for the Prince of Lampedusa, my great-grandfather. But the friends who have read the book tell me that the Prince of Salina has a devilishly close resemblance to me. I am flattered, because I think he is rather nice.

The whole book is ironic, but not devoid of cruelty. It has to be read very closely, because every word is carefully chosen, and every episode has a hidden meaning.' Lampedusa autographs are very rare, and this letter is one of the most important that he ever wrote.

▲ Giuseppe Tomasi di Lampedusa, photograph inscribed on the back, 1920.
► Giuseppe Tomasi di Lampedusa aged sixty, original photograph, 1956.
►► Giuseppe Tomasi di Lampedusa, autograph letter signed, 1955.

Palermo      31 Maggio 1955
via Butera 28

Carissimo Guido,

il mio prolungato silenzio non ha scusa, lo so bene, quindi non mi resta che rimettermi alla tua misericordia e promettere di non peccare più.

Sono stato molto lieto di ricevere pronta la partecipazione al matrimonio di tua nipote; avrei voluto congratularmi e fare gli auguri vivissimamente alla nuova coppia, ma ne ignoro l'indirizzo e ti prego di farlo quindi a nome mio.

Riguardo alle non belle notizie che mi dai nella tua salute ne sono rimasto molto rattristato e ti prego di non volere, per altruismo, risparmiare a darmi quelle migliori notizie nelle quali spero e delle quali sono anzi sicuro.

La mia salute è abbastanza buona; malgrado seguite cure sono molto smagrito ed ho perso 18 chili di peso; un vantaggio non soltanto estetico ma anche igienico perché mi sento più snello ed il cuore si affatica meno. Mia moglie sta bene

*I wish Castro luck too.*
*He's got it rough right now....*

# Ernest HEMINGWAY

## 1899-1961

The most famous American novelist of his time was awarded the Nobel Prize for Literature in 1954, seven years before he killed himself in Idaho. Ernest Hemingway had lived life to the full: during the First World War he served as an ambulance driver in the American army in Italy, then settled in Paris where he mingled with the intelligentsia through the 1920s. He travelled all over the world, returning many times to Spain – a country which he loved passionately – and it was the Spanish Civil War that inspired his most popular novel, *For Whom The Bell Tolls* (1940). He then lived for many years in Cuba, in the famous Finca Vigia, which has now been turned into a museum.

It was here, in April 1959, less than two years before his death, that he wrote the long letter reproduced opposite. He is talking about articles that he was supposed to write for various American publications, but the most remarkable section is a political observation whose significance not even he could have foreseen: 'I wish Castro luck too. He's got it rough right now.' Fidel Castro had just become Prime Minister of Cuba and was at the beginning of his long 'reign'.

The photograph (below right) by the Cuban photographer Alberto Korda, signed by Hemingway, shows the great novelist meeting Fidel Castro. The photograph above is of a young lion that has just killed a zebra, and it is a unique print taken by Hemingway himself. He shot it for the magazine *Esquire* during a trip to Africa in 1933. On the back he has written: 'copyright by Ernest Hemingway' with the number 4 to indicate its position in a sequence of photographs he took for the magazine.

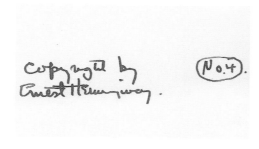

▲ Ernest Hemingway, original signed photograph, 1933.
▶ Alberto Korda, portrait of Ernest Hemingway and Fidel Castro, original print signed by the photographer, 1959.
▶▶ Ernest Hemingway, autograph letter signed, 1959.

April 10 1959

Dear Mr. Peterson:

Thank you for the letter and the book of poems. Will do what you ask.

Please give my best to Tom and tell him I missed him there twice but will try again the next time I'm in Miami.

When I got home here Easter Sunday found galleys of Eastman The Sat. Review had sent asking me to answer (hoping to get newsworthy I guess) for a while I thought of saying I hoped writing that piece made him feel better about what really happened to him and what Perkins really said. Then I thought why should I do even that. Incidentally I wrote their Esquire piece, if you saw it. It was then working for Arnold Gingrich of Esquire. I didn't answer that one either. Hope this isn't a bad seque.

I already said I am to be a review of Michigan — was nearly 4 weeks old when I went there for the first time.

Truck Castro looked too. He's got it rough right now.

Have been away 6 months and am swamped with stuff but wanted to answer your letter before I got into the permanent MUST BE ANSWERED AT ONCE pile.

Best luck always.
Ernest Hemingway.

# *Mae* WEST 1892-1980

# *Stan* LAUREL 1890-1965

# *Oliver* HARDY 1892-1957

Although they never had the mythical status of Garbo and Valentino, there were a few comic actors in the first half of the 20th century who were recognized the world over. They included the Marx Brothers (known as Groucho, Chico, Harpo, Gummo and Zeppo), W. C. Fields (1880–1946), the double act of Laurel and Hardy, and the tempestuous Mae West. The latter defied the strait-laced conventions of a puritanical America, flaunting her ample sexuality and taking risks that no other actress of her time could possibly have got away with. In the course of her long life, she happily signed countless items, but signed photographs from the 1930s – particularly of such good quality as the one on the right – are far from common. The picture shows her decked out in all her finery, and it is dedicated to a journalist who covered the cinema for a Brazilian magazine.

The popularity of Laurel and Hardy during the 1920s and 1930s was matched only by that of Charlie Chaplin and perhaps Buster Keaton (1895–1966). This international fame continued through the 1940s, and the two men were always ready to oblige the hordes of autograph collectors – although there are also large numbers of pieces that have been signed by secretaries or with a stamp. Photographs in postcard format are relatively common (though still much in demand), but large-format pictures like the one opposite are far rarer. This is one of the finest known portraits of the duo, and bears an affectionate inscription written by Laurel and signed by both stars.

► Mae West, inscribed and signed photograph, c. 1932.
►► Stan Laurel and Oliver Hardy, inscribed and signed photograph, 1953.

Stan Laurel.

Oliver Hardy

KINDEST REGARDS &
BEST WISHES ALWAYS
TOM,
SINCERELY —

OCT. 24TH
1953.

*I wish you not to be like me.*

## *Boris* PASTERNAK 1890-1960

## *Vladimir* NABOKOV 1899-1977

These two compatriots, belonging to the same generation, went in totally different directions. After the Russian Revolution, writer Vladimir Nabokov went into exile and lived freely in the West, where he wrote with equal facility in Russian, French and English. Poet and author Boris Pasternak remained in the Soviet Union and was forced to submit to the rigours of the Stalinist regime, which censored his work and made him refuse the Nobel Prize for Literature in 1958, after the astonishing success of his novel *Doctor Zhivago* (1957), which was banned in his own country but translated everywhere else in the world.

The text that Pasternak sent to an American collector just one year before his death, when he was at the height of his fame, is particularly poignant. Isolated in his own homeland, he writes: 'I wish you not to be like me.' He urges him not to cause any suffering to those that are dear to him: 'This is my only misfortune and life torment.' And he finishes on the saddest of notes, referring to this as 'one of my heaviest days'.

At the same time, Nabokov was achieving a *succès de scandale* with his novel *Lolita*, published in Paris in 1955, and banned in several countries on grounds of obscenity. Today it is regarded as a masterpiece. *Lolita* brought fame to a writer whom the critics had long regarded as one of the greatest of his time. Nabokov autographs are rare, and the portrait on the right is certainly one of the best that he ever signed. Taken by *Paris-Photo* at Menton in 1938, it is dedicated to his friend Lisbet Thompson. Nabokov has made a pun on the name of the town, which he calls 'Mentown'.

▶ Vladimir Nabokov, signed photo, 1938.
▶▶ Boris Pasternak, autograph letter signed, 1959.

To Mr L. Robert

Whittemore

18 Febr. 1959. I am really very busy and not always over-happy at all. And in this need and sorrow and haste I cannot devise wishes for you that should not be commonplace and banal. I wish you not to be like me. I wish you, in your seeking to be good to people around you, not to engender and multiply colliding sufferings of your next or dear ones, crossing each other. This is my only misfortune and life torment.

B Pasternak

At the one of my heaviest days.

*…a small drawing: 10 dollars,*
*a small gouache painting: 20 dollars….*

René MAGRITTE 1898-1967

Paul DELVAUX 1897-1994

René Magritte and Paul Delvaux are the best known of Belgium's Surrealist painters. But although their fame is now universal, for a long time their art barely earned them a living, as can be seen from the Magritte letter reproduced on the right.

He wrote it in 1953 to a young Yugoslavian student, fourteen years before he died. The student had expressed his admiration while also bemoaning his own limited means, and so Magritte offered him photographs of his work ('the photographer asks me for one dollar per photo') or, alternatively, some original works: 'a small drawing: 10 dollars, a small gouache painting: 20 dollars…put in your envelope the dollar bills that correspond to the value of what you want to acquire.' His correspondent should not have declined the offer, as he seems to have done: some fifty years later, the little gouache is probably worth at least three thousand times the amount the painter then asked for.

The extraordinary letter opposite, written and illustrated by Paul Delvaux, was addressed to a friend of his youth with whom he had lost touch but, forty years later, located again in Argentina: 'Thank you for your nice letter which has given me the greatest pleasure…it's a real shame that Buenos Aires is such a long way away! But our old friendship will remain intact in spite of the distance….'

The young nude which Delvaux has drawn in ink is typical of the mysterious females that people his paintings. She makes the letter into a work of art in its own right.

▶ René Magritte, autograph letter signed, 1953.
▶▶ Paul Delvaux, illustrated autograph letter signed, 1970.

Boitsfort, le 20-4-70.

Mon cher Jules
Merci pour ta gentille
lettre qui m'a fait le
plus grand plaisir
Merci aussi pour tout
ce que tu me dis. C'est
bien dommage que
Buenos Ayres soit
loin! Mais notre
vieille amitié se
maintient intacte
malgré la distance...
Ma femme et
moi t'adressons
ainsi qu'à ton
épouse notre
vieille et
bien sincère
affection
Peut-être
viendras-tu bientôt
en Europe??
Félici
Paul

*I am utterly lazy*
         *when it comes to writing letters*
         *and also everything else that is not letters….*

# Jorge Luis BORGES

## 1899-1986

For the last twenty years, a few letters and manuscripts by the famous Argentinian writer have sparked off memorable battles in the great auction houses of Europe, and especially London. A wealthy Argentinian collector of German descent has been largely responsible for the rocketing prices of Borges's autographs, and he now has the finest private collection of his manuscripts. However, Borges collectors the world over also covet the many pages that the great author filled with his minuscule handwriting before he went blind at the age of fifty. His mother then wrote at his dictation, until she died in 1975, aged ninety-nine. All the same, Borges had never hesitated to call on his friends to help him write a succession of works after the 1950s.

The autograph letter reproduced opposite is addressed to the Argentinian writer Horacio Ratti, and stems from the 1920s, when Borges first began to have his work published. 'Forgive me for the lateness of this reply. I am utterly lazy when it comes to writing letters and also everything else that is not letters….'

The card reproduced top right is a greeting that Borges's mother wrote for him in 1957, and it is signed with a vague scrawl by the author when he was virtually blind.

The photograph on the right, by Maurice Jaet, bears the microscopic signature of an elderly Borges. He often signed copies of his books when asked to do so by his admirers, and during the last ten years of his life he remained surprisingly accessible to those who came to see him. Enclosed in his dark world, and living alone after his mother's death – except for the presence of his Paraguayan cook – Borges liked to talk to his visitors, and sometimes got them to read out things that interested him.

▲ Leonor Acevedo de Borges and Jorge Luis Borges, letter written by Leonor and signed by Jorge, 1957.
► Maurice Jaet, portrait of Jorge Luis Borges, photograph signed by Borges, 1978.
►► Jorge Luis Borges, autograph letter signed, c. 1927.

Sr. Horacio E. Ratti.

Amigo: Perdóneme la demora de esta contestación. Soy de una haraganería ejercitadísima para la escritura de cartas y de las que no son cartas también. Ahora que me acuerdo, ya debo tener algún retrato de Vd., en grupo campero de jinetes, con nuestro muerto nobilísimo López Merino. Sus dos composiciones me gustan, y más la intitulada Paisaje que Evocación. Me parece ( si me consiente Vd. opinar, con derecho a equivocarme, claro es) que ha incurrido Vd. en la última en la facilidad de definir a un escritor con palabras de él, con imágenes privativas de él. La página Paisaje la encuentro más hermosa y más suya. Llevaré las dos a Síntesis en estos días.

Le estrecha cordialmente la mano. Jorge Luis Borges ✝

s/c Hotel Helder. calle Rivadavia 857. Buenos Aires +

*Sinceramente*
*Walt Disney*
*Rio 8-28-41*

# Walt DISNEY

## 1901-1966

Creator of Mickey Mouse, the cartoon character that conquered the planet, Walt Disney went on to make more than three hundred animated films, and to transform his studio into one of the biggest communications empires in the USA.

Disney autographs are very popular, especially in America, while original drawings are very rare indeed: nearly all of them were executed by several artists working under his direction. These artists were also quite willing to imitate his signature on all kinds of items to be sold to a public that was eager for souvenirs. The handwriting of the Disney signature varies considerably, which has been the cause of much confusion: his authentic signature has sometimes been attributed to his collaborators, and vice versa. Those reproduced here have been authenticated simply by the fact that Disney himself donated all the items – two of them during a trip to Brazil in 1941.

The photograph reproduced opposite is dedicated to a relative of the minister who had invited him to Brazil. Top right is a picture of Donald Duck on celluloid, produced for an animated cartoon and then later framed; it bears an autograph inscription which Disney wrote in red pencil. Below is a short typewritten letter addressed to a Brazilian composer who had offered him some music. As for the signature in capital letters at the top of this page, some experts have attributed similar samples of Disney's handwriting to studio collaborators, but in fact this one is undoubtedly authentic.

▲ ▲ Walt Disney, autograph inscribed and signed, 1941.

▲ Walt Disney, inscribed and signed picture on celluloid, c. 1948.

► Walt Disney, typewritten letter signed, 1941.

► ► Walt Disney, inscribed and signed photograph, c. 1950.

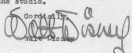

*Rio de Janeiro* September 7, 1941

Sr. J. Sá Róris
Praça S. Dumont 16
Gavea
Rio de Janeiro

Dear Sr. Róris:

May I express my thanks for your gift of records and sheet music of some of your songs. Rest assured that we will listen to them upon our return to the studio.

Cordially
Walt Disney

To
Cuaepp To Alorges Granha
With all Best Wishes
Walt Disney

*Al amigo D˞ Dr. Cervantes Jardim con gran afecto. —
Buenos Aires 5 dic. 1950
Juan Perón*

# *Eva* PERÓN 1919-1952

# *Juan* PERÓN 1895-1974

Few politicians have owed as much to their wives as Juan Perón, who became President of Argentina in 1945. Since then, the myth of 'Evita' has spread far beyond the borders of her country, where worship of the President's wife bordered on frenzy, and where her almost public agony, ending in her death in 1952 at the age of thirty-three, resulted in an unprecedented wave of emotion.

The young actress who espoused the cause of the poor, the *descamisados* [without shirts], also felt herself constrained to act out the role of the beautiful and sophisticated woman, covered with jewels and dressed by the finest couturiers, but this in no way affected her huge popularity. It was in the role of elegant 'First Lady' (in which her dazzling success was a source of great annoyance to the high society of Buenos Aires) that Evita posed for the photograph reproduced opposite, in a Dior evening dress and with a rich 17th-century tapestry in the background. The photograph is inscribed to one of the most important Peronist propagandists, Raul Appold: 'With all good wishes from a Peronist and a friend'.

On the right is the menu for an official luncheon given by the Peróns when they were at the height of their power in 1950. Above is an official portrait of Perón when he was President, with an inscription in his own handwriting.

*Juan Perón*

**ALMUERZO**

Ofrecido
por el Excmo. Señor
Presidente de la Nación
**GENERAL JUAN PERON**
y su señora esposa
**EVA PERON**

En honor de los Delegados
al VII Congreso Internacional
de Cirugía

QUINTA PRESIDENCIAL DE OLIVOS
Año del Libertador General San Martín
5 DE AGOSTO DE 1950

*Eva Perón*

## MENU

Fiambre con ensalada rusa
Empanadas criollas
Canja
Parrillada
Fruta
Mate Cocido

**VINOS**
Tinto y Blanco, "Cuesta del Parral"

▲ Juan Perón, inscribed and signed photograph, 1950.
► Juan and Eva Perón, signed menu, 1950.
►► Eva Perón, inscribed and signed photograph, 1950.

Para Raul Apold con toda mi
simpatia de Peronista y amiga

Eva Perón
4/9/50

# Louis ARMSTRONG 1901-1971

## Duke ELLINGTON 1899-1974

Duke Ellington and Louis Armstrong figure prominently in the pantheon of great jazz players who took this form of music to an artistic peak while also changing it radically.

As pianist and composer, Ellington formed a band that made recordings from 1924 onwards. The nickname 'Duke' did not come about by chance. His music is unequalled in its sophistication, and the distinctiveness of his style, which could only be captured by his recordings (for the scores themselves could never convey it), made him the aristocrat of a form of music that he himself played a major role in creating. His work in the 1930s was even compared to that of the French composers Ravel and Debussy, and it certainly revealed the influence of contemporary composers whom he had met during his tour of Europe in 1933. His career did not end until shortly before his death at the age of seventy-five, and he was still giving triumphant concerts during the 1960s.

It was at this time that the cinema offered Louis Armstrong the ultimate form of recognition, by transmitting all over the world his unmistakable voice along with the sight of the trumpeter blowing his instrument. For many of his contemporaries, and for subsequent generations too, these were and still are the true symbols of jazz. Armstrong enjoyed phenomenal success from the 1930s onwards, and this redoubled in the 1950s, when he was able to spread his music all over the world through hundreds of recordings and a number of films. The photograph (opposite) of him wearing a white turban was taken by Louis Goldman. The large format and the informality of the picture make it quite exceptional. It is signed in green ink, which was the colour that 'Satchmo' always preferred to use.

▲ Duke Ellington, signed photograph, c. 1960.

► Louis Goldman, portrait of Louis Armstrong, original print signed and inscribed to the photographer by Armstrong himself, c. 1965.

To Lois
Goldman
Best Wishes
Louis Armstrong

*Lebeau ...... la souffrance humaine?*

## Albert CAMUS 1913-1960

## Jean-Paul SARTRE 1905-1980

Albert Camus and Jean-Paul Sartre were the most influential French authors and thinkers in the period just after the Second World War. The existentialist movement, of which Sartre was the leading light, was then at its height, whereas Camus – who had made his name especially with *The Outsider* (1942) and *The Plague* (1947) – was opposed to both its political and its philosophical precepts. His work won him the Nobel Prize for Literature in 1957. When Sartre in turn was awarded the same prize seven years later (by which time Camus was

dead, having been killed in a car accident), he decided to refuse it.

The rare photograph above, taken by Lipnitzki, shows Sartre working at his desk. He dedicated it in 1949 to a Brazilian admirer who happens to have been the recipient of the portrait of Camus reproduced opposite. The great photographer Izis shows Camus, also in 1949, checking proofs at his desk. The quality of the picture, and the charming manner in which Camus has written the inscription on an open page in front of him, makes this one of the finest known signed portraits of him.

The autograph question at the top of this page was part of Sartre's notes for a lecture on Titian that he gave in São Paulo in 1960: 'Does beauty heal human suffering?'

▲ ▲ Jean-Paul Sartre, autograph sentence, 1960.
▲ Lipnitzki, portrait of Jean-Paul Sartre, inscribed and signed by Sartre, 1949.
► Izis, portrait of Albert Camus, inscribed and signed by Camus, 1949.

## Orson WELLES 1915-1985

## Rita HAYWORTH 1918-1987

At the age of twenty-six, Orson Welles directed a film that has remained a cult classic for critics and moviegoers alike: *Citizen Kane*, one of the most admired films of all time.

To his immense and universally recognized talent as a film-maker, one can add a certain gift for drawing, as can be seen from the delightful picture opposite. On a booklet published for his old school, the Todd School in Woodstock, Illinois, for a production of *The Merchant of Venice* which Welles directed, he sketched two characters from the play, with an inscription to a friend. One is tempted to think that the figure on the left is a self-portrait.

In the year in which he probably drew this picture, 1938 – the date when the booklet was published – Welles had already created a sensation in the USA with his radio adaptation of H. G. Wells's *The War of the Worlds* (1898). No radio play had or has ever created such a furore. Despite an explicit announcement beforehand that this was a work of fiction, Welles's adaptation was so realistic, almost journalistic, that listeners actually thought it was real, and there were astonishing scenes of panic in New Jersey.

Rita Hayworth married Orson Welles in 1943, three years before her great triumph in *Gilda*, which established her as 'the most beautiful girl in the world'. The inscribed portrait on the right dates from 1947, when the couple were divorced. Above is a photograph signed in the 1980s, showing Welles in the role of Citizen Kane.

▲ Orson Welles, signed photograph, c. 1980.
► Rita Hayworth, signed photograph, 1947.
►► Orson Welles, signed drawing, 1938.

*A page from my personal notebook*

*[signature: Jack Kerouac]*

## Jack KEROUAC 1922-1969

## William S. BURROUGHS 1914-1997

Together with Allen Ginsberg (1926–97), William S. Burroughs and Jack Kerouac were the leading lights of the Beat Generation, a literary movement that dominated American culture in the 1950s and the influence of which is still strong even today.

Burroughs came from a very rich family, which very soon disowned him. His experiments with all kinds of drugs led him to north Africa, and he lived in Tangier from 1955 till 1958, sometimes half-paralysed by narcotics, spending 'a month in a tiny room in the Casbah staring at the toe of my foot'. The remarkable document reproduced opposite dates from this crucial period of his life: it is his identity card from his stay in Morocco, signed by him and showing the face of a man then in his forties. Having come back from the abyss, Burroughs subsequently managed to lead a comparatively normal life, and lived for another forty years as the great surviving guru of the group.

Jack Kerouac's *On the Road* became the work that everyone associated with the Beat Generation, and admiration for this highly original novel, written in a single creative burst, has continued to grow in the USA. The tormented life of Kerouac, whose ancestors were from Brittany, his ambiguous sexuality, and his early death make him a fascinating figure for many readers. Autographs are rare and in demand, and at a public sale in 2000, the manuscript of *On the Road* fetched a record-breaking price of over one million dollars. The page on the right was torn from a notebook, as he informs us in the statement reproduced above and written on the back of the page. It concerns Jean-Paul Sartre, the relationship between money and literature, and Kerouac's disdain for the authors of best-sellers.

◄ Jack Kerouac, autograph page signed, c. 1960.
► William S. Burroughs, document signed, 1955.

N.° 705

النسب بروغس

Nom BURROUGHS

الاسم وليام سيورد

Prénoms William Siward

المهنة

Profession Employé

Arrivé le 18/1/55 وصل بتاريخ

Nationalité américaine الجنسية

Passeport 32 الجواز عدد

Delivré le 21/11/55 منح بتاريخ

à TANGER طنجة المغرب في

Domicilié 6 terrasse الساكن بـ
Renschaussen

Autorisation valable jusqu'au لغاية

19 JANVIER 1958

Coût Frs. 100 الثمن فرنك

Signature امضاء

William Seward Burroughs

Delivré à Tanger le منح في طنجة
21 JANVIER 1957

عز عامل طنجه وناحيتها
P. Le Gouverneur de Tanger
et de sa Province

MOHAMMED AKALAY

TANGER
20F

تجديد يد الاقامة
Prorogation de validité

du من

au الى

Fait à Tanger le حرر بطنجة في

عز العامل
P. Le Gouverneur,

المملكة المغربية
ROYAUME DU MAROC

وزارة الداخلية

MINISTÈRE DE L'INTÉRIEUR

عمالة طنجة
AMALAT DE TANGER

بطاقة الاقامة
CARNET DE RESIDENCE

MOUNIRIA
Calle Magallanes no 1

*I believe Dad paid for this*
*[the car] by check.*

# John F. KENNEDY 1917-1963

## Jacqueline KENNEDY 1929-1994

President Kennedy and his wife were the most attractive, most famous and most popular couple in the world during the 1960s. The unique blend of power, money and elegance that marked them out fascinated a whole generation of Americans. The brutal assassination of John F. Kennedy in Dallas, after a presidency of just a thousand days, made an indelible mark on the minds of all who heard the terrible news.

Kennedy was always a wealthy man, and Jacqueline's – or Jackie as she is more widely known – extravagance was legendary. The letter reproduced opposite, addressed to the young senator by his father's accountant and with an additional comment by 'Jack', reveals quite a lot about the carefree lifestyle of the young couple a few years before they became the youngest occupants of the White House. The document lists their various personal expenses, and one can't help noticing a sum of over $11,000 spent in department stores – the equivalent today of some $150,000 – over a period of just nine months. The most surprising item, however, is the handwritten note by Kennedy himself, who is clearly not altogether sure who paid for his car: 'Tom: This is incorrect. I believe Dad paid for this by check.'

The inscribed photograph reproduced above shows Kennedy when he was a senator. The letter from Jackie Kennedy reproduced on the right was written a few months after her husband's assassination. She is thanking a judge from the Supreme Court for his donation to the Kennedy Library, which had just been set up. The inscribed photograph above the letter dates from 1975 – when the death of her second husband, Greek businessman Aristotle Onassis, made her a widow again. She has signed with the names of both her husbands.

Kennedy autographs are the most sought-after of all American presidents in the second half of the 20th century, while those of his wife are rare and always in demand, especially in the USA. However, the correspondents (and heirs) of the famous couple have recently been more inclined to get rid of the letters addressed to them by one or the other. As a result, in a manner quite common among contemporary celebrities, more of their writings came onto the market after they had died than while they were still alive.

▲ John F. Kennedy, inscribed and signed photograph, *c.* 1957.
◄ Jacqueline Kennedy (Onassis), inscribed and signed photograph, *c.* 1975.
► Jacqueline Kennedy, typewritten letter signed, 1964.
►► John F. Kennedy, autograph comment signed, on typewritten letter, 1955.

OFFICE OF
JOSEPH P. KENNEDY
230 PARK AVENUE
NEW YORK 17, N.Y.

MURRAY HILL 9-2220

October 14, 1955

Mr. John F. Kennedy
277 Park Avenue, Apt. 8-G
New York 17, New York

Dear Jack:

According to our records, you spent the following amounts during the nine months ended September 30, 1955:

| | |
|---|---|
| Travel and hotel | $ 7,462 |
| Medical | 20,485 |
| Department Stores | 11,704 |
| Household expenses | 4,244 |
| Automobile | 2,470 |
| Insurance | 374 |
| Cash withdrawals | 1,048 |
| Miscellaneous | 4,652 |
| | $ 52,439 |

Tom: This is incorrect I believe Dad paid for this by check — Jack.

If you would like more details on any of the above items, kindly let us know.

Sincerely yours

Thomas J. Walsh
per GB.

TJW:GB

Thomas J. Walsh

# Federico FELLINI

## 1920-1993

Few creative artists have fashioned a world so special that a new term has to be coined in order to define it. Fellini, however, was one: his name gave rise to the adjective 'Felliniesque', which passed into the vocabulary of cinema-goers and even some dictionaries – a sure sign, if one were needed, of the impact his films made on his contemporaries.

Federico Fellini's talents were not limited to film-making. The great director was an extremely generous artist who would spontaneously give away his drawings to those close to him. Many of them were created simply with a ballpoint pen, but sometimes Fellini drew more elaborate pieces using crayons or felt-tips. This is the case with the picture reproduced opposite – an exceptionally fine piece which actually contains a self-portrait. He is the little figure on the right, wearing a scarf and – like a lion-tamer, wielding a chair and a trident – struggling to ward off a gigantic creature who has all the Felliniesque attributes.

Fellini's finest drawings have been collected in large illustrated volumes, published in Italy and distributed all over the world. This one, however, has never been published. It was drawn on the back of a page from a screenplay, and comes from the collection of a close friend; the drawings that Fellini had given him were scattered after they had been put up for sale. Most were explicitly erotic sketches, in which Fellini created a dialogue between different parts of the body of a nude man who gives every sign of being an alter ego.

The autograph letter on the right was written one year before his death to an old German colleague. He promises to consider the 'talented lady' recommended by his correspondent.

The inscribed photograph at the top of the page was one of Fellini's favourites, and may well have been the one that he signed most often. It shows him hard at work in about 1972, at the peak of his career.

▼ Federico Fellini, inscribed and signed photograph, c. 1972.
◄ Federico Fellini, autograph letter signed, 1992.
► Federico Fellini, signed drawing, c. 1980.

# *Glenn* GOULD 1932-1982

## *Maria* CALLAS 1923-1977

These two cult figures from the world of music were not only hugely talented in their respective fields of piano and singing, but also shared a reputation for being 'difficult'. Their comparatively early deaths only reinforced their legend.

Maria Callas was by far the most media-conscious opera singer of her time. Her spellbinding beauty on stage, her mastery of tragedy, her impeccable technique, and the range and inimitable timbre of her voice made her the most passionately admired diva since the 19th century. Recordings of her finest concerts have wiped out the memory of the vocal problems she suffered during the last fifteen years of her life, just as photographs of her in her prime have effaced the image of the young and overweight singer that she once was.

Items signed by Callas are much sought-after. On the right we see her in the role of Italian composer Vincenzo Bellini's (1801–35) *La Sonnambula* at the Scala Milan *c.* 1954, at the height of her beauty and her career, when she was still including her husband's name in her signature: Maria Meneghini Callas.

Autographs of Glenn Gould are much rarer than those of Maria Callas. The inscribed photograph reproduced opposite is of particular interest: Yusuf Karsh, the celebrated Canadian photographer, shows Gould at the piano, and the portrait contains a long and affectionate inscription to Dick O'Hagen, 'whose kindness and friendship made my visits to Berlin so very enjoyable'. At the time, Gould was already regarded as one of the most brilliant pianists of his generation.

TEATRO ALLA SCALA
MARIA MENEGHINI CALLAS
ne «LA SONNAMBULA»
foto PICCAGLIANI

▶ Maria Callas, signed photograph, *c.* 1954.
▶▶ Yusuf Karsh, portrait of Glenn Gould, original print inscribed and signed by Gould, 1958.

For Dick Gilbert
whose kindness and
friendship made my
visits to Buffalo so very
enjoyable — all good wishes
Glenn Gould
Feb. 1958

# THE BEATLES 1961-1969

## THE ROLLING STONES 1962-

The success of the Beatles during the 1960s remains a unique phenomenon. The Rolling Stones are the only group to have achieved anything like it, and at least they have the advantage of longevity. The meteoric career of the Beatles lasted for just nine years, but the astonishing popularity of the 'lads from Liverpool' ('We're more popular than Jesus now,' said John Lennon) is simply reaffirmed by each new generation.

There are large numbers of signed items in circulation, but such is the demand (especially for pieces signed by all four) that the market has been flooded with forgeries over the last fifteen years or so. Despite the vigilance of the experts, dubious items still come up for sale even in the most reputable places. The photograph reproduced opposite was given by the Beatles' secretary to the daughter of a Spanish friend, and the signatures are certainly authentic. (The print was slightly damaged because the girl put it in her school exercise book.)

The murder of John Lennon (1940–80) sent prices of autographs rocketing, although they had been common enough before that. The signed snapshot on the right (c. 1976) with Yoko Ono (b. 1933) was probably worth the price of a sandwich at the time, but today would buy you dinner for two in the best restaurant.

Autographs of the two most famous members of the Rolling Stones, Mick Jagger and Keith Richards, are far more common than those of the Beatles, but their value goes up when they are on photographs of a live performance, as in the example reproduced top right.

▲ Mick Jagger and Keith Richards, signed photograph, 1973.
◄ John Lennon (with Yoko Ono), signed photograph, c. 1976.
► Paul McCartney, Ringo Starr, John Lennon and George Harrison, signed photograph, c. 1964.

# TRANSCRIPTIONS AND TRANSLATIONS OF ORIGINAL DOCUMENTS

This section contains transcriptions in full
of the English documents reproduced both
partially and in their entirety in this book, and
translations of non-English originals. Printed
matter, dedications and texts of just a few
words have not been transcribed or translated,
nor has the correspondence of Greta Garbo
and James Joyce for copyright reasons.

# TRANSCRIPTIONS AND TRANSLATIONS

*The following notes apply to the transcriptions and translations of the documents reproduced in this book:*
- *Illegible words have been replaced by square brackets.*
- *Deletions made by the writer of a document are represented by a strike-through.*
- *A vertical rule within a text denotes a line break in the original.*
- *The various ways of signing off letters in non-English-speaking countries have been translated literally.*

## LUIGI PIRANDELLO – PAGE 2

Do not seek anything that does not come from yourself. | Luigi Pirandello | Rio de Janeiro, 15 September 1927.

## CARLO GOLDONI – PAGE 4

Excellency | My wife is very proud and I am quite mortified. She has a letter that honours her, and I have well-founded reproaches. My wife humbly thanks you, and I beg your forgiveness. Perhaps I deferred writing to your Excellency because I simply wanted to have the consolation of saying something amusing to you about the two little farces; but as I am obliged once more to defer the dispatch of these, I can no longer keep silent. You will definitely have them, but it is impossible for me to send them before Lent, because the Théâtre de France is keeping me extremely busy and, to tell the truth, has kept me busy since my comedies started to find favour. You have learned from me about the success of *The Loves of Harlequin and Camille*. That of *Harlequin's Jealousy*, a comedy written immediately after the first one, was the same and perhaps even bigger. If you read the *Mercure de France*, you will see praise for the one and the other. Next Tuesday, the third following on from the two above-mentioned plays is to be performed, and it will be entitled *Camille's Concern*. The actors consider it to be superior to its two sisters; if the public is of the same opinion, the trilogy will be good for me. For the carnival they want some more things from me; they are right to want them, and it suits me to work. For this reason I have had to let down the Court of Lisbon, who wanted a comic opera, and the Theatre San Luca, who were expecting something from me and to whom I have so far been able to send only one comedy. Of all these discourtesies, the most painful for me would be to fail to do my duty towards Your Excellency, but the hope of doing it consoles me, and of doing it on time with a little bit of help on the part of your patience, which I hope will be understanding if you deign to reflect on the conditions I am under. I hope that my three comedies will go to the Court, i.e. the first, which has already been requested, and the two others if the first should happen to please Versailles as it has pleased Paris. I have not yet sought to be presented at Court, and I have even refused the means and the opportunity to present myself there; and if I had had the misfortune of my plays not meeting [with success] in France, I would have left without worrying about it. I am neither a knight nor a man of letters. The only reason why I might be well received by someone is that they know my comedies. Without that, I am worth nothing at all, and that alone might give me

the courage not to expect but to request. The services are done to attract favours but not compliments. It would mean little to me to say, 'I visited the King of France'; but it would mean a lot to me to be able to say, 'The King of France did me some good'. With all these fine appearances, I still don't know if I shall stay or if I shall leave Paris at the end of these two years. Man can easily delude himself, but self-love does not blind me to the point of believing myself to be indispensable in any place. At Easter I think I shall know my destiny. I am not asking for it, but I do my duty, as much in order to improve my condition as to preserve the little reputation that I have earned for myself. If all my affairs went really well and I acquired the biggest fortune in the world, I would consider myself unhappy to have the disgrace of displeasing Your Excellency. I speak sincerely, and I would be ashamed to say this in the guise of a compliment. I hope that this case will never arise. You like me and you understand me, and I shall serve you as quickly as I can. I am enclosing a copy of a letter that I have received from our friend Voltaire. I have also received one from Monsignor Paradisi, who is very dear to me: it is one of those letters that honours both he who writes it and the person to whom it is written. I beg you to pay my respects to Madame the young Countess Orsi, and to give me news of her health, which I wish and hope has recovered. What will be done next year with the new Théâtre de Bologne? Will it be the same society as last year, in the mood to honour its country? Monsignor the Marquis Francesco Albergati has been ill for a few months because of some medicines. Now that he's not having any treatment, he's a lot better. He has decided to go back to Canada. He has made me a flattering offer with regard to my nephew, and I may perhaps be inclined to let him go with him, with the backing of one of his friends, a very rich merchant. The country is a good place for anyone who is willing to work, and a young man of average talent and adaptable character might make his fortune there. If that happens, the name of Albergati will, in another part of the world, be to the honour and the good of my house. In the sixth volume of my new publication, you will see in the preface to the comedy entitled *The War* a letter which does some justice to the knight of whom I speak. I am very respectfully Your Excellency's | very humble, very devoted and very affectionate servant. | Carlo Goldoni | Paris, 10 December 1761.

## CHARLES BAUDELAIRE – ERNEST FEYDEAU – PAGE 6

My dear Baudelaire | I have received the *Paradis artificiels* and thank you for it. | The book has been read and annotated. If you are curious about the notes, come and see them this or any other evening. | All in all I found the thing very interesting. It is well executed and very strange. | Voilà. Good day. | E. Feydeau | Saturday | Autograph all the more curious as I never asked M. Feydeau for his opinion anyway.

## JEAN TINGUELY – PAGE 8

Dear Richard Hamilton, thank you for your letter: agreed for Saturday (what about Rosemarie?).

If I am not there – if I am not there leave me a message where I can reach you. I send you greetings: | Jean Tinguely

## THOMAS CARLYLE – PAGE 9

Quit that of "Autographs", dear young lady; that is a weak pursuit, which can lead you to nothing considerable! – | T. Carlyle (with true good wishes for your young life and you) | Chelsea, 8 February 1872.

## MADAME DE STAËL – PAGE 10

Paris, 24 April 1807 | It seems to me, sir, that from one end of the Earth to the other everything that concerns love of liberty and of justice owes you homage. If I were not the daughter of M. Necker, I should think my name to be too little known for you to recall it, but I am sure that you love my father because you comport yourself as he does. I shall dare to send you my son next year, under the protection of one of the most honest men I know, M. Le Say. Please be so good as to welcome him kindly. I hope that in the middle of this oppressed Europe we all have English and American blood in our veins. I take the liberty of sending you a piece that I have written, which is all that one can write these days. If I were sixteen years old like my son, I would leave for Philadelphia, but allow for a moment that my esteem and my admiration for you transport me there. Keep your country for us, so that all the sentiments of morality and liberty should not be taken for chimeras. The time is not far off when in our old world these ideas will pass for inanities. | Please accept, sir, the compliment of all the forms of respect that your name awakens in my soul. | Necker Staël de Holstein

## PAUL VERLAINE – PAGE 11

Monsieur Prudhomme | He's earnest, he's mayor and family head, | His stiff collar rises and swallows his ear, | While his eyes float in deepest dreams without fear | And light from flowered spring on his slippers is shed. | Does he care for the gold star, the bower overhead | Where birds sing in shade, for the skies blue and clear, | And the green fields where wandering lovers appear? | Monsieur Prudhomme wants his daughter to wed | That young and well-bred Monsieur That-and-this, | He hates Victor Hugo, purrrsues prrrejudice, | He's materialistic, and as for the shower | Of oafs writing verse in their ivory tower, | He pities them all, but gives judgment a miss, | And his slippers shine with springtime in flower. | Paris, 29 March 1862 | Paul Verlaine

## G. W. F. HEGEL – PAGE 11

For the theology student Herr Karl Hermann Friedrich Hahn, born in Pomerania, who registered on 30 September 1829 at this University, it is hereby certified under the signature of the Rector and the seal of the University that nothing untoward is known about him, and also in particular that, as far as the University is aware, he has never been a member of any banned association. | Berlin, 15 March 1830 | the Rector of the

University | p.p. | Hegel Certificate of Morality for theology student K. Hahn, Pomerania.

## PHILIP II – PAGE 16

Sire | having learned of the death of the Count of Portalegre (which weighs heavily on me because Your Majesty has thus lost so old a servant), I cannot but beg Your Majesty with all my heart to grant me the favour of replacing him in his office with Don Francisco de Silva, for (even though the fact that he did not grow up in this kingdom might cause some difficulty) it would be better that this office should remain in the house where he has also been employed for so many years performing the great services that have been rendered to King Don Manuel, whom God preserve, and which oblige us equally, Your Majesty as son and myself as grandson, to pay particular attention to his successors. Added to this are the obligations that I have towards Don Francisco for his services and his person. Your Majesty will therefore understand the intensity of my plea, as Don Cristobal de Moura will explain better to Your Majesty, whose royal personage may Our Lord protect as I desire. De Pardo, 17 November 1579 | The good nephew of Your Majesty | I the King

## FREDERICK THE GREAT – PAGE 16

Monsieur my cousin, I have seen from the letter that Your Royal Highness was so kind as to write to me that the Comte de Grün has fulfilled my mission well. He would not be able to put into words the esteem and tenderness that I have for your person. I felt this feeling when seeing you in Berlin and it will never leave me, I beg you to be persuaded of this and to believe that on all occasions I shall derive a sincere pleasure in convincing you of these feelings, being for ever, my dear cousin | the very good and very affectionate cousin | of Your Royal Highness, | Frederick

## ANTOINE-LAURENT LAVOISIER – PAGE 16

To Monsieur Parisis Jr, la place de Villers-Cotterêts. I have the honour to send you, Monsieur and dear relative, the receipt for 24,132 pounds for the acquisition of Paleine. This acquisition will turn out well in time. As soon as the notice appears for Valséry Abbey and its outbuildings, would you please send me the details, and then I will settle on the price that you can bid to. I have nothing else of importance for you at this moment, and I shall postpone doing my calculations until I have precise information. | I have the honour to be, with most perfect attachment, Monsieur and dear relative, your very humble and very obedient servant. | Lavoisier | 23 March 1791

## PIERRE CURIE – PAGE 16

Science Faculty of Paris | 12 rue Cuvier | Paris, 1 April 1906 | Laboratory of General Physics | Monsieur | My colleague M. Laborde has boiled the water in the bottles that you were so kind as to send us. The gases extracted during boiling have been examined from the point of view of radioactivity. They do not contain any emission of radium – the gases and the baths have not been examined from any other point of view than that of radioactivity. | Allow me, Monsieur, to join those who congratulate you on your perceptiveness as regards that distressing and revolting tragedy of Courrières.

I am among those that read the articles of such clarity and precision that you send to 'the Journal'. | Yours sincerely | Monsieur, P. Curie.

## THOMAS MANN – PAGE 17

Kilchberg Am Zürichsee | Alte Landstrasse 29 | 14 June 1954 | Dear Mr Aita, | It is virtually pointless to tell you that I was profoundly touched by the news that the PEN Club of Buenos Aires is planning a meeting that would deal sympathetically with my person and my work. I know of no better way to express my gratitude than to send to the Argentinian members my most sincere good wishes for the success of the efforts they are making to serve freedom of thought and the glory of their country. | Yours, | Thomas Mann.

## LUDWIG WITTGENSTEIN – PAGE 17

13.8.40 | Dear Hänsel, | I hope these lines will reach you; they are just to tell you that I still think of you all with the same feelings. May we see one another again! Give my warmest regards to your dear wife and children! As ever, your old | Ludwig Wittgenstein | Send your reply under my full name, to the address Postfach 560, Lisbon.

## YUKIO MISHIMA – PAGE 17

Hotel New Japan | Dear Mr. P. Penner da Cunha: Please forgive me for not writing to your kind letter. I have been too busy with preparing the new novel by having trips and meeting people. I am very delighted at your kind request to publish "After the Banquet". | Please be in touch with my agent in Tokyo: Mr. TATSUO IWASE | c/o Orion-Press Fnc., | 34 Building, | 4,3 Chome, Kanda-Agawamachi | Chiyoda-ku, Tokyo-Japan. He will be very pleased to treat the publication right in any foreign country but United States and England. | Yours sincerely, | Yukio Mishima | April 9, 65

## HEINRICH SCHLIEMANN – PAGE 17

My dear Mr. Evans Pray do us the favour to dine with us tomorrow Tuesday 20th September. Yours very truly. | H. Schliemann

## JOHN MAYNARD KEYNES – PAGE 18

King's College Cambridge | 24 July 1911 | My Dear Francis, | You've found material for a much more amusing letter from Lausanne than I can hope to produce from this decrepit place. There's not a cock stirring, there's not a human being except Freddie, Frankie Bisch, Iolo and a few ones whom I know even by sight. And when work and Chianti have sapped my forces too greatly, I slip up to London and view the divine Mr. Nijinsky for an hour or two. There's really nothing else to tell you, except that Mr. Nijinsky was sacked from the Imperial Ballet at Petersburg because one night, the Tsar happened to drop in and found him dancing in the altogether. Justin Brooke's been here – but you don't know him. I'm going at the end of the week to stay with the Berensons where I shall find not only Karim but Phil. Gerald has gone off a long time, and I don't know what he's doing. I went up with him to see the Spirits against the Americans, where we both wept with excitement and only M. Bertie Revillon could remain cool and collected. | Mr. Oakfield is on the Litt. offer for the long but has not appeared yet. Rupert

has a column of poems in the press. Good night. You see I've nothing nearly so amusing to tell you as the doings of M. Alexander or the comings of the abominable Alfred. | Yours | JMK

## D. H. LAWRENCE – PAGE 18

Lerici per Fiascherino | Golfo della Spezia | Italy | 18 December 1913 | Dear Davies, | After that last letter of mine, I wanted to kick myself. What right have I to talk to you from the top of a stool. Don't bear me a grudge, will you. I do wish things could go well with you. | We shall be here till the end of May, and shall be frightfully glad when you come. You would travel by the ordinary route, over Paris, Milan, Parma, Spezia and it costs about £4. But you could come by ship to Genova as to Leghorn [Livorno] – they are both fairly near. You must think about it, whether you would like to come by sea or on land. We should like to come to England in June, I think, by ship from Genova – I should like the voyage. You might go back with us, unless you want to walk in the Apennines. We haven't got anybody coming for Christmas, but we shan't be lonely. The Italians are very jolly – they come and play with us and sing to the guitar at evening. You must learn some Italian when you come. And here in the harbour there's Italy's biggest naval arsenal – war ships with search lights and cannon at night, and submarines nosing up and down. It is really jolly. The country is quite wild behind, really wilder than Wales, but not so gloomy. | You didn't tell me how the work was going. I hope you'll have a good time in Wales. All good wishes from both of us | Yours, | D. H. Lawrence

## ERIK SATIE – PAGE 18

Monsieur Ricardo Viñes | Tuesday | You are invited, dear and delightful companion, tomorrow Wednesday to dinner at Madame Edwards's (8 pm). | There will also be Valentine, Picasso & A. Paul Hinn-Air, the celebrated critic. | I have been given the task of inviting you to this gathering. Great joy for me. | Lots of love. ES

## ALEXANDER POPE – PAGE 18

Sir, | I take this opportunity of assuring you, you have, at the place from where this letter is dated, a friend and servant, | A. Pope

## CARL GUSTAV JUNG – PAGE 19

Küsnacht-Zürich | Seestrasse 228 | Prof. Dr. C. G. Jung | February 1st 1949. | Mr. P. M. Shankland | Hamburg | Dear Sir, | Your proposition is indeed most interesting, but it will be equally difficult to translate such a thing as my ESSAYS ON CONTEMPORARY EVENTS into the language of the film. I must confess that I have not the slightest imagination in this respect. What I think I would do would be : I should give my little book to a number of better-class writers that are interested in the film and I should even start a competition among them in order to see what kind of dramatic phantasies they develop while reading the Essays. My mind doesn't function along these modern ways, but I could imagine that a fertile and dramatising mind could get the necessary kick out of my peculiar way of looking at things. | I'm going to hand your letter around among my colleagues here and if something turns up that might be of use to you, I will let you know. | Yours very truly, | C. G. Jung.

## FRANKLIN D. ROOSEVELT – PAGE 19

The White House | Washington | February 24, 1943. | Dear Mr. President | I am sending herewith a photograph taken of us on my recent trip. I thought you might like to have a copy. | With my warm regards, | Always sincerely, | Franklin D. Roosevelt | His Excellency | Getulio Vargas | President of the United States of Brazil.

## FILIPPO TOMMASO MARINETTI – PAGE 20

Here it is my dear colleague, | With all my deepest sympathy and my warm handshake. | F. T. Marinetti

## TRUMAN CAPOTE – PAGE 21

Our parrot is proud of her vocabulary | Mrs. Farrish who lives next door to the family I was visiting last summer has rather an eccentric old parrot whose name is Cotona. The bird was purchased from an Indian in Brazil, who captured it far up in the jungle on the Amazon River. | Cotona was first taught to speak a Spanish-Indian dialect; apparently she hated to hear English spoken as she went into a frenzy every time every time she was spoken to. When Mrs. Farrish landed in New York with Cotona, she created a pandemonium at the dock, with her wild screeching and talk that no one could understand. The custom inspector was sure Cotona was hurling awfully incomplimentary words at him, but he could not be sure. | The parrot seemed to be much happier when she arrived at the Farrish home in the south and at once formed a great liking for the youngest of the Farrish children, named Mildred. Every morning, when Mildred started to school, Cotona would set up an awful fuss. Soon she could say school and hello. | Mildred asked her mother one day if she could take Cotona to school with her. The teacher had given her permission for the bird to be brought. When Mildred arrived at school the next morning with the parrot, the children all crowded around and took turns trying to teach the parrot more words in English. But Cotona would not speak a word. She was so quiet, the teacher said that Mildred could bring her to school whenever she liked. After taking Cotona to school several times, every one began to laugh and would say Mrs. Farrish was having her parrot educated. One day during spelling class, the teacher asked Mildred how to spell cat, before she could answer Cotona croaked C-A-T. Every one laughed and the parrot started preening herself and very important after that she learned many words. She can repeat like school and is very proud of her vocabulary. | The End | Truman Capote

## HENRY VII – PAGE 22

Trusty and well beloved friend. We have understood not only by the rapport of our [...] by the bearer there of but also by the other the continual good mind and loving heart [...] towards us for which we [...] thank you, and pray you of continuance and [...] trust that we have in you and thank you whole that one shall so remember you a [...] think the often that you have done us, We bestowed and employed in out [...] such as out said [...] shall show you on our behalf. We pray you to own credence ever. Under our signet at our Castle of Kenelworth the 20th day of [...] | Henry R.

## LOUIS XIV – PAGE 23

Holy Father. The commendatory abbey of Aubasine, order of St Bernard in the diocese of Tulle, being at present vacant owing to the change of state of Monseigneur François de Sourdin, the last commendatory and gentle possessor of the same, and being well informed of the good life, morals, piety, sufficiency, ability and other virtuous and praiseworthy qualities that are to be seen in the person of Monseigneur Pierre Blouin, clerk to the diocese of Paris, We nominate and present him to Your Holiness, that it may please him on our said nomination, presentation and requisition to take up the power of the aforementioned abbey, granting him and issuing to this end all bulls and apostolic provisions required and necessary, following the memoranda and most ample supplications that will be presented to Your Holiness. Whereupon we pray to God to preserve You, Most Holy Father, for long years to rule and govern our Mother Church. Written at Versailles, the twenty-eighth day of April 1686. | Your devoted son, the King of France and Navarre, | Louis | (countersigned) | Phélipeaux

## GREGORY XIII – PAGE 23

1 April 1581 | For Bernardo Olgiatto and P. Bandino & Company, tenderers of the domains of Rome. | Our agent Bernardo Olgiatto will be paid two thousand five hundred pounds of money towards what is due to him [...] for the rent of [...]. From my palace. 30 March 1581 | Gregory pp XIII

## BERTOLT BRECHT – PAGE 26

Who does it for silence? | Bertolt Brecht | 1955.

## PROSPER MERIMÉE – PAGE 28

52 rue de Lille | 8 June 1855 | Madame, You have given me a good laugh with your scruples, or rather with the scruples of your friends. I should very much like to know which charitable souls have given you this fine information about me? From where and how do they know me? What is more, you have time to decide. I have shown my apartment to Mr Senior, who will give you an account of it. There are no trap doors, and no walls covered with tapestries hiding secret doors. There are three beds of which one is good and one is very bad; two quite cheerful rooms, quite a lot of books and two divans with some Turkish and other pipes. I think I shall start out for I don't know where towards the beginning of July. Before leaving, I shall let you know, and if between my departure and the time of my return your heart tells you to do so, you have only to write to my maid to get the apartment ready for you. If it might help you make to up your mind, I am sending you via Mr Senior the portrait of the present master of the house, with whom you will be dealing during my absence, and whom I recommend to you in a very special way. Mr S. will also hand over to you a book which will amuse you, I think, although it is a little naughty – I do not dare to say because it is a little naughty. I am very ill, and I think I shall soon deprive the sun of my presence. Furthermore, I have the blue devils continuously, and man delights me not no woman neither. Lady Ashburton is here, who seems to me to be a little more cross than she was a few years ago, and Lady Holland is

ever more charming. We still have a large number of foreigners and provincials. | I have just been paying court to a Spanish lady who arrived with three daughters (including a niece, as an Irishman would say). That makes eight eyes of which each is worth half a dozen. The unfortunate thing is that one of these pretty people who has come to Paris for a throat disease is in the last stages of consumption, according to the doctor I recommended to them. They speak terrible French, and the doctor, who hardly knows how to make himself understood, has charged me to tell the mother that her daughter only has a few months to live. What do you think of the commission? I don't think anyone ever has an illness of the chest in Spain, but they do of the heart, an internal organ that is unknown or shrunken north of the Pyrenees. In my journals I have several lamentable cases of such illnesses, including those of two people who loved each other and who died within a week of each other. What will be very surprising to you is that they were not husband and wife, or rather they were a husband married to another woman, and a woman married to another husband. They had the temerity to love each other in spite of their situation, and so they were in a great hurry. Let us hope that they are roasting in a place that I shall not name and which has been established for such great felons. | Since you like Viardot so much, allow me to send you her portrait. I think you will find it's a good likeness. It's a long time since I last saw her, but her features remain engraved on my memory. | We have here a Madame Ristori who is causing a sensation in a detestable tragedy by someone called Alfieri. It's the tale of a certain Myrrha who had some bad tendencies. The women who claim to know Italian, and there are many of them, swoon with admiration, as do the romantic young people. | I quite like the actress, but the play seems very boring to me, even though it's immoral. My Lady Mayor is delighted with her stay in Paris, but she finds that people don't eat often enough, and indeed lunch hasn't yet been imported over here, which is a great pity. My Lord Mayor takes his mace with him wherever he goes. The other day, they tried to plant it behind his chair at dinner, but there was no way. | We still have a very nice little king of Portugal who looks like a jolly German student, that is to say, *picked out of ten thousand*, because the German student is usually melancholy and weeps at the sight of the moon. | I should like to see the Millais picture you have told me about. There are some of his at the exhibition, and they are not lacking in a certain *je ne sais quoi*. But it seems to me that he works with microscopic brushes, and he does everything – the main subject and the incidentals – in the same manner. If I am not mistaken, there is an Ophelia by him who is in the process of drowning, and it made a pretty powerful impression on me. It is a figure one doesn't like to remember when one is about to go to sleep and has turned out the light. How do you have the courage to suggest that I should drink an eau-de-vie in order to cure myself? You accuse me of Satanism, but it's a lot more in your case. Mr S. has lent me some notes on Algiers which I found very interesting. In two months he saw what many of our great men have not been able to see in twenty. If the Emperor did the right thing, he'd make him governor. I congratulate you on the nice things that he brings you, but there are even nicer things at the Turkish and Indian exhibition. It is said that the people in the Company are furious that the Indian princes kept all that, instead of sending it to the Crystal Palace as loyal subjects ought to have done. Farewell, Madame, I hope that you have not yet spoken your final word and that you will come and see all of this. Please give my kindest regards to Mlle Mimi, after all my respects and also my reproaches.

### ALFONSO VII OF SPAIN
#### ALFONSO IX OF SPAIN – PAGES 40–41

In the name of God, I, Alfonso, by the grace of God Emperor of the Spains, give to you Fernando Guterriz this letter of donation and confirmation of ownership of the place known as Gracho Rego in Val de Salze, with everything that appertains to it, including the lands cultivated and uncultivated, the vines, the pastures, the rivers and the mountains, the production and the divisions within all its boundaries. This heritage is given to you, Fernando Guterriz, so that you and your descendants should keep it by the right of perpetual inheritance. This heritage is situated in Val de Salze. And if anyone on my behalf or someone else's behalf should wish to invalidate this act, may he be cursed and condemned to Hell along with Judas, the traitor. This letter has been written when the said Fernando has participated at the side of the Emperor in battles against the Muslims in Cordoba. On the tenth day of the month of September 1187 [1149] by the Emperor Alfonso, king of Toledo and of León. I, Alfonso, have ordered that this letter be written and I have confirmed my hand. (Sign of the Emperor). Arnaldo, Bishop of Santa María de Asturias, myself, Don Fernando, I confirm that the following witnesses were present: Don Pedro, Don Apontius, elder of the House of the Emperor, Poncius de Menerbe, Don Manrique, Commandant at Balza, Don Ramiro de Asturias who bears witness.

In the name of Our Lord Jesus Christ, Amen. I, Alfonso, by the grace of God king of León and Galicia, by means of this document which shall be valid in perpetuity, for the present and for posterity: I give to you, by hereditary right, both to the monastery of Carriao and to you, Countess Doña María, as well as to all your successors, the property called Viveiro with all its borders and demarcations ancient and new, so that you and the monastery of Carriao may possess it for centuries to come. I do this for the salvation of my soul those of my parents, and so that the said monastery may have its share. If anyone, no matter who it may be, whether of my people or a stranger, should seek to invalidate this act, may he meet the wrath of God and the fury of the King for his temerity and his audacity. This letter has been given to Benevento, on the tenth day of [...] in the year 1231 [1193] of the Christian Era, and I confirm my authority... | The Archpriest of Compostella, Count Gomez, Commandant Manrico, The Bishop of León, Count Horta Astias, Jean Ferdinand, Major Domo to the King, Loup, Bishop of Asturias, Pedro Fernandes de Benevides, Gonzalo [...] witnesses.

### CHARLES V OF FRANCE | CHARLES VI OF
#### FRANCE | KING EDWARD IV – PAGES 42–43

From the King | Maître Guy Troche. We request of you but nevertheless demand of you, by all the love and loyalty that you owe to us, that in order to cover the cost of this present army and passage that we intend at the pleasure of our command to undertake in our person to England, you lend us the sum of one hundred francs and send this through the good offices

of our well-loved and faithful counsellor Maître Nicolas de Plancy [...] the 18th day of this present month of September in order to register it with the Receiver [...] and our aforementioned counsellor will register it for you in the schedule of taxation so that you may recover it from us [...] in force on the said day in person for our benefit, no matter where we are, for the advance which you have given to me, and do not fail...that you doubt that you will incur our wrath, and write back to us by the bearer of this present missive what you intend to do. Given at Annecy the IX day of September. | Charles

Dear loved ones. We have heard that you or some people in your Faculty have [...] endeavour that a bull issued by Barthélemy de Mariz [?] at the Saint Juge de Rome, which quite recently was fraudulently presented to the Rector [...] read out in public before a full assembly of which we have had news [...] should not receive or publish letters of any kind from the said Mariz [?] the reading or publication of which might engender [...] also we demand [...] and in order to demonstrate our wrath, that you should on all counts prevent the writing or publication of the said bull or other letters of any kind by the said Mariz [?], and furthermore we forbid you from now on to receive any, for you could not cause us greater displeasure and we shall make haste to provide such remedies as these connections require [...] which may not be pleasant for us and will set an example to all, and in order that you may be more certain [...] of our will, we have undersigned our name in letters. Given at Montargis, the XX day of November. | Charles

Very dear Prince, relation and friend. I wish you good health and an increase in your prosperity. The captain and soldier Robert Chamberlain Miles has been obedient to us for many years and has served us in a friendly, honest, courageous and faithful manner. And as the aforementioned Count Robert, by his services, has been welcomed among us and considered as a very intimate and very dear member of our household, we beg Your Serene Highness that he may be received by you with the deepest respect. You have expressed the desire that he should accomplish a special favour [...] at the Visere Palace. He is effectively of noble blood, a valiant knight, well practised in the military arts and welcomed by us to one of the most respected positions. Whatever favour or benefit may be given to him, it will also be seen as being given to us. From our city of London, 22 May 1482. Edward, by the grace of God, King of France and England and Lord of Ireland.

### ISABELLA I OF SPAIN
#### FERDINAND II OF SPAIN – PAGES 44–45

Don Ferdinand and Doña Isabella, King and Queen, by the grace of God, of Castille and León, of Aragon, of Sicily, of Grenada, of Toledo, of Valencia, of Galicia, of the Balearic Islands, of Seville, of Sardinia, of Cordoba, of Corsica, of Murcia, of Jaen, of the Algarve, of Algeciras, of Gibraltar, of the Canary Islands; Count and Countess of Barcelona and Seigneurs of Biscay and Molina, Dukes of Athens and of Neopathia, Counts of Roussillon and of Cardonia, Marquis of Oristono and of Graciano. To you the counsellors, mayor magistrats, bailiffs, provosts, judges and other officers of justice in the towns, villages and seaports and territories of our kingdoms and seigneuries; to the captains, masters, mariners and navigators of all boats and ships; to the

inhabitants and original natives of our aforementioned Realms; and to all those whom the content of this letter may affect directly or indirectly, we wish good health and the grace of God. Know you all that the vessel named Santa Cruz [...] the captain and master is Iñigo de Artieta, who honours our kingdoms. We wish it to be known that when no matter what merchandise is to be loaded in any of the ports of our kingdoms where this vessel may happen to be, this vessel is to be loaded first and before all others. It is therefore necessary that the masters of other ships refrain from loading them before the aforementioned ship, as the merchants will not in any way be disadvantaged in so far as their merchandise will be more securely and better transported. And we are giving you these letters in our name so that our orders may be carried out. To each and every one of you in your towns and your fields of jurisdiction, on every occasion when the aforementioned Iñigo de Artieta (or his representative) makes a request to you, you will respect it and will carry out the content of this letter in all that it contains, and will not contest anything in the tenor or form of it, under pain of our displeasure and a fine of ten thousand maravedis for every offence. To those who refuse this letter, fifteen days will be allotted to appear before the court, and we command all lawyers who are summoned upon this matter that they bear witness with their seal so that we may know how our orders have been executed. Given in the town of Medina del Campo, the 20th day of the month of June of the year of the birth of Our Lord Jesus Christ one thousand four hundred and ninety-four. | I, the King | I, the Queen | I, Fernando Alvarez de Toledo, secretary to the King and Queen, I have written this letter by their command.

The Queen | Sancho de Paredes, my Chamberlain, I command that of the three hundred and eighty-seven thousand five hundred maravedis that you have received, following my orders, from the Treasurer Morales in the city of Seville, there should be given and paid immediately to Hernán Martínez Guijarro eight thousand seven hundred and forty-two and a half maravedis which are due to him because of the eight thousand two hundred and seventy-five glazed tiles which he gave on my orders in the aforementioned city of Seville to be passed on to this city of Grenada, of which three thousand five hundred and fifty-six are large, costing three and a half blancas each; five thousand two hundred and four are medium-sized, and the remaining four thousand seven hundred and nineteen are small, each costing one and a half blancas, amounting to three thousand five hundred and thirty-eight and a half maravedis, so that the sum total amounts to eight thousand seven hundred and forty-two and a half maravedis. Also give him eight thousand four hundred and ten maravedis so that he can pass them on to Iñigo López Espartero for ninety-four [...] of the said tiles. And give the above-mentioned maravedis immediately to the same Hernán Martínez Guijarro. And take [...] of [...] in the same way that you have received, with which and with this document I order those responsible for the accounts to receive you and to include in the accounts all the sums mentioned, and I order the clerks of my chamber to give you [...] from where you have charged them. Done at the Alhambra in Grenada, on the twenty-fifth day of August in the year one thousand five hundred. | I, the Queen | By order of the Queen.

I Hernán Martínez Guijarro acknowledge having received from you, Sancho de Paredes, by the command of Our Sovereign Queen, the eight thousand seven hundred and forty-two and a half maravedis that are due to me for [...] of the tiles in conformity with the above-mentioned order from Her Highness. I also acknowledge receipt of eight thousand four hundred and ten maravedis to be given to Iñigo López [sic] Espartero who shall have them for what he has done for [...] the said tiles, the total being ten thousand one hundred and fifty-two and a half maravedis, which I declare I have received. [...] by this contract signed with my name. Done at the Alhambra in Grenada, the XXVth day of the month of August in the year one thousand five hundred. (Initials) To be given to Guijarro [...] for tiles given and [...] ninety-five.

## | RAPHAEL – PAGE 47

Ferdinando Ponzetto, archdeacon of Sorrento, | General Treasurer of the Apostolic Chamber of Our Lord Most Saintly and Eternal, | To the respected lords Master Augustino Chisio & his colleagues, | depositaries of the money of the companions of the Holy Crusade. Salvation in the Lord. | By the authority of our office of Treasurer, we confide and send to you a sum for you to dispose of. Pay fifty ducats, or ten carlins per ducat at the rate of the old money, for the excellent master of painting Raphael of Urbino for his provisions, | sum | assigned to him by our Very Holy master, for a month to be counted from the first day of the month of last June, for the painted works in the palace of our Very Holy master, and also for the necessary paints, as it appears in the register kept in the hands of the rev. master of the house of His Holiness, and which has been shown to us. | And we charge these ducats to your audited accounts. | Given in Rome, in the Apostolic Chamber, the first day of the month of July 1516, | the third year of the pontificate of our Very Holy master Pope Leo X | Luc. de Carl. | G. Blondo

I, Raphael, painter, have received the fifty ducats for this month of June.

## | FERNANDO DE ROJAS – PAGE 49

The [...] day of the month of August in the year five hundred and nine, I, the honest man Gonzalo Suares de Talavera, in the name of my nephews, the children and heirs of Alonso Sedeño – glory be to him – as the former executor to Hernando de Avila, the Old, whom God protect, on the one hand and Diego Hernandes, his lawyer, on the other have together examined the expenses and receipts of the said executor. In the light of all the papers and their contents, and comparing the amounts of the two parties, a difference has been noted [...] Hernandes [...] to the above-mentioned heirs one thousand two hundred maravedis more than the above-mentioned receipt. Thus remaining debtors, they propose to pay in the course of the month of August the account that has been verified [...]. The lawyer Fernando de Rojas, inhabitant of this town of Talavera, has been chosen as third party to examine the case and arrange settlement. Thus he has appended his signature to those of the parties. The receipt therefore amounts to thirty thousand three hundred and fifty-three maravedis, and the above-mentioned expenses to twenty-nine thousand one hundred and fifty-three maravedis, and all the parties sign it with their names. The lawyer Fernando de Rojas | Gonzalo Suares | Diego Hernandes

## | CESARE BORGIA – PAGE 51

Cesare Borgia of France, by the grace of God Duke of Romagna [...] Prince of Adria and Venafro; Lord of Piombino; Gonfalonier and Captain General of the Holy Church. To our loyal Andrea Gianpetro da Imola [...] our [...] Vicar, greetings! The sincerity of the faith that you show towards us and our state [...] confirms you in the same function as you have fulfilled up to the present and [...] we consider the good deeds [...] for you [...] to [...] And that is why we confirm it [...] to Saint Andrew [...] as Vicar of our aforementioned [...] for the trimester, [...] with the honours, responsibilities, power, salary and customary emoluments [...] As regards [...] the delegates [...] and the ceremonies [...], it is from you [...] and not from another [...] that they will receive permission and it is right that they should obey you, in the same way as for the favours [...] opportune; and they will draw neither the salary nor the aforesaid revenues. And let this be done by those who are meant to do it, in conformity with the time. Given [...] in our Council, the year of the Lord 1503 and the third of our Duchy [...] Cesare

## | QUEEN ELIZABETH I – PAGE 53

Elizabeth | By the Queen | Trusty and well beloved we greet you well letting you know that our will and pleasure is you continue the exercise of the office of our attorney general in the same sort as you did heretofore in the time of our deceased sister the Queen late dear Mary, doing and executing all manner of things to the same office pertaining as amply as you were wont to do until you shall be otherwise advised from us in this behalf and this our bull shall be your sufficient warrant and discharge in this behalf. Given under our signet at our manor of Hersfield this 20th day of November this first of our reign.

## | SAINT VINCENT DE PAUL | SAINT FRANÇOIS DE SALES – PAGES 54–55

From Paris, 29 October 1659 | Monsieur | the grace of Our Lord be with you for ever. I cannot offer M. Michel my help in the affairs of his mother, not being in a position to devote myself to it, and besides M. Michel has written to me that his presence there is absolutely necessary in order to prevent this good mother from being ruined. That is why I have told him to go there and finally put things in order, and then to come back to you as soon as possible. He informs me, however, that you will be able to do without him. | I am sending you a packet for M. Lambin. I beg you to have it delivered precisely to one of those to whom it is addressed. I am in Our Lord, | Monsieur, Your very humble servant | Vincent de Paul +++D.L.M. | Text [...] of the banquet, I shall reply on the verso | I have just received your latest. In reply, I would say that you did well to see Monsieur Cabel.

In the name of Our Lord, Amen. | I hereby declare, I Notary public of lower rank, the eleventh day of the month of July 1667, in the ninth year of the Pontificate of the Very Holy Father and Lord in Jesus Christ, Clement, Pope by divine providence: firstly, that the Right Reverend Father Antoine Gilles, Frenchman, member of the minor order of Saint François de Paul and moderator [...] of the convent of the Very Holy Trinity of Mont Linceo in Rome, known [...] to me, and the Reverend Father Jean-François Artaud, from the

city of Aix-en-Provence, priest belonging to the said order in the said convent [...] and elsewhere in the best manner [...] and middle [...], have sworn with hand on heart, in the manner of priests, have said and declared [...] that the letter written by both parties and to which a page has been attached, was written in his own hand by Saint François de Sales, and they have recognized it as such, swearing with hand on heart, not only by reason of the aforesaid similitude, but also by all the best means [...]. Given in Rome on the aforesaid day [...] by the most illustrious and very Reverend Cardinal Vicar [...] authentic. We, Marzio, by divine mercy Bishop of Porto, cardinal of the Holy Roman Church, and | Gennaro, Vicar of our Most Holy Lord the Pope [...] and of the Roman Curia, and twice ordinary judge of the aforementioned [...] we authenticate and declare that the aforementioned [...] Lord Martius, notary, and Antonio Francesco Marias, administrators of [...] and who [...] have both sworn under signed oath that they have been and are public notaries of our tribunal, legal, authentic and worthy of trust, qualified to draw up all public writings [...] In faith of which [...] this day, 2 July 1667 [...]

## | PETER PAUL RUBENS – PAGES 56–57

Most illustrious Lord, | the successful rescue of the English has fooled no one, because it was judged to be impossible after the news that the hamlet was well defended and that the harbour walls had held out against the Emperor, even after the storm, without regard to the fact that the delay gave the King and Monsieur Cardinal Richelieu time to calmly deal with all the inconveniences that might arise on all occasions. It is reckoned that this rescue was only the cause of and the epilogue to the tragedy and that, once this obstacle has been eliminated, the differences between the Crowns of France and England, which incidentally are not very fundamental, will be swiftly ironed out. It is certain that His Majesty finds himself under a great obligation to the English with their unfortunate invasion of the Île de Ré, which gave him an excellent reason to lay siege to La Rochelle and to take it, to their great displeasure; and it would be a very fine jewel in the triumphant crown of His Majesty if, by freeing himself from internal war, he managed to employ his forces elsewhere, and if – as I think he should – he paid attention to the affairs of Italy. We know that the siege of Casale is proceeding slowly, with very few troops available, to the effect that over half of the place is not being defended. It seems that the climate in Italy means nothing to Don Gonzalo and that he could lose the glory gathered in Germany with Tilly, which is not unimportant. | It is true, according to what has been written to me, that the Duke of Savoy, having taken Trino, is going to join up with Don Gonzalo. But it could also happen that the Duke of Mantua, in laying siege to Cremona, wanted to push him into coming to the rescue of this important place which, in my view, is not a cat that will let itself be captured without a pair of gloves. The surrender of Trino was really strange. The Duke (of Mantua) imposed a tax of seven thousand pistols on the citizens, and allowed the Jews to be robbed by the soldiers. This decision resulted in a greater loss for the Christians than for the Jews, because the houses of the latter were full of objects that the Christians had pawned for sums of money that the Jews are allowed to lend at high rates of interest.

Passing through here is the most illustrious Count Carbil, who is going to Lorraine and Savoy, and perhaps even further, without any particular commission for Madame the Infanta; and I am pretty sure, if I am not mistaken, that while passing through Brussels he will go and greet Her Highness. It is believed at the moment that the Marquis of Spinola has departed at this time from the Court of Spain, although we do not yet have any news of his departure. But His Excellency wrote on 7 May that it would be pointless writing to him, or at least that one should no longer address letters to Madrid. It seems that the Dutch are busy preparing for an enterprise that no one has yet succeeded in identifying, but if we are to judge by certain clues, it is believed that they are now basing their parade ground near the fortress at Saint-André, not far from the town of Bolducy. These states are conducting a disastrous war against the King of Spain, subsidized by private financiers, especially those of the West India Company, and if I am not mistaken they have just sent a very powerful fleet to the bay of Todos los Santos in order to attack the town of San Salvador, which they had already taken once by treachery. And having nothing else to tell you, I conclude by humbly kissing the hands of Your Lordship and of My Lord your brother.

From Anvers, | the first of June 1628. | The very affectionate servant of Your Most Illustrious Lordship | Peter Paul Rubens | I did not write to Your Lordship last week because I was making a small journey off the main road and I was not able to do any correspondence.

### LOUIS XIII OF FRANCE
### CARDINAL RICHELIEU – PAGES 58–59

From Abbeville, 14 June 1630 | I am very pleased that your miner is at last happily ready for action! You can activate M. Lambert's mine when you feel the time is right, without waiting for any moment other than when it is ready. No thought at all has been given to fortifying your lines against the cannon, but they should be organized in such a way that the musketry can have free and comfortable play behind. As for the fortresses, it has been thought necessary to fortify them, and it never did any harm in winter to have a bit of padding on a camisole. I admit, as you do, that it does not appear as if the enemy are going to attack [coded name] while they have two leagues of open country to negotiate in order to capture a place, but that also entails the necessity of covering this open country so well that it cannot happen. | I owe the success I have had in my life, firstly to the benediction of God, and secondly to the care that I have taken to prevent bad accidents, and to a certain caution bordering on timidity, but useful in that [...] to convince me that I would be sheltered if, though it may not be raining at all in my chamber, a gutter might fill my room with water. As a result, I have not forgotten to cover both the one and the other. I have no doubt at all that we shall soon take Hedin, but you will see with M. de Noyers what must be done in order to play at [..] in this opening-up of two leagues, and everything that you decide with him will be regarded as good. To God. Rejoice and be assured of my affection | Cardinal Richelieu

19 March 1628 | My Cousin, I have seen the judgment that you made against Mr de la Meilleraye, Camp-Master in my army, found guilty by way of the duel

he fought against a cavalryman from La Rochelle. I have nothing but praise for the care that you are taking over the discipline of my army, sparing not even those that belong to you, and I am greatly pleased by this example; but valuing as I do the courage of La Meilleraye, who committed this fault only [through] ignorance and courage, I lift the penalty imposed upon him by the judgment made against him, and desire that he resume his post in order to serve as he has done before, and there being no other purpose for this letter, I shall always pray to God that he should keep you in health for as long as I desire it. | Louis | Paris, XIII March | 1628 | To my cousin the Cardinal Richelieu.

### PETER THE GREAT – PAGES 60–61

Colonel | Proceed quickly with the construction of the diversion of the water. Send some new workers immediately. I want the whole Empire to be able to drink water from this fountain in February. | Peter | 25 November 1717 | To be delivered at the barracks of the Preobranjenski Regiment of the Royal Guard. 1718.

### CHARLES DE MONTESQUIEU
### DENIS DIDEROT – PAGES 62–63

Received from Monsieur Le Breton, for copies, art fees and memoirs, in continuation of the same extracts from the archives of the Science Academy, philosophical inscriptions and transcriptions inserted into the three following volumes, i.e. the 3rd, 4th and 5th of the encyclopedia, four hundred and fifty pounds, these volumes having become a little less substantial than the first two. Paris, the [...] | Diderot

Monsieur de la Condamine, of the Science Academy | Paris, | 13 June 1753 | On arriving at the Academy yesterday, I found few people. I spoke to Abbé Sallier, who told me that you should be put forward. But without all these restrictions, I therefore put you and Abbé de Condillac forward; Abbé de la Tour had already been suggested. All I can tell you is that the proposal was very favourably received, and *cum elogio*. It is for your friends and yourself to say what you want said on behalf of Abbé Trublet. As for Monsieur de Buffon, it is better than you should not speak to him. Everyone knows that you did not present yourself until after his message. I will therefore say on Monday, unless I have contrary instructions from you, that you do not wish to compete to the detriment of Abbé Trublet. I embrace you with all my heart, my dear La Condamine, whom I also love with all my heart. | Montesquieu | Sunday 17 June 1753 | It seems to me that I can already see the Archbishop of Sens in you.

### VOLTAIRE – PAGE 65

Monsieur | I beg you to be so kind as to give eight cups of wheat to Madame François, baker at Ferney, who has great need of it in order to practise her trade. I should be most grateful to you. I have the honour to be, with respectful attachment | Monsieur | Your very humble and very obedient servant Voltaire | Ferney 19 Nov 1772

### MARIA THERESA OF AUSTRIA – PAGE 67

Luxemburg, 8 May | Madame my dear daughter. I wrote to you on the 3rd by post, complimenting you on your arrival in your kingdom and paying my respects to your dear husband. I wish that he should

find in you not merely a spouse but his wife, and then you will have accomplished perfectly all of your painful and difficult journey in this new condition which, may God grant you, should be as happy and blessed as mine has been. You have everything needed to make a husband happy, and so it is at this time your sole aim to please him and to be of use to him, to attach him to you, to amuse him and to have no other thought or purpose but him. You have a perfect model before your eyes in your sister-in-law; no moods, no impatience, always merry, always tender – those are the only bonds by which we can gain and maintain the respect and affection of our husbands, who alone are able to make us happy, as far as one can be happy in this world, as you well know. Nothing is perfect in this world, and all states have their painful side, but having gone through them all, I can assure you that that of a good marriage is far preferable to all others, and it bears with it some consolations of which the others are deprived. And so, my dear, kind daughter, take courage. Every beginning is difficult. The good Lord has called you and chosen you for this state, and so follow precisely the ways of Divine Providence and have no regrets, not even thoughts, concerning that which you have left. It is little compared to what you have at this time to care about and which the good Lord has lavished upon you, though not in order to win you over. Think of me to inspire you to do your duty and to console an old mother who loves you tenderly but who has [...] every reason, because you have exceeded my expectations by your conduct throughout this journey. You also win nothing but approval and hearts wherever you go. Is not the little inconvenience that you are caused well recompensed by the general approval, and by your own satisfaction, for you must feel it, that one has when one does one's duty, and the comfort that you have given to me and to all the family by having succeeded so perfectly? But do not be proud, and acknowledge your weakness before God, for without His divine assistance you would not have been able to achieve everything, nor without the good advice of Madame de Paar, which you have followed so well. Is it not a great gift from God that all the people who spend even just a little time with you love you immediately and so tenderly? The example of Paar, of Trautmansdorf, of [...] Pallavicini, even of Aya must inspire you. I flatter myself that my dear son – for I regard him as such, hoping that you are his wife – will do the same, what joy for you and for me! I am told that I am putting on weight, that my face is better since you have made me so happy, so radiant with all that reflects on me. Thus you will make me live to a hundred. There is only the separation from your brother and sister, who currently are such a support for you, that still weighs on my heart. It will be a difficult time but it is predictable, and they will not leave you without having given you enlightenment or advice which you will follow to the letter. If only they could find you a lady like la Paar, for every person at every age has need of advice and is happy to find a true friend, and you all the more so at your age with the spirit and the fire that you have with your inexperience of the world. Regardless of that, they are sacrificing their tender children and affairs of state for you, and they cannot do so for too long in accordance with time and reason. And so it is this moment, which I do not yet know, which worries me very deeply on your behalf. You will never be able to show them sufficient gratitude and consideration, but you must not abandon yourself to excessive sadness, for this could displease your husband, who must hold you fast at this time of all times, and fix your desires and happiness. My dear, kind daughter, I give you my blessing. The Emperor is very well; on 4th, I had news of him. | Prayers continue for you and I am always | your faithful and dear | Maria Theresa

### JEAN-JACQUES ROUSSEAU – PAGES 68–69

Paris | 9 October 1751 | I flattered myself, Madame, that I had a soul that was proof against praise; the letter with which you have honoured me teaches me to have less faith in myself, and if I must see you, that gives me more reasons to have even less faith in myself. Nevertheless, I shall obey, because it is up to you to tame the monsters. I shall therefore submit to your command, Madame, on the day that it will please you to set for me. I know that Monsieur d'Alembert has the honour of paying court to you; his presence will not drive me away at all; however, do not think ill of me, I beg you, if any other third party should make me disappear. | I am with profound respect | Madame | Your very humble and very obedient servant | J.-J. Rousseau

Mr Rousseau...1200 | In consequence of the decree issued by the Bureau de la Ville on the twenty-third of the present month of July, Mr Denouville will pay to Mr Rousseau the sum of twelve hundred pounds for the reasons contained in the said decree and repeated in the attached note, and on the return through the aforementioned Mr Denouville of the present executory formula and receipt from the aforementioned Mr Rousseau, the said sum of twelve hundred pounds will be passed and allocated to him in the expenditure of his accounts without hindrance. Done at the Bureau de Ville, 24 July 1753. | De Bernage | Received by J.-J. Rousseau | It has been decreed at the Bureau de Ville, 23 July 1753, that the fees both for the words and for the music of the play *Le Devin du village*, of which Monsieur Rousseau is the author, remain fixed at the sum of 1200 pounds, the payment of which shall be ordered for the benefit of Mr Rousseau.

### LOUIS XV OF FRANCE | MADAME DE POMPADOUR | COMTESSE DU BARRY – PAGES 70–73

I am very upset at having broken my word to you on paying the interest on the debt I owe you. But the return of funds on which I was depending has been postponed until next month. Thus, Monsieur, you are too honest to wish for my happiness. Accept my apologies and the assurance of the feelings I have for you. | La Ctesse du Barry. | 11 October 1779.

My brother, cousin, and son-in-law, | I have seen the copies that M. de Crussol sent to M. de Saint-Contest. I hope with all my heart that you have made the right decision, and that the king your brother approves of your reasons, myself desiring above all else your happiness and your repose, loving you truly, and with all my heart, even though I am deprived of the satisfaction of knowing you in person. And now I pray to God that he has you, my brother, cousin, and son-in-law, under His holy and worthy protection. | Crécy, 11 June 1752. | Your good brother, cousin and father-in-law | Louis

I have had the honour, Madame, of presenting to the King the letter that you made me that of writing to

me [*sic*]. His Majesty gave no answer, and it would have been against the respect that I owe him for me to insist. I am absolutely, Madame, your very humble and very obedient servant. | Marquise de Pompadour. | 20 October 1761 | To Madame de Voyer

To Monsieur le Comte d'Argenson | I offer all my thanks to Monsieur le Comte and I have the honour of informing you that running round the apartments in Versailles is a certain Milord Gordon who is stark raving mad and who [...] not a month ago. There is no sort of lunacy that he has not indulged in here. I do not like to see him close to the King or behind the Dauphin, especially with the taste that he has declared for drinking human blood. He is in the Royal Scottish regiment. And so I think it wise for Monsieur le Comte at least to send him to his regiment.

### GIACOMO CASANOVA – PAGES 74–75

Monsieur le Comte | At the very moment when you perform a generous action on my behalf, for which I thank you, you are pleased to write me a fine and mortifying letter. It is so true that I have not taken you for my guarantor, that I have written to M. de Bellegarde himself. Did I do wrong to send you my letter to find out if you approved? What you have just done demonstrates that you would have disapproved of me had I sent it to him. I could forget everything, I know, but unfortunately, I have little affairs which keep my memory in a constant state of alertness. In any case, Monsieur le Comte, if my conduct in this affair, which is so small for Monsieur le Comte de Bellegarde and quite big for me (pity the poor human species), has not pleased you, have the kindness to forgive it in a situation which does not allow me to follow the same sentiments as those which you cherish and which, in other circumstances, would be my models. I shall have the honour of thanking you at dinner. | Have you read my letter to M. de Bellegarde? Think a little, and you will see that I am very worthy of being honoured by your esteem, and of signing with the greatest sincerity, | Monsieur le Comte, | Your very humble and very obedient servant | Casanova

### CATHERINE THE GREAT – PAGES 76–77

By the Grace of God, We, Catherine II, Empress and Absolute Sovereign of all Russia *et aliis*. Let it be known to everyone that on the first day of January in the year one thousand seven hundred and eighty, We have very benevolently accorded to Vassili Selevine, who serves us as captain, in view of the devotion and fidelity that he has shown to us, the rank of Our Second Major. And since We desire and declare it thus, We order all Our subjects from now on to respect and recognize Our designated Second Major as such; also We hope that, in his new rank, generously bestowed by Us, he will continue to serve Us faithfully with the devotion suitable for a good and loyal officer. And in order to certify this, We here sign with Our own hand, ordering that the imperial seal be applied. Drawn up in the city of St Petersburg, the year 1781, 31 December. | Ekaterina

Monsieur le Maréchal de Castries. I have just received your letter from Eisenach, dated 13 Nov. You owe me nothing, Monsieur le Maréchal, I stand with the King

your Master. I flatter myself that you have long considered me among the most constant and most unwavering friends of His Majesty. I pray as you do to Heaven to restore King Louis XVIII to the throne of his ancestors as soon as possible, and to set you to work, using your brains, your experience and your abilities for the restoration of your Motherland which so many scoundrels have been devastating for so long. | Catherine | 14 December | 1795.

### THE MARQUIS DE SADE – PAGES 78–79

You will be pleased, Madame Sade, my wife, on reception of these words, without delay or deduction to extract from the funds passed on to you by the family gathering for our common upkeep, in currency having weight and validity in the kingdom, the sum of three hundred and thirteen pounds twelve sols, which you will have delivered into the hands of Mr Boucher, equerry for the department of State prisons and first assistant to Monseigneur the lieutenant-general of the Paris and Suburban Police. The purpose of all this is to satisfy Monsieur Fonteillot, Surgeon Major on the place de Vincennes, specially attached to the prisoners whom the justice of the Ministry detains in the aforesaid prisons of the royal keep of the aforesaid place and at the garrison of the junior officers, mainly detailed to guard and secure the said delinquents. The said payment having two faces, the first being to fulfil the gratification of the usage accorded to the execution of beards, as operated by the said gentleman under the tolerance and protection of the Magistrate, and the second [is] settlement for the supply of milk to myself administered by the horned beasts of the government. – Drawn up under the intentions and with the approval of Monsieur de Fougemont, Knight of the Royal Order and soldier of Saint Louis, lieutenant for the king of the said Citadelle de Vincennes and governor surviving of other places or fortresses of the Monarchy. In witness whereof, this twenty-sixth of April in the year of grace seventeen hundred and eighty-two, at eleven o' clock in the morning, enjoying our full health and reason, we have signed these words, to serve the necessary purpose. | The prisoner Sade

I beg you, Monsieur the lawyer, to be so kind as to send me the rest of what belongs to me, which is at la Coste – my effects, my rags, papers relating to my administration, the accounts of debts paid by my mother on my behalf, letters addressed to me, and everything of mine that you find. I should be infinitely obliged to you, and am most absolutely, Monsieur, your very humble and very obedient servant. | Montreuil de Sade | 2 April 1790
(To Monsieur Gaufridy, lawyer at Apt)

23 February 1771 | Convinced of your zeal and devotion to my interests, my dear Sir, I entrust to you with pleasure the responsibility for my property and estate at Mazan, which your uncle Taulier looked after, whose loss I assure you could not have been more painful to me. I hope that you would like to take his place, not only in his offices but also in his real devotion to my person. I urge you to arrange a service which I demand and which I insist that one must hold for him at my expense in the church where he has been buried. | I am absolutely, Monsieur, your very humble and very obedient servant. | de Sade
(To Monsieur Ripert)

LOUIS XVI OF FRANCE | MARIE ANTOINETTE
| MAXIMILIEN DE ROBESPIERRE – PAGES 80–83

Memorandum of expenses on behalf of Louis Capet
and his family, during the month of December 1792.
According to the requests submitted to the Conseil du
Temps by Cléry, in service at the Tower. December 1792

| | | |
|---|---|---|
| 4th. A phial of essence of soap......... | 4 | |
| Two balls of cotton................... | 1 | 16 |
| 17th. Two shopping trips to the Luxembourg...1 | 1 | 4 |
| A phial of lemon balm..................... | | 12 |
| Two rolls of grained barley water......... | 3 | |
| 12th. Half a hundred cut feathers......... | 4 | |
| Two pots of almond paste.................. | 14 | 8 |
| 14th. Paid to the piano maker.............. | 6 | |
| Two shopping trips......................... | 1 | 4 |
| 19th. A portfolio in morocco.............. | 18 | |
| A bottle of ink................................... | 1 | 4 |
| Twelve packs of large-sized letter paper.... | 16 | |
| 20th. Shopping at the Luxembourg.......... | | 14 |
| 24th. Two balls of cotton................. | 1 | 16 |
| 28th. Pen and paper of different sizes....... | 16 | |
| 31st. Six pounds of fine powder............. | 3 | 12 |
| Two jars of pomade.......................... | 6 | |
| Essence of soap, two phials.................. | 6 | |
| Half a pound of soap........................... | | 14 |
| Total | 106 | 4 |

It is with the greatest pleasure, my dear brother-in-law,
that I inform you that the Queen has very happily
just given birth to a boy whom I have named Duke
of Normandy. I know well enough your friendship
towards me, my dear brother-in-law, to be certain
that you will share all my satisfaction. I hope that you
will never doubt any of my feelings or the tenderness
with which I embrace you, my dear brother-in-law. |
Louis | Versailles, 27 March 1785, at eight o'clock in
the evening.

Monsieur my Brother, Cousin and Brother-in-Law |
The interest that I take in the events that touch Your
Majesty should convince him of all the satisfaction
that I feel today on hearing the news, of which he
has informed me by his letter of the 26th of last
month, of the birth of the Prince whom the Queen
my very dear Sister has just brought into the world.
I beg Your Majesty to be persuaded of the pleasure that
I have in finding such agreeable occasions for his heart,
and to renew the sentiments of tender and constant
friendship with which I am, Monsieur my Brother,
Cousin and Brother-in-Law, | the good Sister, Cousin
and Sister-in-Law | of Your Majesty. | Marie Antoinette |
Versailles, 24 September 1788 | To Monsieur my Brother,
Cousin, and Brother-in-Law, the King of the Two Sicilies.

I have received your little letter of apology, and you
will see from this that it was not necessary: you got
the date wrong. And so I do not know which day it
refers to, but what gives me pleasure is that I see the
bishop has arrived. Adieu, that is all for the moment.
| 12 December.

Extract from the Registers of the Committee for Public
Safety of the National Convention, of the seventeenth
day of the Prairial, in the second year of the One and
Indivisible French Republic. | The Committee for Public
Safety decrees that Delmas and Laubadère, division
generals in the Rhine Army, shall be arrested and
forthwith brought before the *Comité*. | Michault,
general-in-chief of this army, is charged with the

execution of this present decree. Signed in the
register: Billaud-Varenne, Robespierre, Collot d'Herbois,
Saint-Just, Couthon, Carnot, Barère, | For the extract: |
Carnot, Barère, Saint-Just. Collot d'Herbois, Robespierre,
Billaud-Varenne, Couthon.

JOHANN WOLFGANG VON GOETHE – PAGE 85

I should like a thorough inspection of the shops to
take place and I want a precise report on the fine
Muscat wine which is to be found in Adorf. |
Marienbad, 18 August 1821 | J. W. v. Goethe, Privy
Councillor to the Grand Duchy of Saxony-Weimar.

LORD NELSON
| LADY HAMILTON – PAGES 86–87

His Excellency Cavalier Hamilton to Giuseppe Viganoni
for lessons given to Lady Hamilton between
27 December 1801 and 21 March 1803.

| | |
|---|---|
| 112 lessons at half a guinea each | £58 : 16 |
| For printed music | £2 : 16 |
| For the cost of a piano, paid on the | |
| order of Sir William to Mr. Tomkinson | |
| Piano manufacturer on Dean Street, Soho | £30 : 9 |
| Paid to Signor Morelli for the last concert | |
| that Sir William performed before his death | £3 : 3 |
| For my assistance during five concerts, which | |
| Sir William gave after his arrival, on his return | |
| trip from Merton to London | £26 : 5 |
| | £121 : 9 |

The above account is correct to my knowledge |
Emma Hamilton

*Agamemnon*, Alassio, | August 26th 1795
Sir, | The French having taken possession of the town
and coast of Alassio, I cannot but consider it as an
enemy coast. Therefore to prevent destruction of the
town and to avoid the unnecessary effusion of human
blood, I desire the immediate surrender of your vessel.
If you do not comply with my desire, the consequences
must lay with you and not with your very humble
servant. Horatio Nelson. | To the Commander of the
National Corvette

NAPOLEON BONAPARTE
| JOSEPHINE DE BEAUHARNAIS – PAGES 88–93

You promised me that you would take an interest,
my dear Arnault, in Citizen Gasse, husband of Mlle
Jamié. I send you a very special task to solicit the
minister to give him a position; he is an upright and
unselfish man. Accept, my dear Arnault, the assurance
of my tender friendship.
Lapagerie Bonaparte

Monsieur the Minister for War, | I ask for your
generosity towards Mr Fizelier, whose service record
I attach herewith. He is asking for promotion in the
corps in which he is serving, and I recommend him
to you with all the more pleasure as I am profiting
from this opportunity to renew the attachment that
you know I have for you. | Malmaison | 6 November
1812 | Josephine

Monsieur Talleyrand | I received your letter of the 2nd
at 5 o'clock in the morning. I see with pleasure that you
will be finishing; but I advise you expressly not to speak
of Naples. The insults from this wretched queen are
getting worse with every letter. You know how I have

dealt with her. I would be too much of a coward if I
forgave inflammatory excesses such as hers against
my people. It is necessary that her reign should come
to an end and that I should not hear another word
about her, absolutely none, no matter what happens,
do not speak of her, my order is precise. As for the
contributions, I have told you what I want: half. That is
to say, 50 thousand. | Napoleon | Schönbrunn 2nd
Nivôse year 14 (23 December 1805).

French Republic | Italian Army | Liberty Equality |
General Headquarters Milan, 3rd Vendémiaire |
Year 5 of the One and Indivisible Republic | Bonaparte,
General-in-Chief of the Italian Army | to General
Valette | I have received, Citizen General, the letter you
wrote to me. The circumstances in which you found
yourself in Castiglione were difficult, and should in no
way efface the vital services that you have rendered
to the Alpine army in different conditions. I readily
agree to the request you have made of me, to see the
enemy before holding any subsequent discussions. |
Go to Trente: there you will serve under the command
of General Vaubois, who will employ you in the manner
he deems most useful. On the return of the expedition
that is going to take place over there, I shall let you
know the intentions of the government concerning
yourself. | Bonaparte

Liberty Equality | French Republic | One and Indivisible
| Italian Army | General Headquarters in Mantua 18th
Ventôse | Year 5 of the French Republic One and
Indivisible | Miollis | Brigade General | Commandant |
To the General-in-Chief of the Italian Army | The
accused man Pierre Martinot, assistant store-keeper
for supplies to the artillery, has been found guilty
by the Council of War, assembled here on the
seventeenth, of having taken from the store of which
he was in charge twenty sacks of corn from Turkey,
which were stopped by the Guard on two vehicles
covered with manure at the Moliner gate. I ask for
the most exemplary punishment for this crime, which
in our situation is one of the most iniquitous and the
most dangerous, and the flexible execution of your
order relative to the assignment of the place. | Miollis |
The General-in-Chief orders General Miollis to have the
said store-keeper shot, and to share this duty with the
general staff so that it shall be carried out under the
orders of the Army. | General-in-Chief | Bonaparte

To Citizen Junot, Cavalry lieutenant | I inform you,
Citizen, that having just been nominated to the rank
of Brigade General, I have chosen you to fill the post
of aide de camp to me. If you accept, would you join me
as soon as possible. In the contrary case, let me know.
Greetings and fraternity | Buonaparte

Pianosa | Thursday 22 September at six o'clock | My
dear Marshal. The weather being overcast, put the
ladies on the brig to Campo from where they will go
to Porto Ferraio. I will stay another day. The Campo brig
will return here. I suppose that your [...] whom I [...]
here today with your reply. | Send a landau or caleche
to Campo for my return, to the quayside. Let it be there
this evening. Have everything sent back that is at [...]
on horses but a [...]. Also have the furniture at [...] and
have [...] everything | Np.

Monsieur le Comte Bertrand, | [The work that] has
been done here is like everything else on the island –
that is, very bad. The locks on the doors and windows

are dreadful. They have to be redone. The [way in which the] house [has been] painted resembles the worst possible cabaret. What with Madame having a lot of furniture and Princess Pauline expecting several pieces from Paris and Rome, I believe we have enough. I beg you to send the bed placed for the Empress above the gallery, with the curtains, the bedside table, the chests of drawers and generally all the furniture that was in that apartment. Also send 2 beds for the officers, my night clock, the small marble-top table which was at Madame's, some vases to put water in, an earthenware writing case, and 4 oil lamps. As the rooms here are very big, one could put a billiard table in one. Send it. Send the tapestry-making valet to put up some curtains; also send 2 porters; 2 floor polishers and the tinsmith. As Princess Pauline is definitely due to arrive on the 25th, I think it is right to get a move on with her apartment, and if necessary to bring forward the work relating to the downstairs windows. And now I pray to God that he will keep you under His Holy protection. | Longone, | 6 September 1814. | Napoleon | P.S. Herewith the number of people to be lodged in the Palace. It amounts to 16. As I am asking for two more officer's beds, there remain two more to be sent, but we can make up for those with camp-beds, of which we have 10; but we are completely out of mattresses, covers and bolsters; send some. You will decide if it is best to send those that are at the Madonne. There is just the fear that they may get spoilt that might make this removal expensive.

### TOUSSAINT LOUVERTURE
### HENRI CHRISTOPHE – PAGES 94–95

Liberty Equality | Saint-Marc, 9 Thermidor, sixth year of the French Republic, One and Indivisible. | Toussaint Louverture. | General-in-Chief of the Army of Santo Domingo. | To Citizen Hédouville, special agent of the Executive Directoire of Santo Domingo. Citizen agent, you will receive herewith enclosed a letter addressed to me. As its content is not within my competence, I consider it best to pass it on to you. I have simply added my comments, because the position that I occupy obliges me to be truthful. | Greetings and respects. | Toussaint Louverture

Palais de Sans-Souci 15 July 1813. | Year ten of independence. | The King – to the Prince Royal his son: I am happier, my dear son, with your handwriting from the day of yesterday. I urge you to persevere. If you continue to give me such subjects of contentment, I for my part will do myself a true pleasure by procuring for you the satisfactions which are dependent upon myself. | I embrace you and am your good papa. | Henri

### SIMON BOLÍVAR – PAGES 96–97

General Bolivar takes the liberty of offering [to Mr Alexander Cockburn] his horse, which served him throughout the Peruvian campaign. This animal has no distinction other than having borne its master against the enemies of the Motherland. | General Bolivar hopes that Mr Cockburn will grant him the favour of accepting this little token of his friendship. | Caracas, 6 May 1828.

The whole of this note is written in the hand of General Bolívar and is addressed to Mr. A. Cockburn, the British Envoy Extraordinary then at Caracas on his way to Bogota. I was present when Bolívar wrote the note | Robert Ker Porter

### LORD BYRON – PAGES 98–99

La Mira 8 October 1817. | Madame, | I have just received the letter that you did me the honour of writing to me. There is nothing more flattering to me than your permission to meet you, which I shall take advantage of at the first opportunity – Meanwhile, Madame, I take the liberty of informing you that, according to the proposal that Monsieur Hoppner was kind enough to make to me, I already consider myself to be his tenant – and my visit either to Este or to your house in Venice will have as its main purpose to show you how touched I am by the very obliging manner in which Monsieur your husband has allowed me to use the villa. | I beg you, Madame, to accept the deepest respect with which I sign myself | Your very devoted servant | Byron

### GIOACCHINO ROSSINI – PAGES 100–102

Dear marquis and friend | I shall have to deprive myself again this year of the pleasure of seeing you in Rimini. The contrary advice of the faculty and my own weakness oblige me to go to Bologna to take some gentle baths and therefore to forego the happiness of being with you. My gratitude to you will be no less, however, for offering me hospitality with such generosity and delicacy. Do eat some of those famous fish soups for me [...] and pity me!! I hope you will come and see me, at full strength, and that thus you will make happy him who is pleased to call himself your very affectionate | Gioacchino Rossini | Madame Pélissier sends you a thousand nice greetings. It is the Marquis Albergati who will bring you this letter.

Monsieur Le Comte | I am extremely sorry that I cannot accept the offer made by your agent. Please accept my regrets and the assurance of my absolute respect. | O. Rossini. | Tuesday 24 | 5 o'clock

### GEORGE SAND – PAGES 104–105

Madame, | I do not want to delay any further acknowledging receipt of the works that you were kind enough to send me. I do not know them yet, but I know how much they are appreciated. I should have liked to read them before replying to you, but I have so much to do that I shall not be able to read them for several weeks perhaps; and until then, I do not want you to think that I am indifferent to the good memories I have of you or to the precious sympathy that you have shown me. And so please accept my sincere gratitude and my regards in haste. | George Sand | 16 June 56.

Dear Darling, Chopin and his sister arrive in Paris on the evening of the 28th by the [...] train. Make sure the keys are there and they can go to bed. I am not writing to you. I finished my novel yesterday. I am dead, but I assure you I shall write to you. | George | Monday

### VICTOR HUGO – PAGES 106–108

Hauteville House, 16 June | Monsieur, | I have read your last article. No one knows better than you my law which is, for the detail as for the whole, nothing superfluous. Everything must serve the purpose. The purpose – often the poet conceals it and must conceal

it, but the philosopher does not lose sight of it, for the poet is always transparent to the philosopher, the light of the one being made for the eye of the other. You have, Monsieur, that superior penetration which makes the great critic. What you say about Balzac is taken from the very basis of art and of the ideal. I greatly admire your articles, and feel a profound affinity with you. One admires close to oneself. I said this in *L'Homme qui rit*. With a deep and intimate satisfaction I observe this kinship of our minds. When I finished reading this last page, so lofty and so noble, written by you about my book, I looked for your hand in order to shake it. Around me I found solitude. Exile sometimes makes one feel its bitter point. I am your friend. | Victor Hugo
(To Monsieur Jules Levallois)

### RICHARD WAGNER
### LUDWIG II OF BAVARIA – PAGES 110–111

In addition to his annual salary, my treasurer may also disburse a loan, which will be the last, totalling 10,000 florins (ten thousand Gulden) to the composer Richard Wagner, by means of a bill of exchange on Paris. | This new loan, as well as the remainder of the advance which I granted to the composer by handwritten authorization on 27 March last year, should begin to be repaid on 1 April 1869 through regular deduction of 166 fl. 40 kr. per month, or 2,000 fl. (two thousand Gulden). All that remains is for my Court Secretary to make the necessary arrangements. | Munich, 2 March 1869. | Ludwig | A second handwritten letter from H. M. The King 9|3.69.

Most honoured Sir! | I am today in greatest need of 500 francs. If you could once more grant me this small sum, you would be doing me an enormous favour. Whatever happens, I will give it back to you the day after tomorrow. Would you be so kind as to give the money in an envelope to the bearer of this message? Your devoted | Richard Wagner | Paris 14 June 1860, afternoon.

### CHARLES BAUDELAIRE – PAGE 113

Monsieur Bourdilliart – bookshop and printer Dear Sir, | M. Dhormoyr has told me about his desire to meet M. Ferdinand Fougues. M. Fougues is now looking for M. Dhormoyr's address, in the provinces or in Paris. Please be so kind as to give it to him. Your very devoted | Charles Baudelaire. | I forget nothing, and I always dream Wagner and Poe.

To Alphonse Baudelaire | [Lyon]. The 1st day of the year 1834. | Charles the Younger to Alphonse the Elder, | hello and Happy New Year. | Another year gone, in April I shall be thirteen, and two years will have passed far from my brother, from Madame Tirlet, from Paris. Indeed from Paris, which I miss so much. How boring it is at school, and especially at the school in Lyons! The walls are so sad, so filthy, so dank, the classrooms so dark, the Lyonnais character so different from the Parisian character! But at last the time is drawing near when I shall return to Paris. There I shall see again my brother, my sister, Théodore, Mme Tirlet, Eugène her son, Paul and Alfred Pérignon; it is to be hoped that my mother and father will follow me there soon after. I miss the boulevards, and Berthellemot's sweets, and Giroux's general store, and the rich bazaars in which one finds so many things that will make fine presents.

In Lyons, there is only one shop with good books, two for cakes and sweets, and with other things it's the same. Oh! Rari nantes in gurgite vasto, it's certainly the place in which to apply the precept. In this town, blackened with smoke from the coal, you find nothing but big chestnuts and fine silks. | I had promised you presents, and first or second place, but...but...I don't know what to say by way of apology. I don't dare to make any more promises, because if discouragement overcomes me again....This discouragement is quite excusable. Hardly had I got back to the school when I was getting nothing but bad [grades]. Add to that, the memory of my former glory. I mean my strength in class last year. For after all, even though I didn't win any prizes, [I] did shine throughout the year. But let us hope that, in seeing those who were below me now trampling over me, I shall come back to life and, with hard work, will be more deserving of awards. | Give my best wishes for the New Year to my sister and Théodore too. Dad and Mum send their greetings. | Charles

## Gustave Flaubert – page 115

Monsieur and dear Master | Only a few days ago I received *L'Homme qui rit*. That is why I have not thanked you earlier. This memento from you has filled me with pride. I will not extend the impertinence so far as to send you tokens of my admiration. When you appear, we prostrate ourselves. | I am, O Master, | your very humble, very affectionate and devoted | G. Flaubert | Croisset near Rouen | 10 June 69

## Mikhail Bakunin – page 117

25 November 1861 | Boston | Revere House | My dear friend – I cannot leave Boston until Saturday evening. But I hope that without delay you will decide to come yourself. I am in a position to introduce you, beginning with Mr Agassiz, to the best and most intelligent society of Boston, the best in the United States, I think. If you do not come, you will perhaps miss out on a unique opportunity. And so decide, dear friend; the crossing to New York is at 10 o'clock. 'Revere House' is an excellent hotel, and Boston society is well worth coming for. – We shall spend several pleasant days together, and your friend will be very happy about that. Adieu, I am waiting for you. | Your devoted, | M. Bakunin

## Queen Victoria – page 118

Osborne, August 14th 1883 | I have to thank you so very much for giving yourself the trouble of attending to the question which puzzled me & others very much. The second suggestion was just what I wished to express. | Let me now say how much gratified & enchanted I was to have seen you again and to have conversed so freely with you on subjects of such importance. I felt deeply touched by your kindness to me & your true sympathy! I do need it for few have had more trials & none have been or still are in such an exceptionally solitary and difficult position.

It has been my anxious wish to do my duty to my country, though politics never were congenial to me and while my dear Husband lived I left as much as I could to him. Then when He was taken I had to struggle on alone. And <u>few know what</u> that struggle has been....

Friends have fallen on all sides and one by one. I have lost those I cared for at least on [...]! And now again lately, I have lost one who — humble though he was – was the truest & most devoted of all! He had no thought but for me, my welfare, my comfort, my safety, my happiness. Courageous, unselfish, totally disinterested, discreet to the highest degree, speaking frankly the truth fearlessly & telling me what he thought and considered to be "just & right", without flattery & without saying what would be pleasing if he did not think it right. And ever at hand – he was part of my life and quite invaluable!

He has been taken & I feel again very desolate, & forlorn – for what my dear faithful Brown – who was in my service for 34 years and for 18 never left me for a single day – did for me, no one else can. The comfort of my daily life is gone – the void is terrible – the loss irreparable !

The most affectionate children – no lady or gentleman – can do what he did. I have a very dear devoted child who has always been a dear unselfish companion to me – but she is going and I can't darken her young life by my trials and demons. My other children, though all loving, have all their own interests and homes. And a large family is a great anxiety. God will, I trust, give me strength to the end, when I trust to meet again those I have "loved & lost" but only for a while. You were so kind that I have let my pen run so I said more than I intended when I first began my letter, but I wished you to know what I felt unable to say to you the other day. I have preferred writing in the first person as the other form is so stiff & it is difficult to express feelings in the third person. My dear Beatrice returned [...] to my great comfort & much regrets not having been here when you came. Trusting to see you again and wishing to be remembered to Mrs. Tennyson, Believe me yours truly, | V [ictoria]. R[egina]. I[mperatrix].
Alfred Tennyson Esq., Poet Laureate, the Q.

## Charles Darwin – page 121

May 13 | My dear Frank, | Will you try and persuade Mr. Bartlett to do me a great favour (and if he will, report the result to me) – That is to show to the porcupine a live snake and observe whether the sight of the snake will make it rattle the quills in the tail, as Mr. Bartlett showed me that the porcupine does when angered. You can show this note to Mr. Bartlett. | Yours affectionately | C. Darwin

## Giuseppe Verdi – pages 122–123

Piacenza | Saturday | Dear Muzio | I am in Piacenza where I have met Gavignani, to whom I have given the whole of the first act and the finale of the third! They now have something to work with for a while! I have learned, along with Peppina, and with much consternation, of your sufferings during your journey. I have every confidence and hope that the baths and mudbaths will do you good; they are highly recommended, and I hope you will send me your news frequently, which I hope will go from good to excellent in the next few days. If you know of a gallant gentleman who might be able to find fifty or so bottles of Barolo, that is to say good Barolo, real and authentic, send them to me. But be very careful. If you are not sure, absolutely sure that it is real and authentic, pure Barolo, don't send it to me. I can do without it. I like Chianti, and if it's not real Barolo, I prefer to do without

it. Farewell. | Give me some good news, that is to say some sincere news. Yours | Verdi

## Louis Pasteur – pages 126–127

I have received today, 28 January 1885, from the hands of M. Savadon, merchant from Gray, a dog that has been attacked by one that is rabid. It will not leave my kennels, where I shall attempt to make it resistant to the rabies, despite the probable bite of four days ago. | 28 January 1885. L. Pasteur

Paris 22 Oct. 1879 | My dear friend, | Thank you for your kind regards. I am feeling better. Yesterday I was able to go to the Académie de Médecine. At the end of September, I was assailed in Arbois by such a violent intestinal indisposition that you would have said it was cholera. For several days my stomach could not take a single drop of water. Champagne chilled with pieces of ice was the real remedy. As we were under pressure to come back because of the preparations for the wedding on 4 November, I bravely got myself underway for Paris at the first sign of recovery. We arrived on the 14th, and since then I have been regaining my strength, albeit very slowly. I am delighted to hear that you are well and that Madame Cochin is going to make you a father for the third time, with that courage which is customary for her and which is so well reflected in the vigorous beauty of your dear children. I saw with pleasure that your letter to Monsieur Dumas seems to have been appreciated, and its interest understood. My dear master would like to be one of the witnesses for my dear child, and my first visit will be to him. You will certainly be able to submit your work to him for the annals, with every confidence that you will see it in print straight away. I am convinced that he will have welcomed the conclusions with great interest. No-one understands better than him scientific thoroughness and refined, decisive experiments. Looking forward to seeing you again and to resuming work in the laboratory, I send you my most affectionate regards and please give my very respectful greetings to Madame Cochin | L. Pasteur

## Auguste Renoir
## Edgar Degas – pages 128–129

Madame Manet accepts the invitation to dine at the Degas' and so do I | Renoir | To Monsieur Mallarmé

Mont Doré, Sunday | Hôtel en la Poste | Dear Monsieur Alexandre | Please be so kind as to send me at once your article on the Friends of the Louvre. *La Libre Parole* speaks of it, Drumond knows it, and I do not know it. I am impatient to read you, or rather to have you read out to me, that you must not make me wait a single day longer. This morning I lost Zalmeyr, an admirable reader...I still have Sprunk (*Débats*), a mellifluous reader. With greetings to you both | Degas | To Monsieur Arsène Alexandre

## Claude Monet
## Édouard Manet – pages 130–131

Thursday | Mademoiselle Éva, | Are your two pictures finished? You know that if you need me, I am entirely at your disposal. | Édouard Manet

...as has been said above, the purchasers must see to the leases and rentings, which will then be declared, and account to the tenants without reducing the rents received in advance.| Messieurs Manet will subrogate the purchasers in the clauses of termination, but it will be the responsibility of the purchasers to take over the costs of indemnity against termination whatever they may be without reducing the sale price or making claims against the vendors. | Carried out in quadruplicate between the parties in Paris, the twelfth of July one thousand eight hundred and eighty-one. | Read and approved the above document E. Manet | Read and approved the above document G. Manet | Read and approved Ed. Manet | Read and approved the above document G. Besquiel

I, the undersigned Claude Monet, acknowledge receipt from M. Gustave Manet as a loan of the sum of one thousand francs, which will be repayable on the royalties from the sale of thirty-five of my paintings, which is to take place in the course of next February under the direction of Maître Charles Oudart, auctioneer. As a guarantee for this loan, on this very day I deposit eight pictures destined for the above-mentioned sale, and the other twenty-seven pictures (including the one representing a lifesize Japanese woman) are to be deposited by me at the same place as and when they are completed, the last having to be delivered by the first of next February at the latest.

Done in Paris, in the year one thousand eighteen hundred and seventy-five, the eighteenth of October. | Document approved | Claude Monet

## MARK TWAIN – PAGES 132–133

March 5. 1906 | Dear Mrs. Ditson : I am glad to have that speech : it has moved me, and also modified me, in some degree. I don't feel the same passionate appetite for your dog that I felt that evening ; it is probably because I have just had my breakfast. I can't really depend on my reforms. They are so likely to be inspirational and temporary. Therefore for my sake and the dog's, I think it will be better that one of us keep out of the way. | Yours affectionately, | S. L. Clemens

## GUY DE MAUPASSANT – PAGE 135

Monsieur and dear colleague | I thank you most cordially for your fine drama which I have read with great interest. It is powerful and profound, and I beg you to accept with my very sincere compliments the expression of my fraternal devotion | Guy de Maupassant

From Guy de Maupassant to August Strindberg | On the subject of my tragedy, *The Father*

## OSCAR WILDE – PAGE 137

To the manager | Redpath Bureau | Boston, Mass. | Dear Sir. | Will you allow me to introduce to you Mr. Heron Allen who is very anxious to lecture in America. Mr. Allen has in a very short time won for himself a most remarkable position here, through the brilliancy of his books and the charm of his personality, and should you be able to give him any engagements, I am sure that his audiences will derive profit and pleasure from his lectures. He proposes, I think, to speak on the scientific basis of Occultism on Palmistry principally, a subject on which he has written some very remarkable books, and he will illustrate his lectures by numerous examples, anecdotes, and large

diagrams so as to make his address as popular as possible. If he succeeds in exciting as much interest in the States as he has in London he will have a great success. Knowing how important it is to be properly introduced to the American public, I have ventured to recommend him to your well known Bureau, and hope you will be able to give him the opportunity of speaking under your management. | Truly Yours, | Oscar Wilde

## HENRI DE TOULOUSE-LAUTREC – PAGES 138–139

Dear mother | We shall be arriving shortly. Viaud will let you know. With love and affection | Henri

Château de Céleyran 28 April | My dear Godmother | I embrace you with all my heart, and tell me if Mlle. Julie is well, if Arnaud, Justine and Antoine are well. | I embrace you once more and that is all | Henri

## GUSTAV MAHLER | ALMA MAHLER-WERFEL OSKAR KOKOSCHKA – PAGES 140–141

[Hotel] St. Moritz on the Park | New York 18|II|43 | My dear Mrs. Edwards | I thank you so much of sending me the Patriotic Song. I only wished I would have a piano here for playing it. But I read it and find it very interesting | Thank you <u>very much</u> for this new sign of friendship | Cordially yours | Alma Mahler-Werfel

Madame Adèle Marcus | Very dear friend! | It would be the height of ingratitude if I did not address one of these lettercards to you. I presume you have received my brief military commands from Justi? And so all I have to add is that the concert yesterday apparently went very well. During the *Siegfried Idyll*, I realized that for the first time in my life I was making music only for money. Another piece of progress this year! And so soon I shall attain bourgeois respectability! With warmest good wishes, Yours | Gustav Mahler

## ÉMILE ZOLA ALFRED DREYFUS – PAGES 142–146

L'Affaire Dreyfus | An autograph letter of Captain Dreyfus (This identical letter formed part of the evidence laid before the Cour de Cassation). | An autograph letter of Esterhazy | These letters were given me by Madame Dreyfus for the purpose of comparing the pulsetracing in the handwriting of Esterhazy, the Captain and the author of the Bordereau. I discovered that the pulse beat can be found in all handwriting if written slowly, and is characteristic of the writer's pulsebeat. By these means I discovered that the copy of the Bordereau published in France did not show either Dreyfus' or Esterhazy's pulse, and was undoubtedly a tracing taken by a third party over the original document. The letter of Esterhazy's here shown is an order on his Broker to purchase 5000 Italian rentes (consols). The fact that the shares fell in price before settlement day landed him in difficulties, and the theory is that it compelled him to resort to other means to raise the money, by applying to the secret service, which resulted in an infamous plot, the consequences of which are felt to this day. G. Lindsay Johnson. Ll. D. F.R.C.S

Rouen 12 October 1892 | My dear friend, I have received what you sent me. Would you please

buy me 5000 italians tomorrow, Friday, including fifty for the end of October | Yours | Esterhazy

Place Parmentier, Bourges | My dear Paul, Your letter gave me great pleasure, and if you knew the joy that you bring me, you would force yourself to give it to me more often. What is more, you would make me in turn follow your studies a little more attentively, and sometimes give you some advice, as at last I think I have acquired some experience in the matter. Trust in me, tell me all your thoughts, and do not believe that I can make nothing of them. On the contrary, they will bring back memories of my childhood, the same hesitations that I had to go through, the same difficulties that I had to overcome. Your French composition [...] confirms the old saying 'Grasp all, lose all'. The rough copy [...] you then quietly read through again. [...] It is true that I am so little at home that it doesn't matter much to me. [...] Embrace your brothers for me, and accept an affectionate kiss from your dear uncle. | Alfred

The seven-page manuscript, of which four are reproduced on page 145, was used for publication. Therefore it does not contain any variations from the printed version published in 1882: ZOLA, Émile. *Une Campagne* (1880-1991). Paris: G. Charpentier Publisher, 1882. Pages V-X (Preface).

## AUGUSTE RODIN CAMILLE CLAUDEL – PAGES 146–149

19 February 1906 | Monsieur, | Monsieur Rodin is extremely busy and is preparing for his journey to London tomorrow, and to his great regret cannot at this moment arrange any sessions with M. Belleroche. | When he returns from London at the beginning of March, he will do all he can to accommodate you. In the meantime, M. Rodin sends you his warm and cordial regards. | A. Rodin

Monsieur | I was very sorry on Sunday not to have had a visit from you at my studio. Nevertheless, I should be very happy to show you my waltzers and have your judgment, even though it is a very incomplete work. Monsieur Rodin has asked me to send you his apologies, as he was busy on Monday and Tuesday and did not let me know. He joins me in asking you to come next Sunday, if that is possible for you, and to accept an invitation to have lunch with him. Please accept my best regards | Camille Claudel | 113 Boulevard d'Italie

Dear Mademoiselle Jouvroy | If you can find a good expression for the man holding the keys, who weeps, make a study for it and show me the model. Yours from the heart and respectfully, | Rodin

## SIGMUND FREUD – PAGES 151–153

17.8.1929 | Dear Mother | Here are six dollars as a present for next year, when you will be with us in undisturbed joy. I greet you warmly [...], Your Sigm.

For dear Mother, in the name of her youngest great-grandson Gabriel Freud, born 31.7.21, Berlin 18 August 1291 [*sic*] Sigm.

Prof. Sigm. Freud | 20 Maresfield Gardens | Tel. : Hampstead 2002 | London N.W.3 | April 18th 1939 | Dear Mr Challage | Pray excuse my answering you in English which after all is not my native tongue. | I thank you greatly for the present of your book on Nietzsche which I have already started reading. I hope I may some day enjoy the lecture of the book you intend to devote to me, but I am not sure of it, being in rather poor health. By this same reason I suggest, you should for any information you want about my person or about literature apply to two pupils of mine, living in Paris. One of them is Mme Marie Bonaparte (Princess Georges of Greece) 6 rue Adolphe Yvon, the other Dr Heinz Hartmann (6 Villa George Sand, XVIe). I am sure you will get from them all the help you want. | Sincerely yours, | Sigm. Freud

P.S. Permit me to correct what I consider to be an error, in the first chapter of your book. You say Lou Salomé is – or rather was – a Jewess. I have known her rather intimately. We were near friends during her last 25 years she practised psychoanalysis as my pupil. I have learned that she was the daughter of a Russian general of French descent but I never heard her mention anything about being Jewish.

## Claude Debussy – pages 154–155

Wednesday | My dear Monsieur Dernats | Could you let me know the whereabouts or even have sent to me the two scores and orchestral parts of L'Après midi d'un faune. I have urgent need of them, and am very anxious to know whose hands they are in. | Yours | Claude Debussy | 10 rue Gustave Doré

Page 46 of "Jeux de vagues" | My dear Choiseul [musical notes] | I think I forgot the corrections above [musical notes] | which are on the proofs | Thank you and all the best | D.

## Richard Strauss – page 156

Dr. Franz Strauss | Garmisch | Zöpperrizstrasse 42 | Garmisch, 13 march 1948 | Dear Sir, | My father in law, the Composer Dr. Richard Strauss, has send me your letter, asking him for a photograph. But I can not answer your question concerning the National Symphonie, as I never heard the titel, I do not know, what you mean. Would it be possible to send us into this dreadful food misery with two boys, the only grandsons of Dr. Strauss some food package, we would be so thankful. | With kindest regards and many thanks | Yours | Alice Strauss | Bavaria | Garmisch

## Mahatma Gandhi – pages 158–159

(Mr. Ronald Duncan) | Dear friend, | I thank you for your pamphlet. The argument appeared to me to be sound so far as it went. Perhaps there is not sufficient emphasis on personal individual actions irrespective of what society does or does not do. Non-violent action does not depend upon another's cooperation. Violent action is ineffective without the cooperation of others. Here both the forces are conceived in terms of the ultimate good of society. | As at Segoan Wardha | Yours sincerely | M. K. Gandhi | 23-12-36

Patna. | March 16, 1947 | Dear friend, | Of course I knew your brother very well indeed. But I plead with you to spare me at the present moment. I must not divide my attention for things great or small. It will be time for me to consider others also if I come out safe from the fire which I am trying to quench. The odds are so great

that the fire may quench me instead of my quenching the fire it. | Yours sincerely | MKGandhi | Solomon Alexander Esq. | Barrister at Law, | 25, Rue Talaat Harb., | Alexandria. | (Egypt)

## Albert Einstein – pages 160–163

Pasadena, 29.11.32 | Dear Mileva | I already thought that something must be wrong with Tetl, as he had not written for so long. There were also several warning signs in his letters. We must come to terms with the fact that he has a hereditary illness, and we must simply accept it as it comes. I have a very low opinion of psychoanalysis, having seen nothing but bad results among our acquaintances. I consider it to be an extremely dangerous fashion and am totally opposed to it. No one will ever be submitted to this kind of treatment with my consent, and under no circumstances will I encourage it. I think it would be good for Tetl if he came to me in Caputh, provided that he doesn't keep going to Berlin. Life there is quiet and peaceful, and my influence on nervous natures is beneficial, thanks to my calm character. The sailing is good too. From 1 April I shall be in Berlin, and for the whole of May in England. From 1 June until October I shall be in Caputh, and Tetl can come if he wants to, and stay as long as he likes. There is this crisis with its terrible unemployment. Things are being dismantled everywhere, and there is no end in sight. One can rely on nothing whatever except one's own talents and good health. Don't worry too much, but take things as they come. Think of all the tragedies that the world has known, and yet everywhere the flowers go on growing and the birds sing. Nature is not interested in the individual, and man must live out his destiny as best he can. I send my best wishes to you and Tetl, Yours | Albert

Those who know their poetry | Are rarely fond of cookery, | But Lisboa the poetess | Has earthly talents nonetheless: | When she set eyes upon the sage, | Immediately she seemed to gauge | His heart did in his stomach beat, | And so she brought him things to eat – | New works of culinary skill | Devised in the kitchens of Brazil. | And so I thank with happy heart | The noble mistress of the art. | Albert Einstein

...the Sacco and Vanzetti affair; ...we are sufficiently aware of how deep the sense of fairness is in the American people to hope that they will not allow a new miscarriage of justice to take place. Would they want to bear, for many years to come, the same burden of anguish and remorse that weighed on France as a consequence of the Dreyfus affair? We hope with all our soul that the Charlotte verdict will not be confirmed. Please accept my best wishes | L. Lévy-Bruhl | J. Hadamard | Léon Brunschvicg | A. Einstein J. Hadamard, professor at the Collège de France, member of the Science Academy; | 25 Rue Jean-Folent, Paris XIV

## Giacomo Puccini – page 164

Signor Duque Estrada | I have acquainted myself with your literary, theatrical work and have registered the good intentions and the quality. A similar subject has already been proposed to me and I refused because I did not feel inclined to work with Roman costumes. From now on I am about to commit myself to a Marie Antoinette, and I absolutely cannot devote myself to or

even think about anything else. I will send your work back to you. Thank you for sending me your libretto. I was also able to appreciate the talent of a man of letters and the passion of a poet. With warmest greetings from Giacomo Puccini | Buenos Aires, 12 July 1905.

## Grigori Rasputin
## Nicholas II of Russia – pages 166–167

Ukase addressed to the Directorate of Imperial and Royal Decorations of Russia. To express our special benevolence, we generously confer the titles of Knights of our Imperial and Royal Orders on the following officers of foreign armies, wishing to decorate with the Order of the White Eagle the Minister of War of France, General Picquart, and the Minister of War of the Austro-Hungarian Empire, Brigadier Franz von Schönaich. We also wish to decorate with the 3rd degree Order of Saint Anne the warrant officer from the Ministry of War of the Netherlands, Captain Raymond Dufour, and with the 3rd degree Order of Saint Stanislas, created for non-Christians, the Chinese subject Sin-Tsai-Lsu-Khin-Shin. We also give orders to the Directorate of Imperial Decorations that the above-mentioned insignia should be given to these new knights, along with their respective certificates | Nicholas | Tsarskoïe Selo, 8 January 1908 | To the Chief of Staff

Eternal peace is not an isolated glimmer of hope but comes from the shining light of heaven. | Grigori

## Mata Hari – pages 170–171

My dear Jean | I am still not leaving tomorrow morning. I have not had time to pack my suitcases. I will send you a little note. All my good wishes. | Yours | Mata Hari | I have paid the rent, the concierge etc. So you can write to me there, but still only as Lady MacLeod. I have not spoken of Mata Hari.

## Pancho Villa
## Emiliano Zapata – pages 172–173

Private correspondence of General Francisco Villa | Pueblo di Meogui, 7 May 1920 | Mr W. J. Ougtley, President of the Potosi Mining Company, Santa Eulalia, Chile | Respected Sir | All the mining companies in this region of the State benefit from my guarantees, which are most substantial and most complete, thanks to the forces under my command, and all can devote themselves with total confidence to their work. These companies thank me for the guarantees which I give them so that their affairs may function at full capacity, and they give me their support with funds destined for the maintenance of my forces. The Potosi Mining Co. – of which you are president – is a business of very great importance for this State, and if you are working without any problems this is due to the guarantees given to you by my forces. I could still prove to you that other factions are not in a position to guarantee you the same protection. It is therefore right that you should help me, on the understanding that I will provide you with safe-conduct. To this effect, I have authorized W. S. Harrison to arrange this matter with you. I need to inform you that the sum I am asking you for is 50,000 (fifty thousand dollars) dollars. With no other subject-matter, I am your affectionate servant. Francisco Villa

Mexican Republic – Liberation Army of South and Centre | To General Genovevo de la O. in his camp. The village of Ocotepec has complained about the following persons: Juan Cervantes, Atilano García, Lorenzo Balderas, Leandro García and Manuel Paredes, who are said to have been causing damage and appear to have been responsible for the death of Paulino López, a neighbour from the aforementioned village. I therefore urgently advise you to discipline these individuals, because such abuses are not to be tolerated, and to prosecute them so that their guilt can be established. I am communicating this to you so that you may take cognizance of it and act accordingly. Reform, Liberty, Justice and Law. | Revolutionary camp at Morelos, 1 April 1913. | General-in-Chief of Army of South and Centre. | Emiliano Zapata

### LENIN | JOSEPH STALIN – PAGES 174–175

Confidential doc. No. 373 | Communiqué from General Staff of Supreme Command No. 0508 | 25 December 1941, Moscow | The General Staff of Supreme Command has DETERMINED: In view of the extremely important missions which have fallen to the 27th Army Corps, the said Corps shall be renamed the 4th Campaign Army. Incorporated into the 4th Campaign Army will be the 23rd, 33rd, 332nd, 249th, 257th, 358th, 360th infantry divisions. As from 1 January 1942, the salaries of all levels of officers (high-ranking, middle-ranking and low-ranking) of the 4th Campaign Army will be increased by one hundred and fifty per cent, and those of the rank and file troops will be doubled, in accordance with military regulations. Bring to the attention of all units of the 4th Campaign Army. General Staff of Supreme Command | J. Stalin | B. Chaporchnikov

To lawyer | Dr Huber | Kirchstrasse 17 – Rohrschach (Canton Sankt Gallen) Dear Comrade | Allow me to highly recommend the bearer of this message, Comrade Bagotsky, and to ask you to help him with your advice. Comrade Bagotsky is a member of the Social Democratic Workers' party of Russia N. | On behalf of the Central Committee of the Social Democratic Workers' party of Russia | Lenin | V.I. Ulianov in Sörenberg (Canton Lucerne) | Greetings from the party | V. I. Ulianov

### MARCEL PROUST – PAGES 177–181

...made me meet her. But that happened every day, and there was every reason to fear that she was content to reply to my greetings from afar. So much so that it ~~could~~ would go on like this all through the season without my getting any further.... Shortly after the party, one morning when it was almost cold and it had been raining, I was accosted on the 'front' by a girl in red wearing a close-fitting toque and carrying a fur muff, completely different from the girl I had met at Elstir's party – one would have said this was ~~not towards~~ a sketch in which it was impossible to recognize her as the same person, ~~so well that she noticed~~ an operation that I just about attempted, though after a moment of surprise that did not escape her. 'What weather,' she said. 'So you don't do anything here? We never see you at golf, or at the Casino balls; ~~but to encourage you~~ you don't go riding either. How bored you must be. I can see that you're not like me, I love all sports!'

Friday evening, 9 September 1904 | Dear Monsieur de Binibuls | I did not come this evening since said. And so out, and so crisis. And so say if want me Sunday evening (leaving me the chance not to come till Monday if suffering too much). But as letters do not arrive Sunday daytime, send little telegram so that know. - Cwied reading sufferings of my Buncht. How would like to be able to make suffer naughty baddie that tortures you. When Clovis heard the tale of Christ's Passion, he rose, seized his axe, and cried: 'If I had been there with my brave Franks, that would not have happened, or I would have avenged your sufferings.' Which is really pony on the part of the wicked king so and so. But I can't even say that because I could not have prevented and would not know who to punish. not even old P'who wears on her head plumes which would be in place on hearses and as far as decorations, in between the cross of the hundred guards and the blue ribbon of the Children of Mary' (R. de Montesquiou). You know he is finishing a book which is divided into two parts. I) the beauty that does not allow its noble old age to be seen: the Comtesse de Castiglione; and II) the ugliness that exhibits its decrepitude: old P[otocka], a work of which he gave a foretaste the other day in a letter to the Siècle. In Saint Moritz, as someone had lost a superb pair of opera glasses, he said it must be M. de Rothschild – or Mr. Lambert – or M. Ephrussi – or M. Fould. And the following day he said: I had aimed too high, it was M. Untermayer, below M. Mayer, less than M. Mayer, think what it is.

Dear Binibuls, I wish the case of my memory was richer so that I could distract dear little sickie. But know nothing. Just this however. Meyer is as if drunk. He has 'announced' his marriage to all the sovereigns or at least the dukes. His witnesses will be the Dukes of Luynes and Uzès. He met Barrès and told him: I am leaving for Versailles, would you like me to give your regards to my cousin Louis XIV? He wrote to old Brancovan that he was going to make all the Fitz-James come to life, and he's leave the Gaul to his fiancée's brother whom he will attach there while he's still alive. And other idiocies of that kind. He who more pitifully another time told us about his duel, making excuses for his famous display: 'What do you expect, I thought I was going to find a gentleman, and instead I found myself facing a kind of lunatic who could have killed me!' (a saying worthy of M. Jourdain, the other *bourgeois gentilhomme* who also insisted on saving his skin) – It's the same duel about which he said: 'For that to be forgotten, it'll take at least ten years – or a war.' But you know all that, and little kissie of hello from birnuls. At Larsue's (from where crisis and crisis) they played such lovely musicke and everybody and everybody and it was. Because down here all soul. And Antoine Bourbesco said that it was similar to Mozart trios (?).

Dear friend | Your second letter (charming and I thank you for it a thousand times) having corrected what was certainly the erroneous interpretation I had made of your first, we shall come to this; I asked you whether I would be acting against your wishes (to which I already bowed in advance) if I put publication of the 2nd and 3rd parts in the hands of the NRF. You replied through M. Brun that you wanted them to be published by you. And so that is agreed, at least for the first edition. Who wrote that touching doggerel: 'With a word the storm starts, with a word the storm ends, and we finish by being much closer friends.' Allow me

to hope that these lines may apply to our relationship as well, and do please believe me when I say how grateful I am for your so sensitive and friendly letter, and accept my feelings of affectionate devotion | Marcel Proust | What you say about not printing any more since December upsets and above all astonishes me. It was precisely then that the word, I might even say the sensation, began to spread, precisely then that the critics wrote articles of which even the least pleasant have nevertheless 'travelled'. (Thus I was personally very disappointed by Chaumeix's article, but thanks to some well-placed witnesses, I have been able to learn about the effect it has had in St Petersburg and Bucharest and other places too.) As for the manner in which subsequent volumes might be published by the *Nouvelle Revue Française*, you will tell me your views.

### HENRI MATISSE – PAGE 183

silver white | yellow ochre | red ochre | cadmium or yellow chrome | orange chrome | vermilion | ordinary Siena | burnt Siena | ultramarine blue | emerald green | bright red | ivory black | Matisse | 132 Bd Montparnasse Paris | post

### WINSTON CHURCHILL – PAGE 184

Dear Mr. Cappes. | By all means make the announcement at your convenience and keep the advertisement back until this has been done. Some unauthorized paragraphs have been circulated in the press, but I do not propose to send any notice elsewhere | Yours very truly | Winston S. Churchill | 2 September 1902

### GUILLAUME APOLLINAIRE
### MARIE LAURENCIN – PAGES 186–187

10 January 1956 | Dear Madame and Friend | How can I thank you for those extraordinary items 'unknown to the addressee'? How are you? As you see, I have at last got my apartment back. When you are able to, you must come and see your husband's books and the care that I have taken of them – Believe me | Yours | Marie Laurencin

Dear friend | I am ill and have not been able to write my column about novels. Next month you shall have your [...] as detailed and complete as I can make it. Your book is very beautiful. It is powerful, engaging and poetic. I admire your imagination where everything is grace and tenderness, your culture so refined and your wit delightful. I very much like Arlequin, a charming idea, and I regret not being able at all to taste this liqueur. My publisher has dealt very stupidly with you, because I showed him your letter for the address, but emphasized that the book should be sent at my expense. He sent it to you with a demand for payment. As soon as I go out, I shall send you the three francs delivery charge, and we shall be quits and you will forgive me. If your success allows the prospect of a new edition, let me know: I know some lovers of literature who, seduced by the final lists, would I think be willing to subscribe. Marie has neuralgia which refuses to yield to any remedy. She is working a lot and is finishing a picture that is admirable in tone and composition. You offered to introduce me to some influential people in the editorial offices and publishing houses. Do so, dear friend, as you would be doing me a favour. Having retired to Passy, I am working a lot and seeing very few people. Max Jacob seems to have renounced my friendship, and Passy seems to him to be too far away. For my part, I find that there is no comparison between Montmartre and my new environment, which wins from every angle. | I am your very devoted friend | Guillaume Apollinaire

## Colette – pages 194–195

O dear Jef, how I love this second volume! What beautiful work from a man of letters! Great man, it seems to me that I would say it even better to you if you came to see us. The sitting of the seated, and what pleasure I take in a writer who penetrates the femininity of men! When are you coming? Both of us embrace you. | Colette

Formulae 'Her nose, her eyes, her mouth and her ears...' (sounds familiar). They have big noses, for a while, because they uncover their ears, and also because they have damnably slimmed. Such beauty as we have, we who are fifteen or twenty years older, known to be delightfully snub-nosed, short-lipped, a dimple at each corner of the mouth, and Fragonardish as anything, we find it – if we have left it alone for five or six months – big, bony, with the profile of a Luxembourg horse. How did that nose, that sad lip grow, and that high cheekbone of a Mongol tyrant become so long? And it's taken on a big eye, you know. An eye that rolls like a forgotten egg at the bottom of a nest. An eye which confirms its dreadful form as an organ: 'the eyeball'.... And what sort of gums does it reveal to us, our Beauty, when it laughs? Where did it get hold of so many gums? The gums of a pregnant woman in her ninth month. It is not, Lord, possible that we saw it before, such a steppe of cheek between the ear and the nose! Actually, it has changed ears – turn away for a moment from the flat ear, thin and made up – you remember its little edible ear, half veiled by untidy blonde hair? Yes, untidy, my memory is accurate. | Untidy – hair – strange terms, which we risk with modesty before a pale brass helmet, fashioned in irremovable snails, in coagulated waves which not even the breeze can budge? Oh! This coiffure à la once-and-for-all! These large ripple marks that no tide can wipe away! If I want to laugh about it, I must recall a portrait painted once by Marguerite Moreno: 'She wore a wig of sculpted rosewood, laid out in a row of winkles at the front, and a thousand droppings on the nape....' But now that I have laughed, I sit down and weep. Because I expected to console myself with the figure of our Beauty of today, relieved of its carnal weight.... But I cannot console myself. No, I do not like, under the satin veil, to see so clearly the projection of the aborted fins, the hard shoulder blades. No, I do not like, when my former Fragonard crosses a salon, the perceptible play beneath dress and girdle of the bones of its pelvis. Where are the sweet haunches, where, Verlaine, the 'joyous buttocks'? It was not so long ago that I heard, as our blonde passed by, the clicks of the tongue, the eulogies of the horse dealers, which offend and flatter beautiful women. But it is clear that in speaking of her, a cold and robust young man replied: 'Ah no, very little for me. You come away full of bruises up to the iliac bones...' | You will tell me that I am an expert.... Exactly. An 'expert' who, from the height of her seventy-two kilos, listens to the coughing of emaciated youth, looks at the bosoms floating, the stomachs dropping, and swarming

between death and life a host of stars exhausted by grapefruit without sugar, black coffee, *plié* with lemon, salad and other illusions. You know the story of the American woman from whom her firm demanded two more kilos? At first she burst into tears, threw herself onto a cream cake, then a boiled egg, and she stammered through her sobs: 'It's eighteen months since I last tasted an egg.' | The disease is not so old that one cannot trace its source. The sabotage and the great curse on the flesh began with the breasts. Without mentioning maniacs, mental or physical androgynes who couldn't care less about fashion, woman is easily infuriated by her mammary wealth. In thirty years, I have heard passed from mouth to ear formulaic conjurations, recipes to make you tremble, both town and country: 'Make yourself a mattress of parsley, and you lie on it for thirty days....' 'At night you put your breasts on ice, and gradually it kills them off....' 'You take your breast, like this, you fold it from top to bottom, and then you wrap yourself in a strip of rubber that goes under your arms and twice round your body. That dries up the breast, and it shrinks to nothing....' 'Of course it's not worth having surgery....' They talk about it as if it was like treating a persistent cold – or lancing an abscess. It is in order to "have it", the sought-after bosom, that mad women have invented slimming. But they did not realize that there is no such thing as a pretty bosom on a thin body. They did not foresee that the breast, deprived of its comfortable base, its settled voluptuousness, its necessary luxury – a bit of fat – returns to the teat. Unless, overmuscled by certain sports, the lifting of heavy weights, for example, it opts to join the opposite sex and takes on the shape of a masculine nipple, flat and quadrangular. [...] I shall stop. What smiles of hope light up at these words on the faces of my readers... |...Flat, quadrangular, *pliés*, emptied, eliminated, not to say amputated, you return like proud exiles, to the next change of regime, you who were the flower, the fruit, the summit visited by the dawn, you, 'breasts elastic and light | breasts of the unrivalled beauty....' | Colette S.H. – Yes, my readers can write to me at *Marianne*.

## Pablo Picasso – page 199

Vallauris, 6 June 1953, a.m. | My dear Ascher | This is Monsieur Georges Masson who has come on my behalf to talk to you about the Exhibition in Vallauris. | You will be the kind friend that you are | I hope to see you soon here or in Paris | All the best | Picasso

## Ezra Pound | William Butler Yeats – pages 200–201

Stone Cottage | Coleman's Hatch | Sussex | Dear Mr. Herts | On receiving your letter, I wrote to Mr. Watt. | I have received from him the enclosed letter which explains itself. | Yours, | W. B. Yeats | p.p. E. P

13 April | Edtr|Everyman | (" trusting you may find space for ") | I shd. be deeply interested in learning from you or your reviewer where there is any trace of personal antipathy in my "ABC of Economics". And I defy either of you to name a single line in which any such trace of personal feeling is present. | I admit a thoroughly impersonal feeling not only of antipathy, but of contempt for pretended leaders who refuse to look facts in the eye , and who suppress for decade after

decade the discussion of the fundamentals of economics. | Can you indicate to me any single British daily paper which has openly stated the cause of recurrent crisis ? | Or which has admitted that every factory creates prices faster than it distributes the power to buy ? | An antipathy to men who advocate starvation and sabotage has no need of being personal. Yrs. Very truly | Ezra Pound

## Samuel Beckett – pages 202–203

Paris 21.5.65 | Dear Nino Frank | I have received your letter with the article. I am very sorry that you wrote it. I never give interviews, but never. I thought we were simply having a chat, as friend to friend. How could you have done that without talking to me about it first? It makes me sick. Ah, I can tell you, I could have done without that. | Sam Beckett

## Maurice Utrillo – page 205

I asked God to give me Lucie Valore as my wife, and He answered my prayer. | Maurice Utrillo, V, 28-8-1955

## T. E. Lawrence – page 207

Plymouth 12. X. 22 | Dear Benham | I have both your letters, and no *Seven Pillars*. Group Captain Nichol, who said he was sending it back at once, has let me down. It shall follow this letter as soon as it arrives. What a to-do about a wretched book! I assure you, solemnly, that it is not worth any trouble at all. | Yours ever | T. E. Shaw

## Frank Lloyd Wright
## Le Corbusier – pages 208–209

America claims that I make philosophical comments. Well, perhaps in this book there really is a little glance in the direction of wisdom. | To M. Renato Almeida, one of the nicest Brazilians in Rio, December 1929 | Le Corbusier

Dear Anne : Such a nice little letter. | The first to grandfather. And this is the first to grandaughter. She seems to be distinguishing herself as a good actress, letting the glamour girl slide. And I am glad of that. We will be seeing you soon in L. A. of all places. I hope that we can see something of you and go places together a little. We are quite well and hopeful as usual but trying to keep off the war, etc. Give my love to your mother (Taffy at the studio door, etc.) with all affection from | Grandfather | Frank Lloyd Wright | March 21 st, 1944. | And now we've lost your address and must send this care of Lloyd

## Leon Trotsky – page 213

Dear "Sra." Frida, It seems to me that you did'nt receive my cards*) it is the only one reason why I permitted me to cable yesterday. Can you be so kind and send the card to D. Hidalgo? I dont have his adress (la direccion) It rains. It rains. My best thanks and greetings to D. D. and to yourself. Yours | L. Trotsky

P. S. Do you see Natalia ? What about Cristina ? Yours L. T. *) Every thing must be send thruw two or three intermodiarys... Nothing is sure (excuse my english, please) (excuse the two inks)

### DIEGO RIVERA
### PABLO NERUDA – PAGES 214–215

America, I do not invoke your name in vain | When
I hold the sword to the heart, | When I endure the leak
in the soul, | When through the windows | a new day
of yours penetrates me | I am in the light that produces
me, | I live in the shadow that determines me, | I sleep
and awake in your essential dawn: | sweet as the
grapes and also terrible | bringer of sugar and of
punishment, | soaked in the sperm of your species, |
suckled in the blood of your heritage. | Pablo Neruda |
Santiago in Chile | Diego Rivera

### FERNANDO PESSOA – PAGES 216–217

To Her Excellency Madame Ophelia Queiroz |
An abject and miserable individual named Fernando
Pessoa, my dear and very special friend, has given me
the task of communicating to Your Excellency –
given the fact that his mental state prevents him from
communicating anything at all including a dried pea
(prototype of obedience and discipline) – that Your
Excellency is forbidden: (1) to weigh fewer grams
(2) to eat little (3) to sleep little (4) to have fever
(5) to think about the individual in question. For my
part, in my capacity as sincere and intimate friend of
this good-for-nothing, for whom (for a great sacrifice)
I have taken on the task of conveying this message,
I would advise Your Excellency to grasp the mental
image which you will have chanced to build of the
individual in question (and the very mention of whom
is soiling this relatively white piece of paper), and to
throw this mental image down the sink, because of
the fact that it is physically impossible to send to this
well-merited destination the falsely human entity to
which he would aspire if there were any justice in the
world. Greetings to Your Excellency from | Alvaro de
Campos | Naval Engineer | Abel, 25/9/1929

### JEAN COCTEAU – PAGES 218–220

The ~~mystic~~ personality, the wingspan, ~~the de Chirico
large format~~ of our painter his equine figure. his
plaster mask with teeth of gold, his gruff accent, ~~in
brief~~ – his real presence ~~with teeth of gold~~, in flesh and
bone ~~his equine presence~~ | ~~pace the teeth of gold~~, his
presence painted or written in brief this 'large format'
makes small everything ~~that one~~ that one can set
against him that is better painted, more original,
more solid ~~more aggressive more serious~~ more
haunted, more ~~disturbing~~ violent, more ~~rich~~ integral,
stormy, ~~in enigmas~~ | ~~discovered~~ and ~~make~~ makes ~~some
works where he is puzzling and~~ of an attitude which
revolts ~~so full of excessive zeal~~ his old supporters,
of a ~~direction~~ new attitude which he has adopted,
something ~~venerable~~ singular and intriguing at the
same time, in a sphere that is all in all far less seductive
than ~~his mysterious architectures~~ | ~~his myths~~ | ~~his
mythology~~ | ~~manias~~ | ~~and his meetings of objects~~ |
~~familiar accessories~~ the sorcery of his first paintings.

Egoism | Life is an arena where the athletes compete |
Where one throws the discus, where horses paw the
ground | One sees there lions dancing to the sound of
flutes | And negroes suffering new tortures | But what
does the azure or the shining discus matter | The wild
ones bent on savage meals | And the painted singer
motionless on my right | I am the Emperor who does
not look.

### FEDERICO GARCÍA LORCA – PAGES 224–225

Dear Guillermo: Do not treat me as a 'bad guy', and
hear my reasons. I am correcting proofs of my books
and I spend whole hours working on a poem, only to
leave it as it wishes itself to be. I've been suffering from
flu all week. What's more, I did not know what to send
you. Everything that I am producing these days is quite
long, but I will copy out for you some prose dialogues
that I have and that might suit La Gaceta. Buster
Keaton dialogue, photograph dialogues etc. I prefer
to publish prose. I am sending some essays in prose
to the Revista de Occidente, and I would like to begin
in this way in La Gaceta. Would that suit you? Or do you
prefer the poet? It's for that reason that I have not sent
you anything. La Tarjeta Iberica will be sent when
something interesting is produced. Do not forget to
write to me; the letters fill me with immense joy and
affection. And so why are you provoking me? Ah,
perfidious Guillermo! I shall soon take revenge on you!
And the article on the Ode? If you have received it, let
me have it, as I am very anxious to read it. Farewell,
Guillermito. You will soon receive my original material
for La Gaceta. Meanwhile, lots of love, | Federico. |
Write to me!

### ANTOINE DE SAINT-EXUPÉRY –
### PAGES 230–231

Dear friend, | I had completely forgotten, this evening,
a dinner of some importance for my personal affairs,
but I find it in my notebook. I'm sure you will not
be offended if we put off till tomorrow evening,
for example, our dinner at your place. And I hope
that you will kindly telephone me tomorrow morning
to talk about it. Please give my apologies to Madame
Char and trust in my friendship | Antoine de
Saint-Exupéry

### GIUSEPPE TOMASI DI LAMPEDUSA – PAGE 235

Palermo | 31 March 1956 | Via Butera 28 | Dearest Guido.
| There is no excuse for my prolonged silence, and I
know it. All that I can do is throw myself on your mercy
and promise not to sin again. I was very happy to
receive the announcement a few days ago of your
sister's marriage: I should have liked to congratulate
the young couple and present my compliments to
them directly, but I don't know their address and
so I ask you to do this on my behalf. As regards the
dreadful news that you have given me about your
health, I am very sad, and I beg you not to try, in
revenge, to delay giving me better news, which I hope
for and am confident of. | My health is quite good;
thanks to some sensible treatment, I have slimmed
a lot and have lost 18 kilos: an advantage that is not
only aesthetic but also healthy, because I feel more
svelte and the heart gets less tired. My wife is well
too, although she gives herself a lot of work for
psychoanalysis. She has been made vice-president
of the Italian Society, and at present she is in London,
to commemorate Freud's centenary. | The house
(except for the terrace overlooking the sea, which has
been paved and redone, as I think I've already told you)
is in exactly the same state as when you saw it: we
lacked the will, need (and money) to restore the
dilapidated rooms. As you can see, there doesn't
seem to be anything important to tell you about, but
in actual fact two very important events have occurred
(or, to be precise, are about to occur): 1) I have written a

novel; 2) we are going to adopt a son. | I will begin with
the first and less important item. I have no cousins on
the paternal side, by which I mean first cousins. On the
other hand, I have three on my mother's side. For some
years now, these three cousins have been engaged in
intensive artistic activity: one has been busy with
etchings and he has been very successful, both with
the public and with the critics, holding exhibitions in
Rome and Milan. Another, who had been painting all
his life as a dilettante, has at the age of over sixty held
a one-man exhibition: he sold all his paintings in one
week and there he is now, proclaimed as a great artist.
The third (the youngest, but he is 53) has become an
author and printed a small volume of poetry: he sent
a copy to the terrible Eugenio Montale and, by return
of post, he received a letter which dubbed him a
genius; he was awarded a literary prize at S. Pellegrino,
and his poetry is to be published next month by
Mondadori, with a preface by Montale; interviews
in the papers, photograph in Epoca (July 1954) – an
avalanche (buy the volume when it comes out: Lucio
Piccolo, Canti barocchi). | Although I love these cousins
dearly (especially the last two), I must confess that
I felt cut to the quick: I was sure that I was no more
stupid than they were. So much so that I sat down
at my little table and wrote a novel: to be more precise,
three long novellas interlinked. I sent the typescript
to Mondadori with the support of my already
illustrious cousin Piccolo, and a month ago, to my great
surprise...my book was accepted by Mondadori for the
[series] 'Medusa of the Italians'! It goes without saying
that when it is published (i.e. not straight away) you
will be among the first to receive a copy with a
dedication from the author. I imagine that the book
will please you. It will be historical, and will reveal
nothing sensational, but rather the emotional and
political reactions of a Sicilian nobleman to the
Expedition of a Thousand and the fall of the Bourbons.
The hero is the 'Prince of Salina' – a thin disguise for
the Prince of Lampedusa, my great-grandfather. But
the friends who have read the book tell me that the
Prince of Salina has a devilishly close resemblance
to me. I am flattered, because I think he is rather nice.
The whole book is ironic, but not devoid of cruelty.
It has to be read very closely, because every word
is carefully chosen, and every episode has a hidden
meaning. Everyone comes out of it badly; the Prince
and his enterprising nephew, the Bourbon supporters
and the Liberals, and especially Sicily in 1860.
It contains a lot of my personal memories and the
description of certain places is absolutely authentic.
I think it is not too badly written, and I have noticed
that certain sentences have become sayings among
the three or four people who have read it. For example:
description of the garden of a villa near Palermo: 'from
each clump emanated the sensation of a desire for
beauty, swiftly diminished by indolence.' | I see there
is no more room for the story of the adoption. In any
case, it is very long, a real novel. I shall start writing it
straight away and you will receive it promptly. | My
affectionate greetings to you | Your Giuseppe.
To Mr Guido Lajolo

### ERNEST HEMINGWAY – PAGE 237

Finca Vigia, San Francisco de Paula, Cuba | April 10 1959
| Dear Mr. Peterson | Thank you for the letter and the
book of poems. Will do what you ask. Please give my
best to Tom and tell him, I missed him there twice but
will try again the next time I'm in Miami. When I got

home here Easter Sunday, found galleys of Eastman the *Sat. Review* had sent asking me to answer (hoping to get newsworthy I guess). For a while I thought of saying I hoped writing that shit made him feel better about what really happened to him and what Max Perkins really said, but then I thought why should I do even that. Incidentally the *Sat. Review* man who wrote the *Esquire* piece last year (if you saw it) was then working for Arnold Gingrich of *Esquire*. I didn't answer that one either. Hope this isn't a bad sign. I certainly can't claim to be a native of Michigan – was nearly 4 weeks old when went there for the first time. I wish Castro luck too. He's got it rough right now. Have been away 6 months and am swamped with stuff. But wanted to answer your letter before it got into the permanent MUST BE ANSWERED AT ONCE pile. | Best luck always | Ernest Hemingway

## BORIS PASTERNAK – PAGE 241

To Mr. K. Robert Whittemore | 18 Febr. 1959. | I am really very busy and not always overhappy at all. And in this need and sorrow and haste, I cannot devise wishes for you that would not be commonplace and banal. I wish you not to be like me. I wish you, in your seeking to be good to people around you, not to engender and multiply colliding suffering of your next or dear ones, crossing each other. This is my only misfortune and life torment. | B. Pasternak | At the one of my heaviest days.

## RENÉ MAGRITTE
## PAUL DELVAUX – PAGES 242–243

René Magritte | Jette | Brussels | 135 rue Esseghem | 17-12-53 | Monsieur, | I have just received your letter of 5-11-53, and I thank you for the interest you have shown. | I can send you: 1) different photographs of my pictures – the photographer asks me for one dollar per photo. 2) a small drawing: 10 dollars, a small gouache painting: 20 dollars. Write and tell me what you want, and put in your envelope the dollar bills that correspond to the value of what you want to acquire. For more security, send the letter to me by registered post – and I shall send to you, also by registered post, whatever you have chosen. Yours sincerely | René Magritte

Boisfort 20-4-70 | My dear Jules | Thank you for your nice letter which has given me the greatest pleasure. Thank you also for everything you say. It's a real shame that Buenos Aires is such a long way away! But our old friendship will remain intact in spite of the distance. My wife and I send you as well as your wife our old and sincere affection. Perhaps you will soon come to Europe? | Yours, Paul

## JORGE LUIS BORGES – PAGES 244–245

Buenos Aires, December 1957 | Dear friend, | I want to tell you that I am very grateful to you for your generous words and I send you my best wishes for a happy and prosperous 1958 | J. L. Borges | Maipu 994

Sr, Horacio E. Ratti | Friend | Forgive me for the lateness of this reply. I am utterly lazy when it comes to writing letters and also everything else that is not letters. I think I now remember that I must have a portrait of you, in a group of rustic cavaliers with our late, very

remarkable López Merino. I like your two texts, more the one entitled <u>Landscape</u> than the other <u>Evocation</u>. It seems to me (if you'll permit me to express an opinion, with the right to be wrong, of course) that perhaps you have given way, in this second text, to the easy option of defining a writer by his own words and by images which belong to him alone. The piece <u>Landscape</u> is more beautiful, to my taste, and reflects you better. I will take them both to <u>Sintesis</u> in the next few days. I shake you warmly by the hand | Jorge Luis Borges | A|C Hotel Helder | calle Rivadavia 857, Buenos Aires.

## WALT DISNEY – PAGES 246–247

Sr. J. Sá Róris | Copacabana Palace | Praça S. Dumont 16 | Rio de Janeiro | Gávea | September 7, 1941 | Rio de Janeiro | Dear Sr. Róris : | May I express my thanks for your gift of records and sheet music of some of your songs. Rest assured that we will listen to them upon our return to the studio. | Cordially | Walt Disney

## JACK KEROUAC – PAGES 256–257

A page from my personal notebook – Jack Kerouac I was very rich – He also thought same of poor Jean-Paul Sartre ! – Don't they realize the money all goes to the Micheners + Wouks + Alexander Kings for God's sake ? – No, + instead they give me those full envious glances

---

+ don't believe when I protest my "innocence" at riches – if I lived a normal married life in the world I'd be broke already.

---

As it is, what I have saved amounts to only 4 years living expenses – Paul himself made more money than I did last year – so what's all the evil fuss? Because I stay home in my study instead of running around "working"? That's what it is

## JOHN F. KENNEDY
## JACQUELINE KENNEDY – PAGES 258–259

October 14, 1955 | Mr. John F. Kennedy | 277 Park Avenue. Apt. 8-G | New York 17, New York | Dear Jack: | According to our records, you spent the following amounts during the nine months ended September 30, 1955:

| | | |
|---|---|---|
| Travel and hotel | $ 7,462 | |
| Medical | 20,485 | |
| Department stores | 11,704 | |
| Household expenses | 4,244 | |
| Automobile | 2,47 | Tom: This is incorrect. I believe Dad paid for this by check – Jack |
| Insurance | 0,37 | |
| Cash withdrawals | 1,04 | |
| Miscellaneous | 4,652 | |
| | $ 52,439 | |

If you would like more details on any of the above items, kindly let us know. | Sincerely yours | Thomas J. Walsh

June 23, 1964 | Justice and Mrs. Arthur Goldberg | 2911 Albemarle street, N W. | Washington, D.C. | Dear Justice and Mrs. Goldberg | The President's family and I are deeply appreciative of your generous contribution

to the John Fitzgerald Kennedy Library in Boston, Massachussets. It was the President's expressed hope that someday a library might be built and he had planned to devote a great deal of his future time to such a project. The Library will serve as a perpetual memorial to the President and your support helps tremendously toward making our goal a reality. | Sincerely | Jacqueline Kennedy

## FEDERICO FELLINI – PAGE 260

Roma Feb. 1992 | Dear Baldwin | I have received your "simpatica" letter in which you present to me in a very enthusiastic way Miss or Madam Jutta Wubbe. | All right I will consider with particular attention your recommandation. I would like to have some other photos of the talented lady. Can you tell her to send me someone? | Good luck to you, dear friend. How's going? I hope very well and to have the chance to see you soon. | Friendly, | F. Fellini

# BIBLIOGRAPHY

**Albrecht, Otto Edwin, Herbert Cahoon, and Douglas C. Ewing,** *The Mary Flagler Cary Music Collection: Printed Books and Music, Manuscripts, Autograph Letters, Documents, Portraits,* New York: Pierpont Morgan Library, 1970

*Autograph Letters & Manuscripts: Major Acquisitions of the Pierpont Morgan Library, 1924–1974,* New York: Pierpont Morgan Library, 1974

**Ayala, Roseline de, and Jean-Pierre Guéno,** *Les Plus Beaux Récits de voyage,* Paris: La Martinière, 2002

*Les Plus Beaux Manuscrits de la littérature française,* Paris: La Martinière, 2000

*Les Plus Belles Lettres illustrées,* Paris: La Martinière, 1998

*Les Plus Beaux Manuscrits de femmes,* Paris: La Martinière, 2003

*L'Enfance de l'art,* Paris: La Martinière, 1999

**Benjamin, Mary A.,** *Autographs: A Key to Collecting,* New York: Bowker, 1946; rev. ed., 1963

**Bérard, Auguste Simon Louis, et al.,** *Isographie des hommes célèbres, ou collection de fac-similés de lettres autographes et de signatures,* 4 vols, Paris, 1828–43

**Berkeley, Edmund, Jr, Herbert E. Klingelhofer, and Kenneth W. Rendell,** *Autographs and Manuscripts: A Collector's Manual,* New York: Scribner's, 1978

**Blatt, Marvin B., and Norman Schwab,** *Seeing Double: The Autopen Guide,* North Babylon, NY: La La Ltd, 1986

*Books and Manuscripts from the Heinemann Collection,* New York: Pierpont Morgan Library, 1963

**Bresslau, Harry,** *Handbuch der Urkundenlehre,* 3rd ed., Berlin: Walter de Gruyter, 1958

*British Autography: A Collection of Facsimiles of the Hand Writing of Royal and Illustrious Personages, with their Authentic Portraits,* 3 vols, London: J. Thane, 1788–93

**Budan, E.,** *L'Amatore D'Autografi,* Milan: Ulrico Hoepli, 1900

**Cahoon, Herbert, Thomas V. Lange, and Charles Ryskamp,** *American Literary Autographs from Washington Irving to Henry James,* New York: Dover Publications in association with the Pierpont Morgan Library, 1977

**Camner, James, and Neale Lanigan Jr,** *Film Autographs, 1894–1941,* New Jersey: Camner, 1978

**Cantagrel, Gilles,** *Les Plus beaux manuscrits de la musique classique,* Paris: La Martinière, 2003

**Castaing, Frédéric,** *Signatures,* Vallauris: Atout, 1998

**Charavay, Étienne,** *Inventaire des autographes et des Documents historiques composant la collection M. Benjamin Fillon,* Paris: Étienne Charavay and Frederic Naylor, 1877

*Catalogue de la précieuse collection d'autographes composant le cabinet de M. Alfred Bovet,* 3 vols, Paris: Étienne Charavay, 1884–85

**Chauleur, André, and Roger Druet,** *De Dagobert à de Gaulle – Écritures de la France,* Paris: Dessin et Tolra, 1985

**Conches, F. Feuillet de,** *Causeries d'un Curieux. Variétés d'histoire et d'art,* Paris: Henri Plon, 1892

**Corrêa do Lago, Pedro,** *Documentos e Autógrafos Brasileiros na Coleção Pedro Corrêa do Lago,* Rio de Janeiro: Salamandra, 1997

*O Século XIX nos Documentos Latino Americanos,* Rio de Janeiro: Capivara, 2004

**Courvoisier, Dominique, ed.,** *Manuscrits du Moyen Âge et Manuscrits littéraires modernes,* Paris: Societé des Manuscrits des assureurs français, 2001

**Czwiklitzer, Christophe,** *Lettres autographes de peintres et sculpteurs du XVe siècle à nos jours,* Basel: Éditions Art, 1976

**Elvers, Rudolph, and Alain Moirandat,** *Bünte Blatter, Klaus Mecklenburg zum 23 Febuar 2003,* Basel: Moirandat, 2000

**Fontaine, P.-J.,** *Manuel de l'amateur d'autographes,* Paris, 1836

**Friedenthal, Richard, ed.,** *Letters of the Great Artists, Vol 1: From Ghiberti to Gainsborough,* London: Thames & Hudson, 1963

*Letters of the Great Artists, Vol. 2: From Blake to Pollock,* London: Thames & Hudson, 1963

**Gaucheron, Roger, ed.,** *Les Lettres, autographes et manuscrits de la collection de Henri de Rothschild,* Paris: Morgan & Rahir, 1924

**Geigy-Hagenbach, Karl,** *Album von Handschriften berühmter Persönlichkeiten vom Mittelalter bis zur Neuzeit,* Basel, 1925

**Gerigk, Herbert,** *Neue Liebe zu alten Schriften. Vom Autogrammjäger zum Autographensammler,* Stuttgart: Deutsche Verlags-Anstalt, 1974

**Gerstenberg, Walter, and Martin Hürlimann,** *Composers' Autographs, trans. Ernst Roth,* 2 vols, Teaneck, NJ: Fairleigh Dickinson University Press, 1968

**Hamilton, Charles,** *Collecting Autographs and Manuscripts,* Norman, OK: University of Oklahoma Press, 1961

*The Robot that Helped to Make a President,* New York, 1965

*Scribblers and Scoundrels,* New York: Paul S. Eriksson, 1968

*The Book of Autographs,* New York: Simon & Schuster, 1978

*The Signature of America,* New York: Harper & Row, 1979

*Great Forgers and Famous Fakes,* New York: Crown, 1980

*American Autographs,* 2 vols, Norman, OK: University of Oklahoma Press, 1983

**Harris, Robert,** *Selling Hitler,* London: Faber & Faber, 1986

**Harrison, Wilson R.,** *Suspect Documents: Their Scientific Examination,* London: Sweet and Maxwell, 1958

*Forgery Detection: A Practical Guide,* New York: Praeger, 1963

**Hay, Louis,** *Le Manuscrit des écrivains,* Paris: Hachette-CNRS, 1993

**Hector, Leonard Charles,** *The Handwriting of English Documents,* 2nd ed., London: E. Arnold, 1966

**Henn, Walter, Dieter Hoffmann, and Brigitte Salmen,** *Die Handschrift des Künstlers: Bilder und Briefe von Caspar David Friedrich bis Beuys und Penck,* Leipzig: Seemann, 1997

**Jans, Hans Jög, ed.** *Musiker-Handschriften: Originalpartituren aus der Sammlung Dr. h. c. Paul Sacher,* Lucerne: Bärtschi & Hasler, 1973

**Jung, Hermann,** *Ullstein Autographenbuch, Vom Sammeln handschriftlicher Kostbarkeiten,* Frankfurt, 1971

**Kallir, Rudolf F.,** *Autographensammler-lebenslänglich,* Zurich: Atlantis, 1977

**Klinkenborg, Verlyn, Herbert Cahoon, and Charles Ryskamp,** *British Literary Manuscript Series I – from 800 to 1800,* New York: Pierpont Morgan Library in association with Dover Publications, 1981

*British Literary Manuscript Series II – from 1800 to 1914,* New York: Pierpont Morgan Library in association with Dover Publications, 1981

*Les Plus belles pages manuscrites de l'histoire de France,* Paris: Robert Laffont, 1993

*Les Plus beaux manuscrits des romanciers français,* Paris: Robert Laffont, 1994

*Les Plus beaux manuscrits des journaux intimes de la langue française,* Paris: Robert Laffont, 1995

*Les Plus beaux manuscrits du théâtre français,* Paris: Robert Laffont, 1996

**Lescure, M. de,** *Les Autographes et le gôut des autographes en France et à l'étranger,* Paris: V. Gay, 1865

**Lesure, François, and Nanie Bridgman,** *Collection musicale André Meyer: Manuscrits, autographes, musique imprimée et manuscrit,* Abbeville: F. Paillart, [1960]

**Lowenherz, David H.,** *The 50 Greatest Love Letters of All Time,* New York: Crown, 2002

**Marans, M. Wesley,** *Sincerely Yours: the Famous & Infamous as They Wanted to be Seen, in Autographed Photographs from the Collection of M. Wesley Marans,* Boston: Little, Brown, 1983

**Mecklenburg, Günther,** *Vom Autographensammeln: Versuch einer Darstellung seines Wesens und seiner Geschichte im deutschen Sprachgebiet,* Marburg: Stargardt, 1963

**Morrison, Alfred,** *Catalogue of the Collection of Autograph Letters and Historical Documents formed between 1865 and 1882,* 6 vols, London: Strangeways, 1883

**Müller, Arno,** *Berühmte Frauen von Maria Stuart bis Mutter Teresa: Persönlichkeit – Lebensweg – Handschriftanalyse,* Vienna: Braumüller, 2002

**Munby, Alan Noel Latimer,** *The Cult of the Autograph Letter in England,* London: Athlone, 1962

**Muns, J. B.,** *Musical Autographs: A Comparative Guide,* Berkeley, CA: J. B. Muns, 1989; supplement, 1992

**Nichols, John G.,** *Autographs of Royal, Noble, Learned, and Remarkable Personages Conspicuous in English History,* London: J. B. Nichols, 1892

**Nicolas, Alain,** *Les Autographes,* Paris: Maisonneuve, 1988

**Patterson, Jerry E.,** *Autographs: A Collector's Guide,* New York: Crown, 1973

**Rawlins, Ray,** *Four Hundred Years of British Autographs,* London: Dent, 1970

*The Guinness Book of World Autographs,* Enfield, Middlesex: Guinness Superlatives, 1977

**Rendell, Kenneth W.,** *Fundamentals of Autograph Collecting,* Somerville, MA: Rendell, 1972

*Autograph Letters, Manuscripts, Drawings – French Artists & Authors,* Somerville, MA: Rendell, 1977

*The Medieval World, 800–1450,* Somerville, MA: Rendell, 1979

*Renaissance Europe, 1450–1600,* Somerville, MA: Rendell, 1979

*The American Frontier, from the Atlantic to the Pacific,* Somerville, MA: Rendell, 1980

*Forging History: The Detection of Fake Letters and Documents,* Norman, OK: University of Oklahoma Press, 1994

*History Comes to Life,* Norman, OK, and London: University of Oklahoma Press, 1995

**Schang, F. C.,** *Visiting Cards of Celebrities,* Paris: Hazan, [1971]

**Sowards, Neil,** *The Handbook of Check Collecting,* Fort Wayne, IN: the author, 1976

**Stargardt, J. A.,** *Autographensammlung Dr. Robert Ammann,* Marburg: Stargardt, 1961–62

**Sullivan, George,** *The Complete Book of Autograph Collecting,* New York: Dodd, Mead, 1971

**Tannenbaum, Samuel A.,** *The Handwriting of the Renaissance,* New York: Columbia University Press, 1930; reprinted New York: Frederick Ungar, 1967

**Taylor, John M.,** *The Autograph Collector's Checklist,* Burbank, CA: Manuscript Society, 1990

*Trésors de l'écrit – 10 ans d'enrichissement du patrimoine écrit,* Paris: RMN, 1991

**Vallières, Nathalie des,** *Les Plus beaux manuscrits de Saint Éxupéry,* Paris: La Martinière, 2003

**Warner, Sir George Frederick, ed.,** *Facsimiles of Royal, Historical, Literary and Other Autographs in the Department of Manuscripts, British Museum,* London: British Museum, 1899

*Universal Classic Manuscripts,* London and Washington, DC: M. W. Dunne, 1901

**Wiedemann, Hans-Rudolf,** *Altersbriefe bedeutender Menschen in Handschrift und Druck,* 2nd ed., Lübeck: Hansisches Verlagskontor H. Scheffler, 1986

*Briefe Großer Naturforscher und Ärzte in Handschriften,* Lübeck: Verlag Graphische Werkstätten, 1989

*Briefe und Albumblätter großer Komponisten und Interpreten in Handschriften,* Lübeck: Verlag Graphische Werkstätten, 1990

*Briefe Europäischer Baumeister, Bildhauer und Maler in Handschriften,* Lübeck: Verlag Graphische Werkstätten, 1993

**Winternitz, Emanuel,** *Musical Autographs From Monteverdi to Hindemith,* 2 vols, New York: Dover, 1965

**Zeileis, Friedrich Georg,** *Katalog einer Musik-Sammlung,* Berlin: Gallspach, 1992.

# PICTURE CREDITS AND ACKNOWLEDGMENTS

## PICTURE CREDITS

**p. 8** © Jean Tinguely, ADAGP, Paris 2004 | **p. 17** © Estate of Thomas Mann | **p. 17** © Estate of Ludwig Wittgenstein, Trinity College, Cambridge | **p. 19** © C. G. Jung Institute | **p. 20** © F. T. Marinetti, ADAGP, Paris 2004 | **p. 20** © Giacomo Balla, ADAGP, Paris 2004 | **p. 20** © André Breton, ADAGP, Paris 2004 | **p. 21** © Courtesy of the Truman Capote Literary Trust | **p. 29** © Constantin Brancusi, ADAGP, Paris 2004 | **p. 29** © Bob Kane | **p. 29** © Charles Schulz Museum | **p. 29** © Courtesy of the Walter Lantz Foundation | **p. 31** © 2004 The Andy Warhol Foundation for the Visual Arts | **p. 33** © Man Ray Trust, ADAGP, Paris 2004 | **p. 35** © Courtesy of the Society of Authors, London | **p. 37** © Audrey Hepburn Children's Fund | **p. 37** © Cecil Beaton, Sotheby's 2004 | **p. 37** © Henri Cartier-Bresson, Magnum Photos, 2004 | **p. 37** © Bob Penn | **p. 38** © Courtesy of the Academia Brasileira de Música | **p. 38** © Photo Harcourt | **p. 140** © Courtesy of Marina Mahler, Spoleto / Italy | **p. 146** © Courtesy of Joanna T. Steichen | **p. 148** © Camille Claudel, ADAGP, Paris 2004 | **p. 150** © Sigmund Freud Copyrights / Mary Evans Picture Library, London | **pp. 151, 152, 153** © Courtesy of Sigmund Freud Copyrights / Peterson Marsh Ltd, London | **p. 157** © August Sander. Die Photographische Sammlung / SK Stiftung Kultur – August Sander Archiv, Cologne / ADAGP, Paris 2004 | **p. 158** © Elliot & Fry / National Portrait Gallery, London | **pp. 158, 159** © Mahatma Gandhi, Navjivan Trust 2004 | **pp. 160, 161, 162, 163** © Albert Einstein and related marks™ HUJ, Represented by The Roger Richman Agency, Inc., www.albert-einstein.net | **p. 163** © Lotte Jacobi / University of New Hampshire Archives, 2004 | **p. 172** © 2004 Instituto Nacional de Antropología e História, Mexico | **pp. 182, 183** © Estate of Henri Matisse | **p. 185** © Walter Stoneman | **p. 186** © Marie Laurencin, ADAGP, Paris 2004 | **p. 192** © Courtesy of John Stravinsky | **p. 193** © Photo Lipnitzki/Viollet | **pp. 194, 195** © Courtesy of Foulques de Jouvenel | **pp. 196, 197, 198, 199** © Picasso Administration, Paris 2004 | **p. 197** © Joel Mariaud, ADAGP, Paris 2004 | **p. 198** © Herbert List, Magnum Photos 2004 | **pp. 200, 201** © Ezra Pound, Hoffman Agency, 2004 | **p. 202** © Courtesy of Mr. Edward Beckett | **p. 204** © Maurice Utrillo, ADAGP, Paris 2004 | **p. 206** © T. E. Lawrence, Tweedie & Prideaux 2004 | **p. 208** © F. L. C. / ADAGP, Paris 2004 | **p. 209** © Frank Lloyd Wright, ADAGP, Paris 2004 | **p. 212** © Frida Kahlo, Banco de México 2004 | **p. 215** © Diego Rivera, Banco de México 2004 | **pp. 216, 217** © Assírio & Alvim, Portugal © Herdeiros de Fernando Pessoa | **pp. 218, 219, 220, 221** © Jean Cocteau, ADAGP, Paris 2004 | **p. 222** © Courtesy of the Roy Export Company Establishment and Bubbles Incorporated SA c/o Association Chaplin | **p. 222** © The Estate of Alfred Hitchcock | **p. 224** © Federico García Lorca, ADAGP, Paris 2004 | **p. 227** © Library of Congress, Prints & Photographs Division, Toni Frissel Collection | **pp. 228, 229** © Successió Miró – ADAGP, Paris 2004 | **p. 229** © Peter Rose Pulham |

**pp. 230, 231** © Estate of Antoine de Saint-Exupéry | **p. 230** © Roger Parry – Patrimoine Photographique, Paris 2004 | **pp. 234, 235** © Giuseppe Tomasi di Lampedusa, Wyllie Agency, 2004 | **pp. 236, 237** © Hemingway Foreign Rights Trust | **p. 236** © Herederos de Alberto Korda | **p. 238** © Mae West™ Represented by The Roger Richman Agency, Inc., www.therichmanagency.com | **p. 240** © Courtesy of the Nabokov Estate | **p. 242** © Foundation Paul Delvaux, St Idesbald, Belgium / ADAGP, Paris 2004 | **p. 242** © René Magritte, ADAGP, Paris 2004 | **pp. 244, 245** © Jorge Luis Borges, Wyllie Agency 2004 | **p. 246** © Walt Disney | **p. 250** © Duke Ellington, CMG Worldwide, 2004 | **p. 251** © Courtesy of Louis Armstrong House and Archives | **p. 251** © Louis Goldman / Photo Researchers | **p. 252** © Photo Lipnitzki / Viollet | **p. 253** © Izis | **pp. 254, 255** © Estate of Orson Welles | **p. 256** © John Sampas. Reproduced by kind permission. | **p. 262** © Maria Callas™ Represented by The Roger Richman Agency, Inc., www.therichmanagency.com | **p. 262** © Photo Piccagliani | **p. 263** © Courtesy of the Estate of Glenn Gould and Glenn Gould Limited | **p. 263** © Jerry Fielder, Yusuf Karsh Curator. Reproduced by kind permission. | **p. 264** © Rolling Stones | **p. 264** © The Estate of John Lennon | **p. 265** © Apple Corps, Ltd, 2004

## ACKNOWLEDGMENTS

This book, which brings together thousands of facts obtained from countless friends and collaborators, owes a great debt to my wife Bia, and I'd like to thank her for her constant support.

At Editions de La Martinière, Céline Moulard, Carole Daprey and Isabelle Grison all took care of this project. I would like to thank all three for the attention they have devoted to it, and especially Isabelle who had the largest part of the task to deal with. In her role as editor she was able to combine enthusiasm with discipline, and rigour with patience. I thank both her and Delphine Lalire for the many miracles, both large and small, that they have made happen in order to publish this book in three different languages.

For their help with the collection or with the creation of this book, I would like to thank  Roberto Alvim Corrêa, Edgar Batista, Peter Beal, Pierrette and Thierry Bodin, Marquis de Bonneval, Alfredo Breitfeld, Fréderic Castaing, Maryse Castaing, Michel Castaing, Naomi Cohen, Sérgio Corrêa da Costa, André Corrêa do Lago, Beatrice Weiller Corrêa do Lago, Luis Corrêa do Lago, Manoel Corrêa do Lago, José Maria da Costa e Silva, Dominique Courvoisier, Fleur Cowles, Nathalie Desmarest, Alberto Dines, Edemar Cid Ferreira, Christian Galantaris, José Luis Garaldi, Lucía García, Jean Edouard Gautrot, Pierre Georgel, Walter Geyerhahn, Carlo Ginzburg, Elizinha Gonçalves, Michaël Guttmann, Nicolas Kugel, Patrick Lévy, Bernard Loliée, Jim Lowe, George Lowry, Henri Loyrette, Jeremy Markowitz, Klaus Mecklenburg, José Mindlin, Marcos de Moraes, Julio Moses, Maurício Nabuco, Alain Nicolas, Marcos Padilha, Marylou Prado, Stephen Roe, Saul Roll, Hinda Rose, Rosine and Renato Saggiori, Yaen Saggiori, David Schulson, Jan Schultz, Betsy and Richard Smith, Monique Sochaczewski, Benjamin Steiner, Antonio Tavares de Carvalho, Elza Vasconcellos, Hugo Vickers, René Vigneron, María Julieta García Vilas Boas, Jean Claude Vrain, Susan Wharton and John Wilson.

# INDEX

Translated from the French, *Cinq siècles sur papier: Autographes et manuscrits de la collection Pedro Corrêa do Lago,* by David H. Wilson

Original version © 2004, Éditions de La Martinière, Paris

First published in the United Kingdom in 2004 by Thames & Hudson Ltd, 181A High Holborn, London WC1V 7QX

www.thamesandhudson.com

First published in 2004 in hardcover in the United States of America by Thames & Hudson Inc., 500 Fifth Avenue, New York, New York 10110

thamesandhudsonusa.com

British Library Cataloguing-in-Publication Data

A catalogue record for this book is available from the British Library

ISBN 0-500-51206-X

Library of Congress Catalog Card Number 2004109957

Printed and bound in Spain by Artes Graficas Toledo

In di nomine Ego Adefonsus di gra hispaniarū impator

rego de ual de salze cū omnibº ptinetiis suis cū tris

ditatē dono rccedo tibi fernādo guteriz. quātin eā

salice. Siquis aūt de mā gente uel de aliena hoc mō facti

lttauit illo impatore c illos mozmutes in cordoba. Notū die

Ego adfonsus hāc cartā iussi fieri. ppria manu roboraui.

Comite don fernādo                    Conf.

Comite don petro                      Conf.

                                      Conf.

Comite don manric tenete baeza